POWERPOINT

A Quick Reference of More Than 300 Microsoft PowerPoint Tasks, Terms, and Tricks

2002 FROM A TO Z

Stephen L. Nelson

PowerPoint 2002 From A to Z:
A Quick Reference of More Than 300 Microsoft PowerPoint Tasks, Terms, and Tricks

Published by
Redmond Technology Press
8581 154th Avenue NE
Redmond, WA 98052
www.redtechpress.com

Library of Congress Catalog Card No: applied for

ISBN 1-931150-23-0

Printed and bound in the United States of America.

9 8 7 6 5 4 3 2 1

Distributed by
Independent Publishers Group
814 N. Franklin St.
Chicago, IL 60610
www.ipgbook.com

Designer: Minh-Tam S. Le
Editor: Fred Lanigan

INTRODUCTION

You should find *PowerPoint 2002 From A to Z* easy to use. You only need to know that the book organizes its information—key tasks and important terms—alphabetically in order to use the book. You'll find it helpful, however, if you understand what this book assumes about your computer skills, what you should know about the PowerPoint program from the very start, and what editorial conventions this book uses. This short introduction provides this information.

What You Should Know About Windows

You don't need to be computer expert to use either this book or Microsoft PowerPoint. Definitely not. But you want to be comfortable working with your computer and Microsoft Windows.

For example, you should know how to turn your computer on and off, how to start and stop programs, how to choose menu commands, and how to work with dialog boxes. This book, for the most part, doesn't provide this Windows information.

If you need this Windows information, you need to take the Windows online tutorial, get a friend to give you a quick tutorial, or acquire another book on Windows.

TIP *Any short book on Windows will tell you what you need to know, but if you're a business user of Windows 2000 or Windows XP, you may want to look at the* Effective Executive's Guide to Windows 2000 *or the* Effective Executive's Guide to Windows XP. *These books supply a tutorial on Windows geared for business professionals.*

What You Should Know About PowerPoint

You don't need to know anything about PowerPoint to use this book. But understanding from the very start how PowerPoint works and how the PowerPoint program window is laid out will help you immensely in your learning. Let me quickly provide this background information.

How PowerPoint Works

PowerPoint provides tools and prefabricated slides you can use to build a presentation you want to give. The slides in a presentation can look like the one shown in Figure 1 and contain only text. But slides in PowerPoint can also easily show other objects, like tables, charts organizational charts, drawings and pictures, and even clip art.

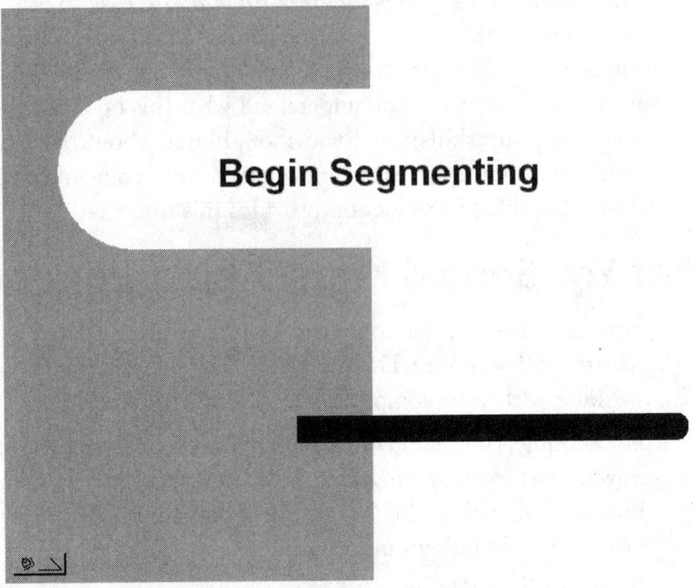

Figure 1 A PowerPoint slide that shows text.

The other thing to note about PowerPoint is that it not only helps you create the slides (such as the example shown in Figure 1), but it also provides tools you can use to present your slides. For example, PowerPoint includes a wizard you can use to create the raw files you need to send to a film company when you want to create 35mm slides. PowerPoint includes tools you can employ to create color transparencies and printed handouts. And PowerPoint includes features that let you easily show the slides you've created onscreen (such as on a laptop) or using a color projector (such as for larger audience presentations).

NOTE *Wizards are little programs that use dialog boxes to collect information from you and then use the information to perform some task. If you have ever worked with Microsoft Excel and created a chart, for example, you have encountered the Excel Chart Wizard. It asks you questions about the data you want to use in a chart, and then it creates the chart for you.*

How the PowerPoint Window Works

Since understanding the Windows program window will make using PowerPoint and this book easier, let me identify some of the more important parts of the PowerPoint program window (see Figure 2).

The program window *title bar* identifies your presentation and provides buttons to resize the window.

The *menu bar* gives you access to the PowerPoint menus of commands and Help.

The *toolbars* provide buttons and boxes for quickly choosing commands.

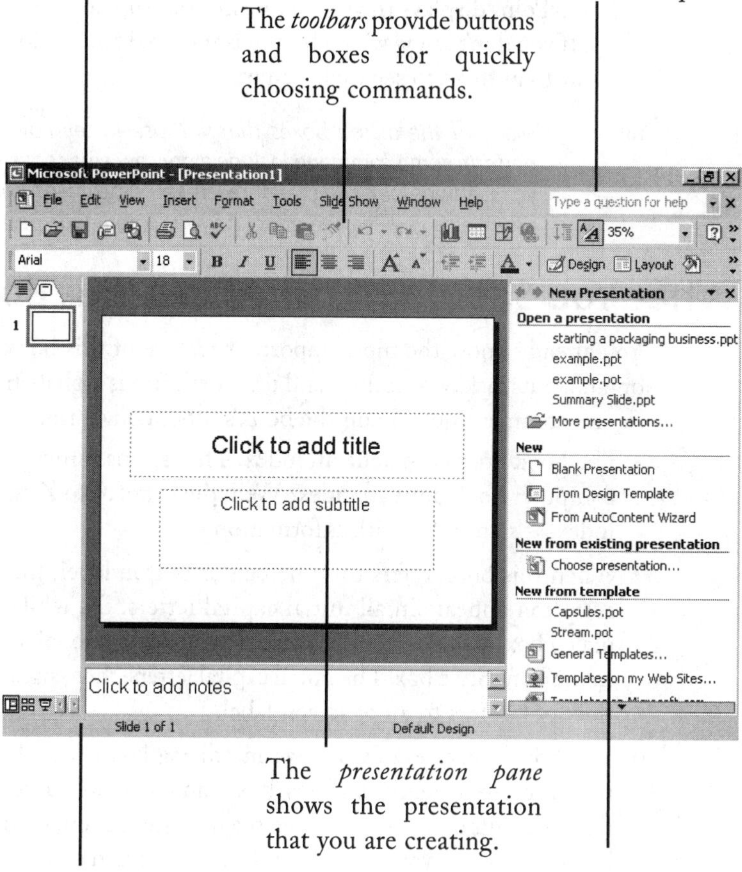

The *presentation pane* shows the presentation that you are creating.

The *status bar* provides information about your presentation and what PowerPoint is doing.

The *task pane* provides hyperlinks to commands and wizards.

Figure 2 The PowerPoint program window.

Let me also point out two important items about the PowerPoint toolbars:

- PowerPoint's toolbars vary greatly in their appearance because PowerPoint personalizes your toolbars so that the buttons and boxes available are those you are most likely to use. Usually, you want personalized toolbars. If you don't, refer to the Personalized Menus and Toolbars entry for information on how to turn off personalization.
- While toolbar buttons and boxes aren't labeled, if you point to a tool, PowerPoint displays the tool name in a pop-up box called a screen tip. If you don't know which button is the Bold button, for example, point to buttons to see their names.

TIP *Many of the dialog boxes that you use to tell PowerPoint to perform some command include a preview area that shows how your settings look and therefore lets you experiment. The preview area helps you see the effect of your command specifications.*

What You Should Know About This Book

You already know the most important feature of this book—that it organizes its task descriptions and term definitions alphabetically. But let me comment quickly on the book's other conventions.

- The book doesn't include an index. That seems funny. How can a computer book omit an index? Well, the list of A to Z entries *is* an index. It's an index with information.
- When this book refers to some box or button label, the label description appears in all initial capital letters. So, while the Font dialog box includes a box labeled "Font style," this book would refer to the Font Style box. The initial capital letters, then, signal you that the book refers to an onscreen label.
- This book's pictures of windows and dialog boxes use a low display resolution to make the buttons, boxes and text look larger. Less information fits on the screen when the resolution is low, unfortunately, but what you see you can read. If the book's screen pictures had used a higher resolution, images would be very difficult to see clearly.

And that's everything you should know to get started.

Stephen L. Nelson

steve@stephenlnelson.com

Seattle, Washington, May 2001

POWERPOINT 2002 FROM A TO Z

35mm Slides

You can produce 35mm slides for the slides that make up your PowerPoint presentation.

If you have a film recorder attached to your network or desktop computer, you can print your PowerPoint slides directly to the film recorder. The film recorder will then create 35mm slides based on the PowerPoint slides. You'll then need to take this undeveloped film to a film processor that will develop 35mm slides you can use in your presentation.

To print slides to a film recorder, take the following steps:

1. Size your slides so that they're appropriate for 35mm slides by choosing the File→Page Setup command. When PowerPoint displays the Page Setup dialog box, choose the 35mm Slides entry from the Slides Sized For drop-down list box (see Figure A-1). Then click OK.

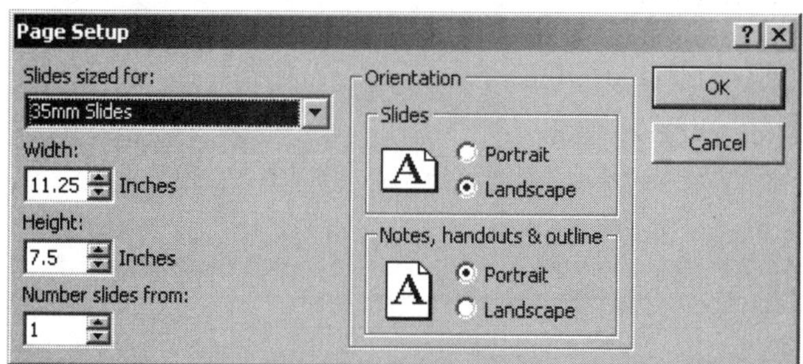

Figure A-1 The Page Setup dialog box.

2. After you size the slides so that they work on 35mm slides, choose the File→Print command. When PowerPoint displays the Print dialog box, choose the Film Recorder entry from the Name drop-down list box. In other words, you print to the Film Recorder. After you do this, verify that the Print What drop-down list box indicates that you're printing slides, and verify that the Color/Grayscale box shows Color—if you are printing to 35mm slides, you want to use color.
3. After you specify how PowerPoint should print, click the OK button. PowerPoint prints the slides to the film recorder. All you'll need to do next is have the film developed.

To create 35mm slides when you don't have a film recorder, send the PowerPoint presentation to a service bureau that will convert your PowerPoint slides to 35mm slides. As you might guess, this just means that the service bureau has a computer attached to a film recorder. You might be able to look up such a service bureau in your local business or telephone directory. You can also use the Genigraphics Service Bureau.

NOTE *To use the Genigraphics Service Bureau, visit the Genigraphics web site at www.genigraphics.com and click the Order Online hyperlink. This starts an online wizard that steps you through process of ordering presentation materials. You can also call Genigraphics directly for information on how to work through the mail. The Genigraphics telephone number is 1-800-790-4001.*

Active Presentation

The active presentation is the PowerPoint presentation shown in the active window.

Active Presentation window

The active presentation window is the document window that shows the PowerPoint presentation that you're currently working on. If you tell PowerPoint to print, for example, PowerPoint prints the presentation shown in the active presentation window.

PowerPoint adds a button to the taskbar for each open presentation. By clicking a document's taskbar button, you can switch to that presentation.

Alignment

You can align the text, tables, and pictures that make up the content of your slides so that the item you're aligning rests against the left edge of the slide, is centered horizontally on the slide, or rests against the right edge of the slide.

Aligning Text

To align text, first select the text. Then use the toolbar's Align Left, Center, Align Right, and Justify buttons to align the text.

If you're using personalized menus and toolbars, these alignment buttons may not all appear. You can still change alignment of the selected text, however, by using the Format→Alignment commands: Align Left, Center, Align Right, and Justify. Simply choose the command that corresponds to the alignment you want.

Aligning Tables

To align the selected table, use the toolbar's Align Left, Center, Align Right, and Justify buttons. Alternatively, choose one of the Format→Alignment commands: Align Left, Center, Align Right, or Justify.

Aligning Pictures

To align a picture, right-click the picture and then choose the Format Picture command from the shortcut menu. When PowerPoint displays the Format Picture dialog box, click the Position tab and then use its Horizontal and Vertical boxes to align the picture (see Figure A-2).

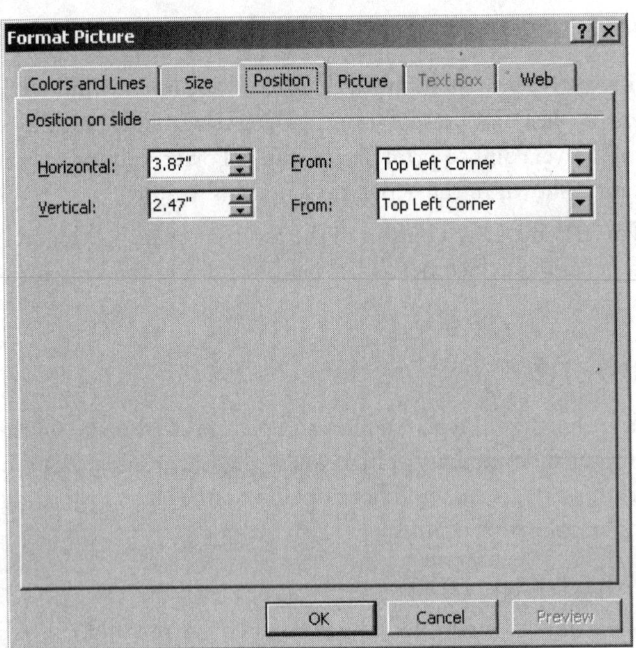

Figure A-2 The Position tab of the Format Picture dialog box.

Aligning Other Graphic Objects

You align other graphic objects—drawn objects, autoshapes, and so on—in the same way that you align a picture. Right-click the object and choose the Format command from the shortcut menu. When PowerPoint displays the Formatting dialog box, click its Position tab. Then use the Position tab's boxes to make your changes.

SEE ALSO *Grids and Guidelines*

Animated GIF

An animated gif file is an image file that shows movement. You commonly see animated gif images on web pages.

SEE ALSO *Animating Slide Text, Sounds and Movies*

Animating Slide Text

You can add movement, or animation, to text. In fact, this will probably be the most common animation you use for your presentations.

Animating title and slide text

PowerPoint provides animation schemes for animating slides. To add animation to your presentation, display the slide you want to animate. Then, display the Slide Design – Animation Schemes task pane and select an animation scheme from the list box (see Figure A-3).

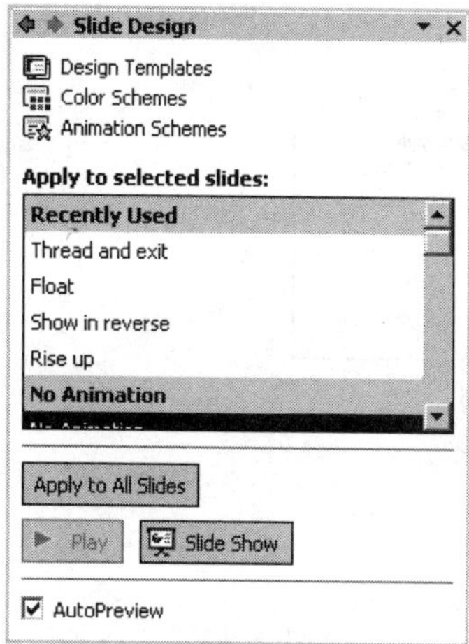

Figure A-3 The Slide Design – Animation Schemes task pane.

TIP *To display the Slide Design – Animation Schemes task pane, click the down arrow button at the top of the task pane and choose the Slide Design – Animation Schemes option.*

When you select an animation scheme, PowerPoint illustrates the animation effects for the selected slides. You can also click the Play button, which appears near the bottom of the Slide Design task pane, to see the animation effects.

TIP *To apply the selected animation scheme to all the slides in a presentation—not just the selected slides—click the Apply To All Slides button.*

Customizing Animation Effects

The Custom Animation task pane lets you control the way text and other object animation works (see Figure A-4).

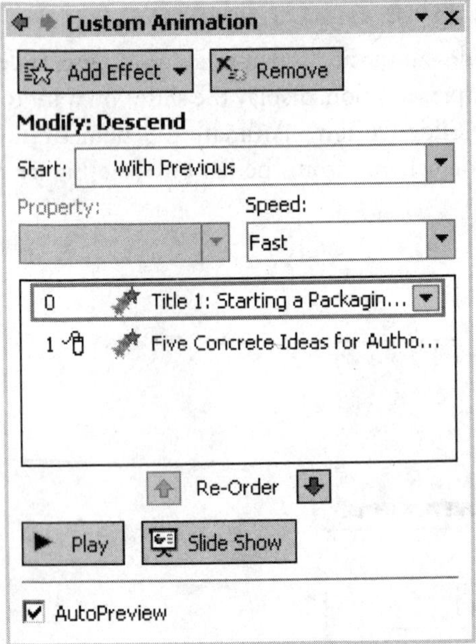

Figure A-4 The Custom Animation task pane.

TIP *To display the Custom Animation task pane, click the down arrow button at the top of the task pane and choose the Custom Animation option.*

You can tell PowerPoint to add four types of animation to the selected slide text: entrance animation, emphasis animation, exit animation, and motion path animation.

To add entrance animation, which is movement that occurs as an item is added to a slide, select the item, click the Add Effect button and choose the Entrance command. When PowerPoint displays the Entrance submenu, choose the entrance animation effect you want to use when PowerPoint displays the item: Blinds, Box, Checkerboard, Diamond, or Fly In. If none of these entry effects is what you want, choose the More Effects command to display the Add Entrance Effect dialog box (see Figure A-5). To use one of its entrance effects, click the button that describes the effect.

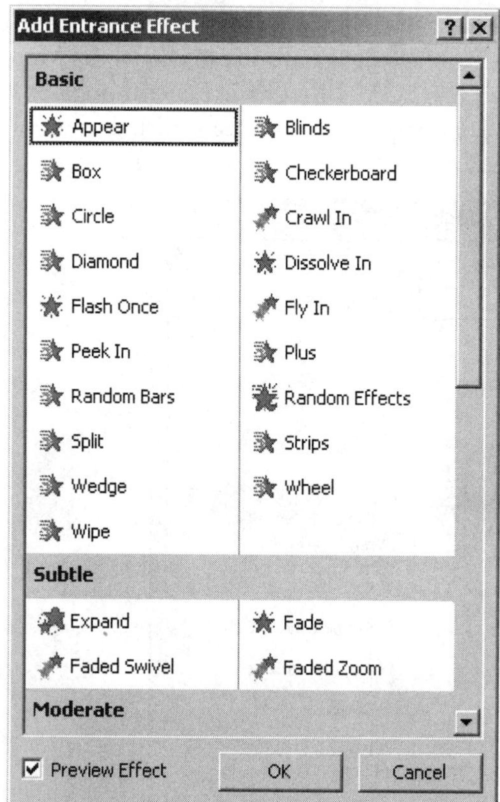

Figure A-5 The Add Entrance Effect dialog box.

NOTE *If you have a question about how some animation effect works, just add the effect. PowerPoint shows the effect as you add it and places the new effect on the list shown in the Custom Animation task pane. If you don't like the newly added effect, select it from the Custom Animation task pane and click the Remove button.*

To add emphasis animation, which is movement that occurs as an item is on a slide, select the item, click the Add Effect button and choose the Emphasis command. When PowerPoint displays the Emphasis submenu, choose the emphasis animation effect you want to use when PowerPoint displays the item: Change Font, Change Font

Size, Change Font Style, Grow/Shrink, or Spin. If none of these emphasis effects is what you want, you can choose the More Effects command to display the Add Emphasis Effect dialog box (see Figure A-6). To use one of its emphasis effects, click the button that describes the effect.

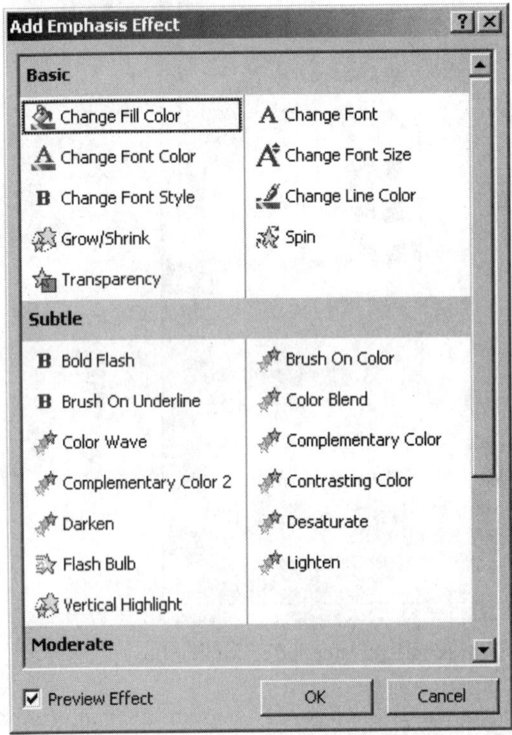

Figure A-6 The Add Emphasis Effect dialog box.

To add exit animation to a slide item, which is movement that occurs as an item is removed from the slide, select the item, click the Add Effect button and choose the Exit command. When PowerPoint displays the Exit submenu, choose the entry animation effect you want to use when PowerPoint finishes displaying the item: Blinds, Box, Checkerboard, Diamond, or Fly Out. (These are virtually the same choices you have for entrance animation.) Again, if none of these entry effects is what you want, you can choose the More Effects command to display the Add Exit Effect dialog box (see Figure A-7). To use one of its exit effects, click the button that describes the effect.

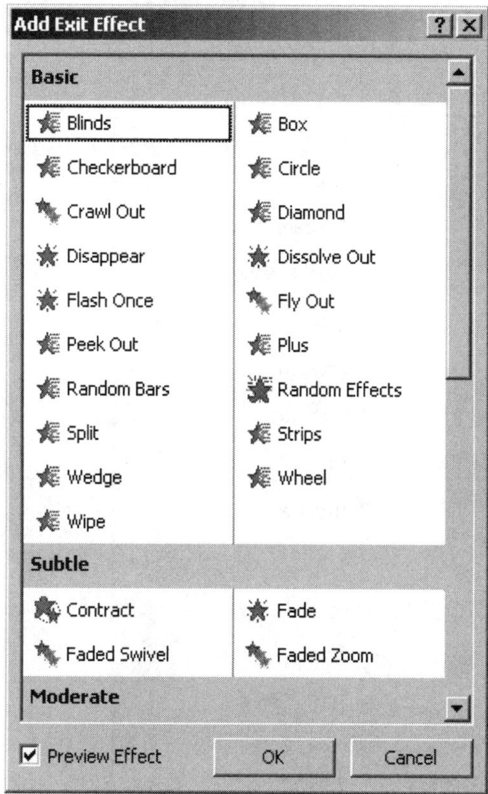

Figure A-7   The Add Exit Effect dialog box.

To specify how an item should move when it moves, select the item, click the Add Effect button and choose the Motion Path command. When PowerPoint displays the Motion Path submenu, choose the motion path effect you want PowerPoint to use: 5 Point Star, Curvy Star, Diamond, Heart, Hexagon, or Loop De Loop. If none of these motion paths is what you want, you can choose the Draw Custom Path command to display another submenu of commands (Line, Curve, Freeform, and Scribble) that actually let you manually draw the motion path you want. Or, you can choose the More Motion Paths command to display the Add Motion Path dialog box (see Figure A-8). To use one of its motion paths, click the button that describes the path.

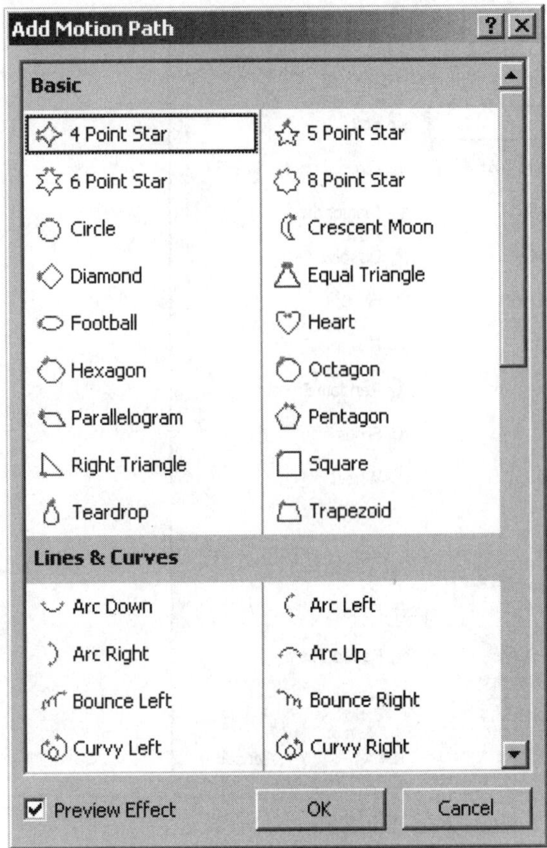

Figure A-8 The Add Motion Path dialog box.

NOTE *To review your all animation effects once you have finished adding them, click the Play button to play the animation effects for the active slide or click the Slide Show to show the entire set of slides including their animation effects.*

Ordering Animation Effects

PowerPoint animates individual objects. This means that you might have several objects on a slide that are all animated.

By default, PowerPoint plays these animation effects in the same order as you added the animation to the slide. You can change this order by using the Animation Effects list box, which also appears on the Custom Animation task pane. This list box lists animation effects in

the order they occur. To change a particular effect's place on the list, click the effect and then move it by clicking the Reorder buttons.

Fine-Tuning Animation Effects

The Custom Animation task pane provides three other boxes for fine-tuning how an animation effect occurs. For example, the Custom Animation task pane provides a Start box that lets you indicate whether the animation effect should start when you click the slide, should start simultaneously with the previous effect, or should start after the previous effect.

The Custom Animation task pane also provides other boxes for controlling other animation effects. Which boxes you see depend on what sort of animation effect you're fine-tuning. If you're fine-tuning the way slide text is moved onto the slide, for example, PowerPoint provides Direction and Speed boxes you use to specify the direction from which the slide text is moved and the speed with which the slide text is moved. If you've told PowerPoint to change the font used for text as an emphasis effect, PowerPoint provides Font and Duration boxes you use to choose the new font and specify how long it is to be displayed.

To learn how any of these boxes work, you can experiment. After you select an animation effect, as mentioned earlier, PowerPoint shows what the effect does. You can also click the Play button to replay all the animation effects for the slide.

Timing Animation Effects

If you right-click an animation effect listed on the Custom Animation task pane and choose the Timing command from the shortcut menu, PowerPoint displays the Timing tab of the effect's options dialog box (see Figure A-9). The Timing tab lets you control how quickly the animation occurs.

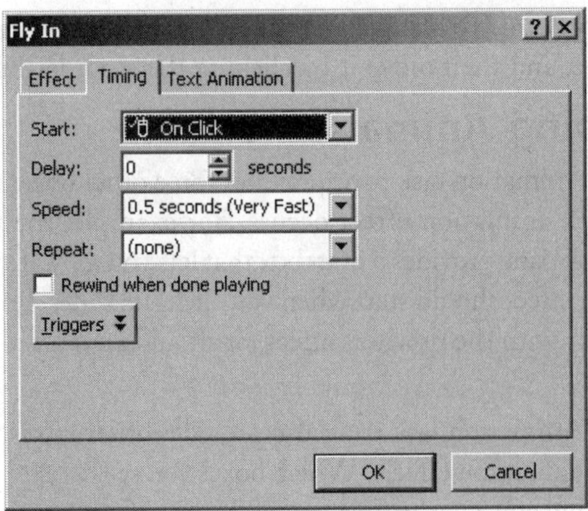

Figure A-9 The Timing tab.

The Delay box lets you specify a delay before the animation starts. The Speed box lets you specify how long an animation takes. The Repeat box lets you specify how many times an effect repeats. The Triggers command button adds buttons to the Timing tab that let you specify how mouse clicks control the animation.

Other Effects Options

If you right-click an animation effect listed on the Custom Animation task pane and choose the Effects Options command from the shortcut menu, PowerPoint displays the Effect tab of the effect's options dialog box (see Figure A-10). The Effect tab lets you further control the actual animation or movement used for a slide.

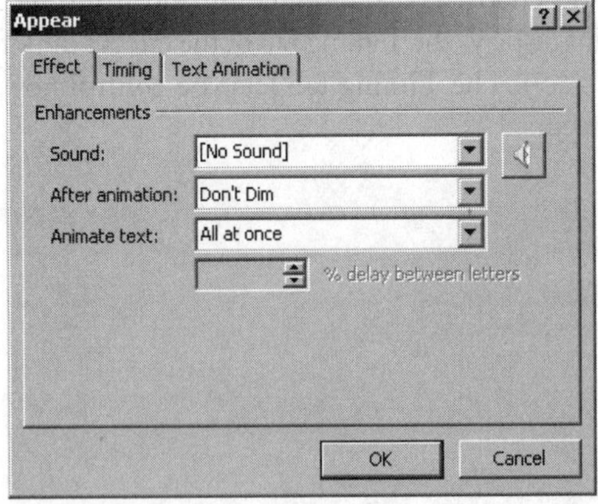

Figure A-10 The Effect tab.

Typically, you can add sound to an animation effect using the Sound box on the Effect tab. Depending on the animation effect, you may also have options such as describing what should happen after the animation and whether text should be animated letter-by-letter or word-by-word.

SEE ALSO *Sounds and Movies*

Animation see Animated GIF, Animating Slide Text

Application

An application is a program such as PowerPoint, or Microsoft Word. Operating systems such as Windows XP aren't considered applications. Operating systems are operating systems.

Application Window

The window that a program such as PowerPoint displays is called an application window. Document windows, which show the presentation, appear inside application windows.

Arrows

You can add arrows to your presentation. Arrows are drawing objects. To add an arrow, first display the Drawing toolbar by choosing the View→Toolbar→Drawing command. Next, click the Arrow button on the Drawing toolbar. Then click at the point where you want the arrow to start and drag the mouse to the point where you want the arrow to end (see Figure A-11).

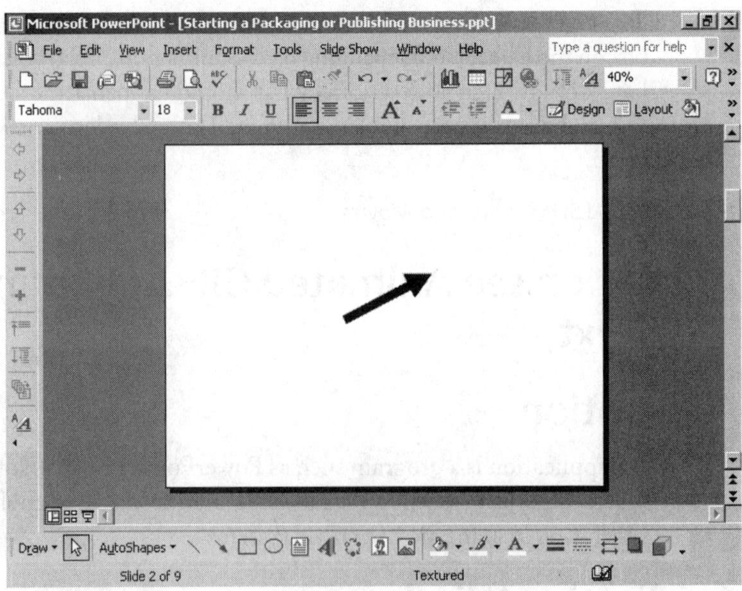

Figure A-11 An arrow created with the Drawing toolbar.

You can move an arrow by selecting it and then dragging it. To change the appearance of an arrow, right-click the arrow and choose the Format AutoShape command from the shortcut menu. When use PowerPoint displays the Format AutoShape dialog box, experiment with its tabs until you get the arrow you want (see Figure A-12).

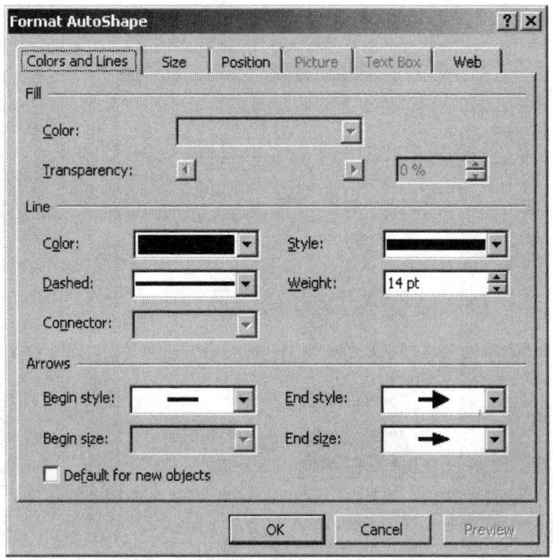

Figure A-12 The Colors and Lines tab of the Format AutoShape dialog box.

Audience Handouts

PowerPoint lets you print handouts for your audience. The handouts show pictures of the slides in your presentation and can provide space for people to jot down notes (see Figure A-13).

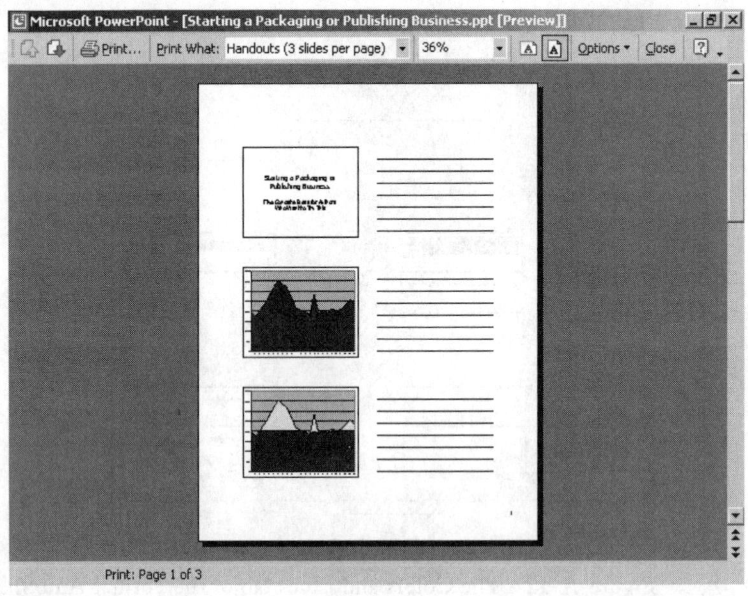

Figure A-13 A handout page shown in the Preview window.

To print handouts, choose the File→Print command, select Handouts from the Print What list box, and click OK.

SEE ALSO *Presentations*

Audio see Sounds and Movies

AutoContent Wizard

The easiest way for new PowerPoint users to create an outline is by using the AutoContent Wizard. To use the AutoContent Wizard, follow these instructions:

1. Tell PowerPoint that you want to use the AutoContent Wizard by clicking the From AutoContent Wizard hyperlink, which is shown in the New Presentation task pane (see Figure A-14). PowerPoint starts the AutoContent Wizard (see Figure A-15).

Figure A-14 The New Presentation task pane.

TIP *To display the New Presentation task pane, click the down arrow button at the top of the task pane and choose the New Presentation option.*

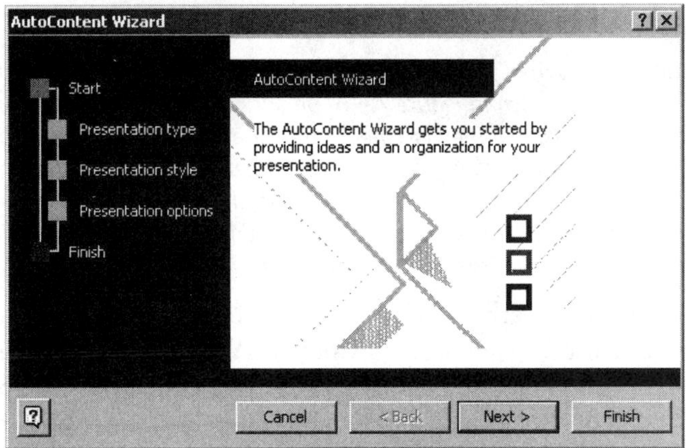

Figure A-15 The first AutoContent Wizard dialog box.

2. When PowerPoint displays the first AutoContent wizard—which simply introduces the AutoContent wizard—click the Next button to display the second AutoContent Wizard dialog box (see Figure A-16).

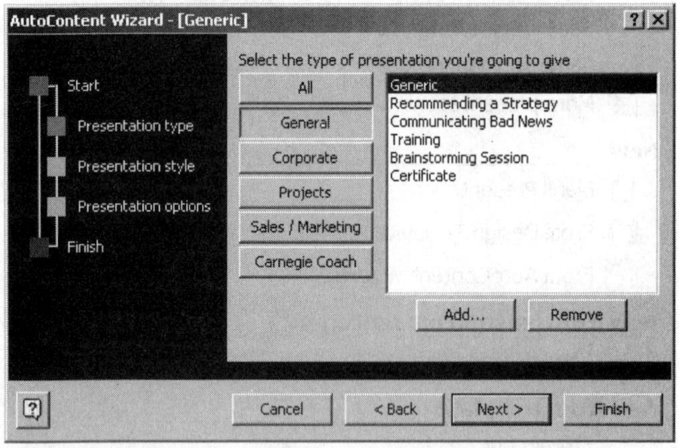

Figure A-16 The second AutoContent Wizard dialog box.

3. Click the button that best describes the general category of presentation you want to create (see Figure A-16). This dialog box provides several buttons and category combinations: General, Corporate, Projects, Sales/Marketing, and Carnegie Coach. When you click a button, the AutoContent Wizard displays a list of prefabricated presentations within that category. You select one of these presentations—they're really just partially structured presentations—by clicking it. Click the Next button to continue.

TIP *When you are working with the AutoContent Wizard dialog box shown in Figure A-16, be sure to explore the presentations in each of the five categories—or at least do this the first few times you use the AutoContent Wizard. The AutoContent Wizard supplies a rich set of thoughtful, well-structured presentations, and—especially as you are starting out—you can benefit by using these presentations as models for your own.*

4. When PowerPoint displays the third AutoContent Wizard dialog box, use it to tell the AutoContent Wizard how you'll deliver your presentation (see Figure A-17). If you will deliver your presentation onscreen using your laptop computer, for example, mark the On-screen Presentation button. Alternatively, if you are going to publish your presentation to the Web—this could be either an

Internet or intranet web site—you mark the Web Presentation button. When you finish providing this information, click the Next button to continue.

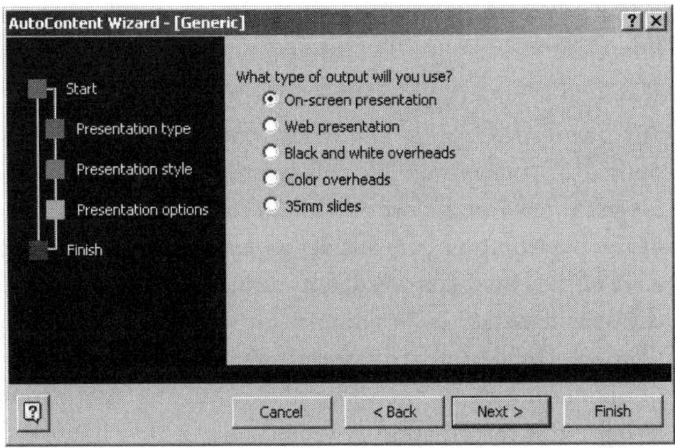

Figure A-17 The dialog box that the AutoContent Wizard uses to ask you about how you'll share your presentation

5. When the AutoContent Wizard displays the fourth dialog box, use the Presentation Title box to name your presentation (see Figure A-18). Optionally, use the Footer box to provide a footer that will appear at the bottom of each of the slides you create. If you want the footer to include the date the presentation was last modified, or updated, and the number of the slide, mark the Date Last Updated box and the Slide Number box.

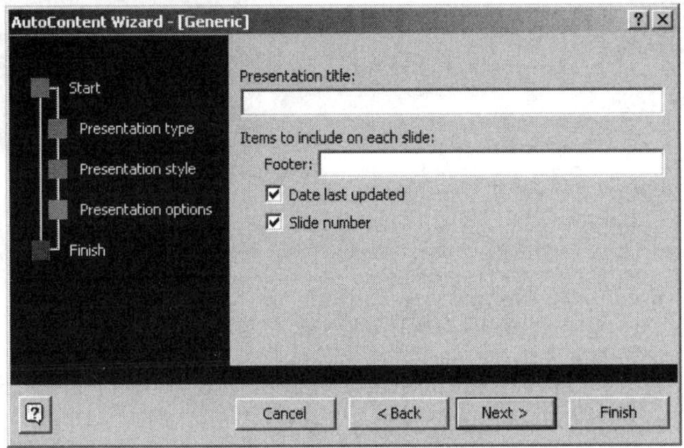

Figure A-18 The dialog box that the AutoContent Wizard uses to ask you for general information it will place on each slide.

NOTE *You might use the footer to name the presenting organization. You might also use the footer to record a copyright notice or a confidential notice.*

6. After you've finished filling in the boxes and marking the check boxes provided by the Presentation Options dialog box, click the Next button. Then click the Finish button.

   After you click Finish, the AutoContent Wizard creates a rough outline of your presentation and opens the presentation using its Normal view (see Figure A-19). Normal view includes the outline of the presentation (the outline appears in the pane along the left edge of the PowerPoint Program window). Normal view also shows the selected slide in the main pane of the PowerPoint program window. You'll be able to identify the slide because you'll see your presentation title on the slide. If you chose to enter a footer, you'll also see this information at the bottom of the slide.

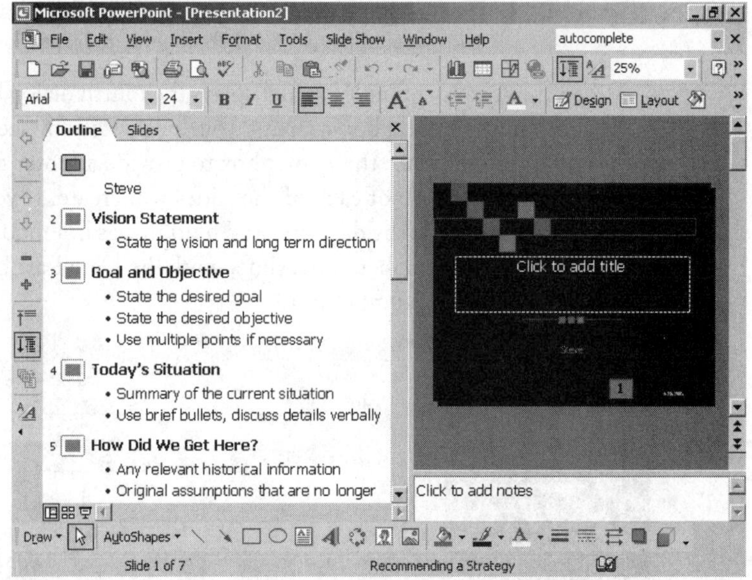

Figure A-19 Normal view showing an outline created by the AutoContent Wizard.

7. After you've used the AutoContent Wizard to create a rough-cut outline for your presentation, add slides, add and edit slide text, and remove unneeded slides.

AutoCorrect

AutoCorrect fixes common typing mistakes. PowerPoint already knows about many of the typing mistakes that people commonly make. For example, PowerPoint knows how to correctly capitalize the first letter of a sentence and how to spell commonly misspelled words.

You don't need to do anything special to use AutoCorrect. PowerPoint's corrections of your spelling and typing mistakes will occur automatically. (Try typing the word *and* as *adn* to see how AutoCorrect works.)

If you want to change the way that AutoCorrect works, choose the Tools→AutoCorrect Options command. When PowerPoint displays the AutoCorrect dialog box, use it to describe how AutoCorrect should operate (see Figure A-20).

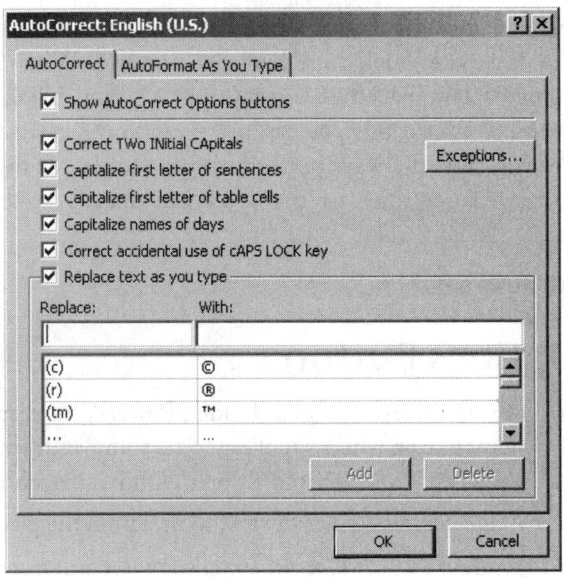

Figure A-20 The AutoCorrect tab of the AutoCorrect dialog box.

The first checkbox, Show AutoCorrect Options Buttons, lets you tell PowerPoint whether to display the AutoCorrect Options buttons. The AutoCorrect Options button, which appears whenever PowerPoint autocorrects some bit of text, displays a menu of options you can use to adjust the autocorrect changes.

You can check and uncheck the next five check boxes listed to specify whether PowerPoint should or shouldn't fix common capitalization errors. Usually you want PowerPoint to make such fixes.

You can use the Replace Text As You Type check box to turn on and off automatic spelling correction and typo correction. The list of corrections PowerPoint will make shows in the list box at the bottom of the dialog box.

To add an error to AutoCorrect's list, enter the erroneous entry in the Replace box and the correct entry in the With box.

SEE ALSO *AutoCorrect Options button*

AutoCorrect Options Button

If PowerPoint autocorrects something you enter, point to the corrected item and click the small blue bar that appears. When you do, PowerPoint displays the AutoCorrect Options button. Click it to display a menu of commands you can use to undo the correction, tell PowerPoint it should always perform the correction, or display the AutoCorrect dialog box so that you can specify exactly how AutoCorrect should work.

SEE ALSO *AutoCorrect*

AutoFit Options Button

If you copy or move text in a placeholder, PowerPoint displays the AutoFit Options button which supplies several commands you can use to specify how PowerPoint should fit text within a placeholder:

- *AutoFit To Placeholder* adjusts the text to fit within the placeholder.
- *Stop Fitting Text To This Placeholder* tells PowerPoint not to fit the text to the placeholder.
- *Split Text Between Two Slides* tells PowerPoint to move roughly half of the text (usually half of bullet points on the slide) to a new slide.
- *Change To A Two-Column Layout* tells PowerPoint to use two columns of text in the placeholder.
- *Control AutoCorrect Options* displays the AutoCorrect Options dialog box, which you can use to control how autocorrect works.

Automatic File Saves

PowerPoint regularly saves a copy of the presentation you're working on just in case Windows or PowerPoint crashes. It's this saved presentation that opens the next time you start PowerPoint after the crash.

To specify how often PowerPoint should automatically save this copy of your presentation, choose the Tools→Options command and click the Save tab (see Figure A-21). Check the Save AutoRecover Info Every box and then specify how often PowerPoint should save the copy. By default, PowerPoint saves the AutoRecover copy every ten minutes.

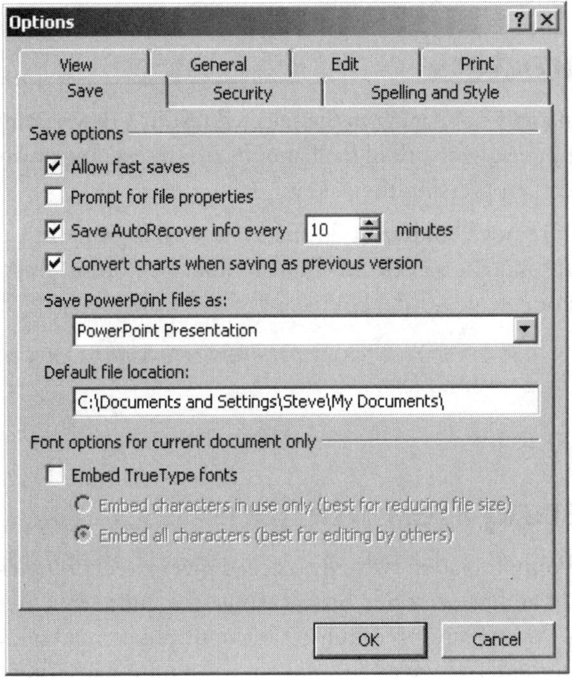

Figure A-21 The Save tab of the Options dialog box.

AutoRecover see Automatic File Saves

Backspace Key

The Backspace key erases the character or object that's just before the insertion point. In comparison, the Delete key erases the character or object that's just ahead of the insertion point.

Backup Copies

You can make a backup copy of presentations yourself simply by saving an extra copy of the presentation.

SEE ALSO *Fast Saves, File Extensions*

Bold Characters

You can apply boldfacing to the selected text in a PowerPoint presentation by clicking the Bold toolbar button or by holding down the Ctrl key and then pressing the B key.

You can remove boldfacing in the same way. If you select the boldface text and then click the Bold toolbar button or press Ctrl+B, PowerPoint removes the boldfacing.

NOTE *You can also use the Format→Font command to apply and remove boldfacing text.*

SEE ALSO *Fonts*

Broadcasting Presentations

PowerPoint includes two advanced delivery technologies: online meetings and presentation broadcasting. An online meeting lets you show a PowerPoint presentation on multiple computers, if all the computers are connected to a network. An online meeting also provides a white board you can use to collect comments from the meeting participants.

A presentation broadcast lets you deliver a presentation over a network. PowerPoint comes with the tools and software you need to deliver a presentation broadcast to as many as 15 people over a network. But Microsoft sells another product, Net Show Server, which runs on a Windows 2000 server (and in the future presumably on a Windows

XP server) and lets you show presentation broadcasts to much larger groups of people.

For more information about online meetings and presentation broadcasts, refer to the *PowerPoint User's Guide* or PowerPoint's online help.

Bulleted Lists

PowerPoint slides typically show words or phrases in bulleted lists (see Figure B-1).

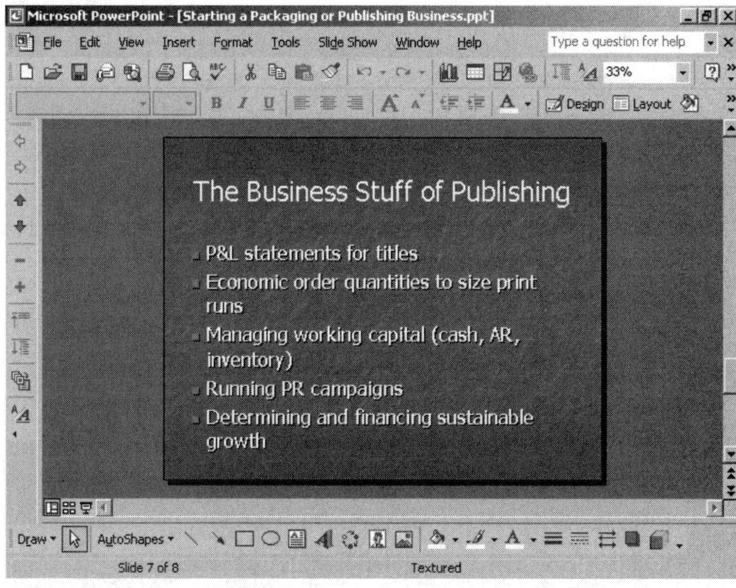

Figure B-1 A PowerPoint slide with a bulleted list.

To specify what these bulleted lists should look like, choose the Format→Bullets And Numbering command, and then click the Bulleted tab. When PowerPoint displays the Bulleted tab of the Bullets And Numbering dialog box, click the box that shows the bullets you want (see Figure B-2).

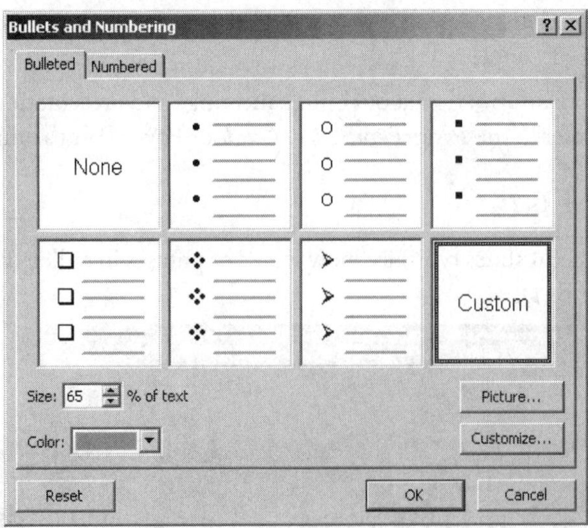

Figure B-2 The Bulleted tab of the Bullets and Numbering dialog box.

You can change the bullet symbol by clicking the Bulleted tab's Customize button. When PowerPoint displays the Symbol dialog box, use the Font box to select the font set with the symbol you want to use as the bullet (see Figure B-3). Then, select the symbol by clicking.

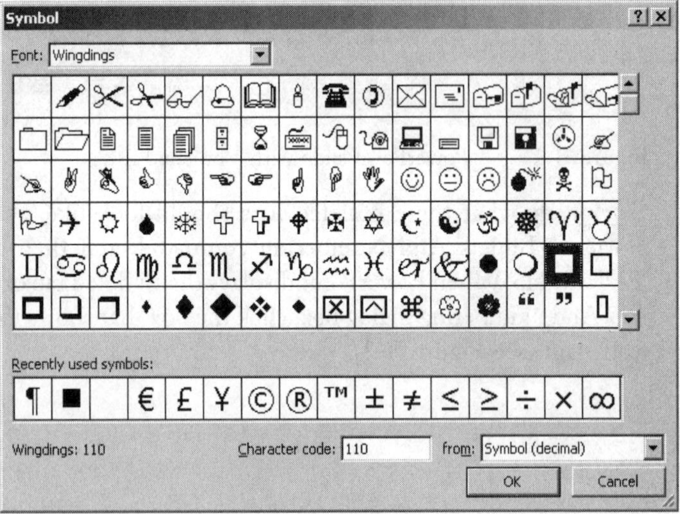

Figure B-3 The Symbol dialog box.

TIP *The Wingdings and Dingbats font sets provide the richest sets of symbols.*

You can use a picture for the bullet symbol by clicking the Picture button. When PowerPoint displays the Picture Bullet dialog box, click the picture bullet you want (see Figure B-4).

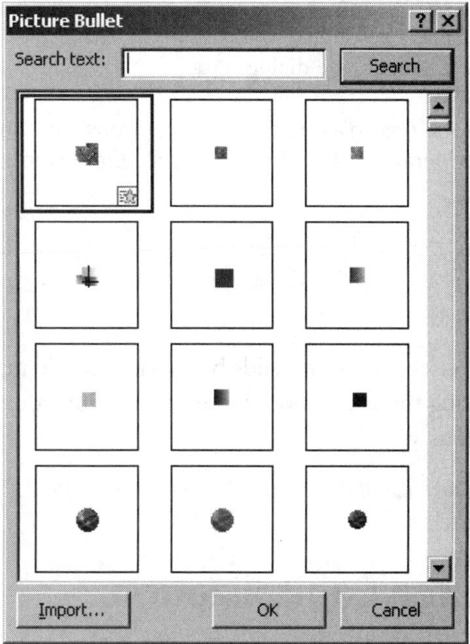

Figure B-4 The Picture Bullet dialog box.

Capitalization

The Format→Change Case command lets you change the capitalization or case used for the text in the selected text placeholder. You can also use the Change Case command to change the case of just the text that is selected. When you choose the Change Case command, PowerPoint displays the Change Case dialog box (see Figure C-1). All you do is mark the Option button that corresponds to the capitalization or case rule you want to use.

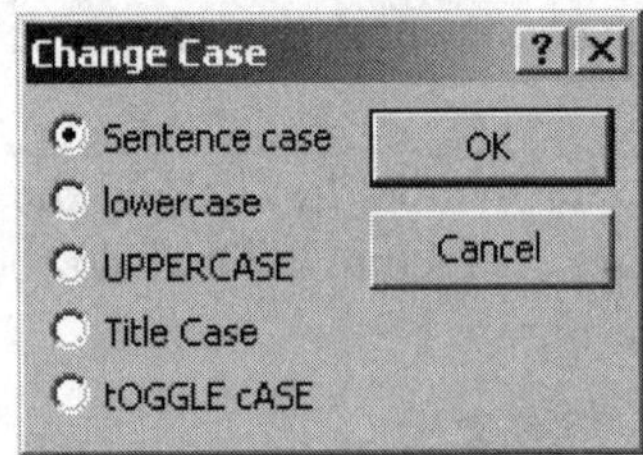

Figure C-1 The Change Case dialog box.

NOTE *The Change Case dialog box's option buttons are labeled using words or phrases that show the case for the option.*

CDs see Music

Centered Text

You can center the selected text in a slide by clicking the Center toolbar button or by pressing the Ctrl+E key combination. Press the Ctrl and E keys simultaneously.

NOTE *You can also use the Format→Alignment→Center command to center and align text.*

Changing Case see Capitalization

Character Formatting

You can change the formatting of a character by selecting the character and then choosing the Format→Font command. PowerPoint displays the Font dialog box (see Figure C-2). Use the Font dialog box to choose a font, font style and point size, font color and any special effects such as underlining or shadowing.

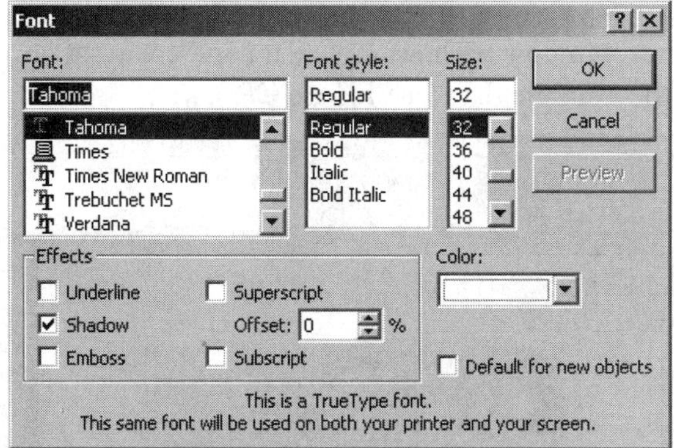

Figure C-2 The Font dialog box.

SEE ALSO *Animating Text, Character Spacing, Fonts*

Charts

Microsoft Office programs like Word and PowerPoint come with a separate, small program called Microsoft Graph that you can use to create charts which can then be used in your documents. The advantages of Graph are that it's very simple and that once you learn to use it, you can use its charts anywhere. The disadvantage of Graph is that it's not a very powerful or flexible charting tool.

Using Excel's ChartWizard

If you already use Excel's ChartWizard, you'll find the ChartWizard the easiest way to create charts for PowerPoint presentations. First, create the Excel chart. Then, select the chart, choose the Edit→Copy command, open your PowerPoint presentation, position the insertion point at the location where you want the chart, and choose the Edit→Paste command. PowerPoint, with the help of Windows, pastes the Excel chart object into your PowerPoint presentation.

Using Microsoft Graph

To create charts for PowerPoint presentation using Graph, follow these steps:

1. Choose the Insert→Chart command. PowerPoint opens the Graph data sheet window with example data and creates a chart object using the example data (see Figure C-3).

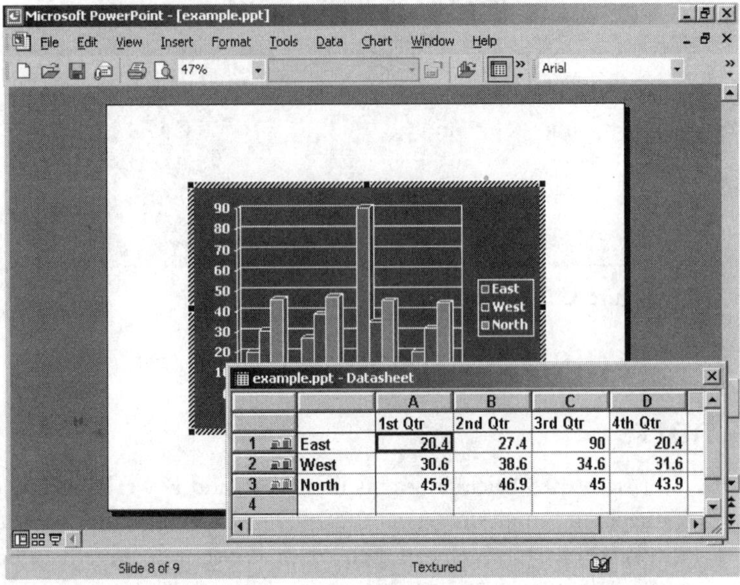

Figure C-3 The Graph datasheet window and chart object.

2. Replace the example data shown in the datasheet with the data you want to plot in a chart. To replace the contents of a datasheet cell, click the cell and then type the replacement text or value. Be sure to replace both the actual values, which you'll plot in the chart, and the text labels, which Graph will use to label your data series and your data categories (see Figure C-4).

example.ppt - Datasheet

		A	B	C	D
		Year 1	Year 2	Year 3	Year 4
1	Revenues	100	200	150	225
2	Expenses	90	150	120	175
3	Profits	10	50	30	50
4					

Figure C-4 The datasheet window after entering new data values and text labels that identify the data series and data categories.

TIP *In order to use Graph comfortably, you should understand three key charting terms: data values, data series, and data categories. Data values are the values you plot in a chart—the numbers that appear in the datasheet window. Data series group the data values into sets—for example, sets of revenue data values, expense data values, and profit data values, as shown in Figure C-4. Data categories order, or organize, the data values within a data series—for example, if a chart shows how some data series' data values change over the years, years are the data category, as shown in Figure C-4. The datasheet window includes text labels that name the data series and the data categories.*

3. Close the datasheet by clicking its Close box. (To later reopen the chart object, right-click the chart object and choose the Datasheet command from the shortcut menu.)
4. Right-click the new chart object and choose the Chart Type command from the shortcut menu. When Graph displays the Chart Type dialog box, select a chart type and a subtype (see Figure C-5). To see what your chart and subtype look like, click the Press And Hold To View Sample button.

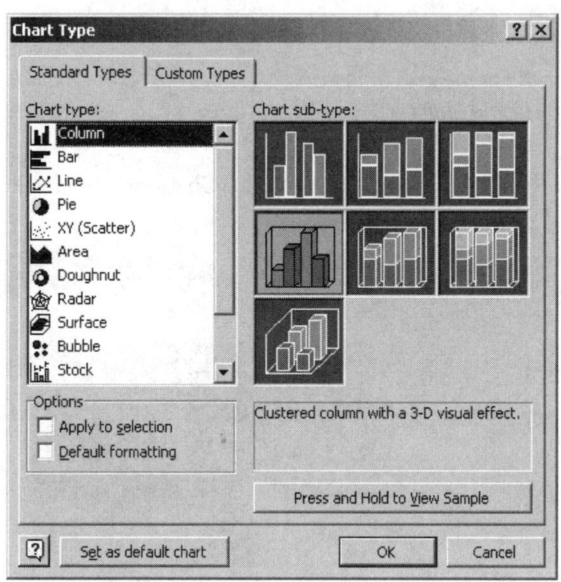

Figure C-5 The Chart Type dialog box.

5. Right-click the new chart object and choose the Chart Options command from the shortcut menu. When Graph displays the Chart Options dialog box, click the Titles tab (see Figure C-6). Use the titles tab to add descriptive text to the chart, the category axis, the value axis and, in the case of three dimension charts, the series axis.

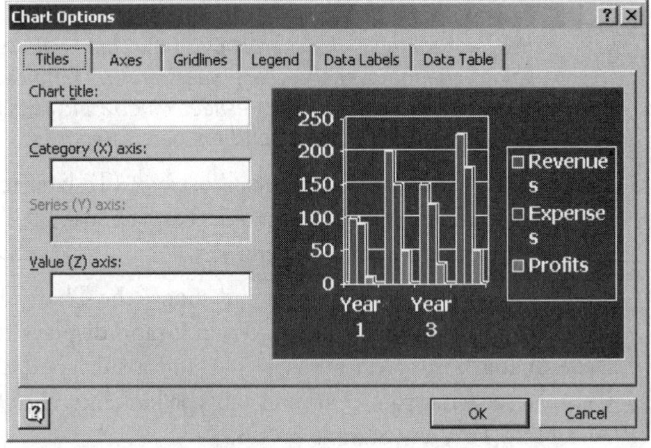

Figure C-6 The Titles tab of the Chart Options dialog box.

TIP *All of the tabs of the Chart Options dialog box include a preview of the chart object. Use this preview to see the effect of your changes.*

6. Click the Axes tab (see Figure C-7). Check and uncheck the boxes to add or remove axes from your chart.

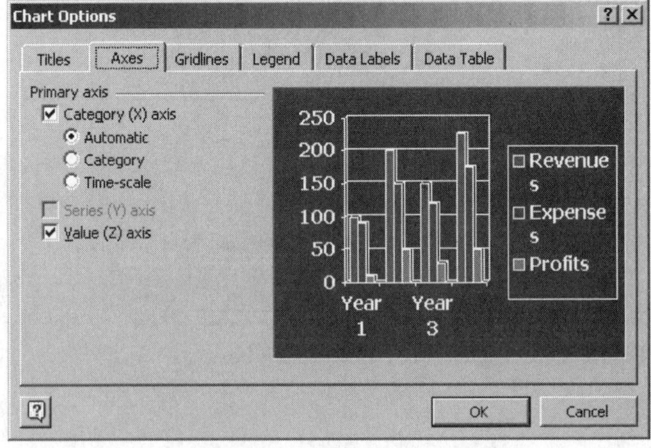

Figure C-7 The Axes tab of the Chart Options dialog box.

7. Click the Gridlines tab (see Figure C-8). Check and uncheck boxes to add and remove gridlines from the chart. The Gridlines tab also provides a 2-D Walls And Gridlines box to turn the chart into a two-dimensional object.

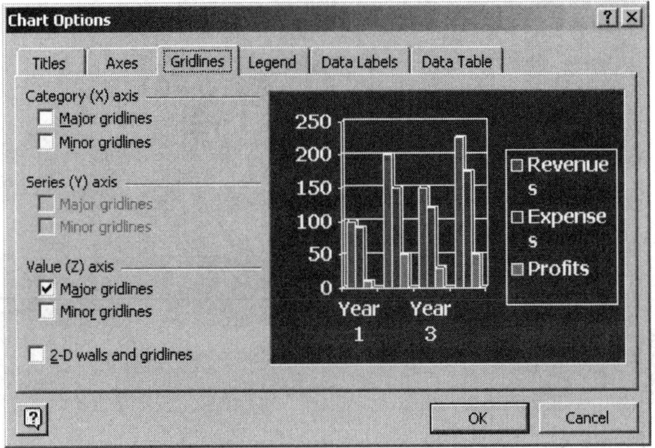

Figure C-8 The Gridlines tab of the Chart Options dialog box.

8. Click the Legend tab (see Figure C-9). Check the Show Legend box to add a legend to your chart object. Use the Placement buttons to position the chart object.

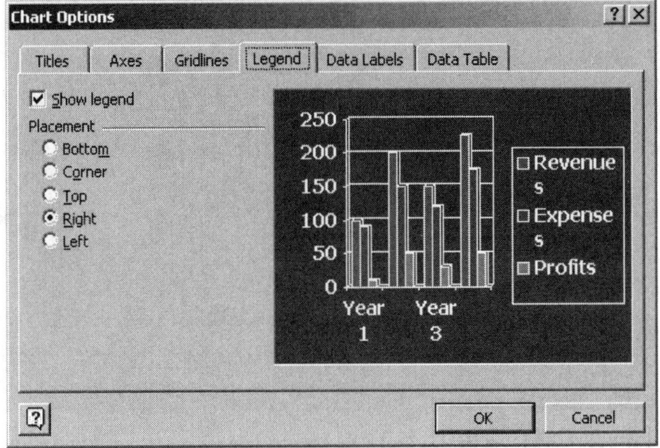

Figure C-9 The Legend tab of the Chart Options dialog box.

9. Click the Data Labels tab (see Figure C-10). Check and uncheck the Label Contains boxes to add descriptive text to the chart that gives the series name, the category name, or the plotted value.

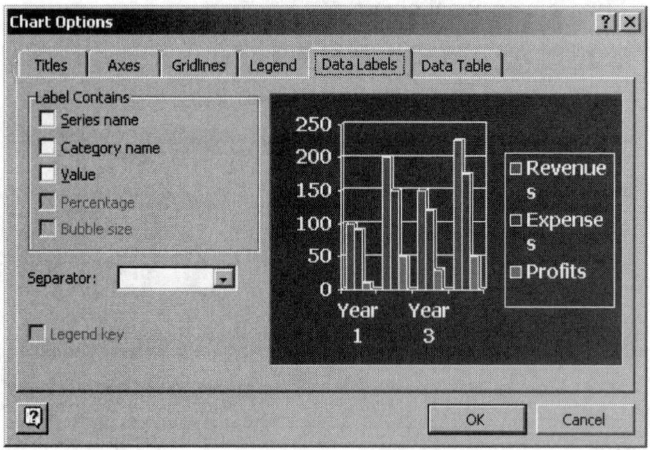

Figure C-10 The Data Labels tab of the Chart Options dialog box.

10. Click the Data Table tab (see Figure C-11). Check the Show Data Table box to add the datasheet to the chart object. Click OK to close the Chart Objects dialog box.

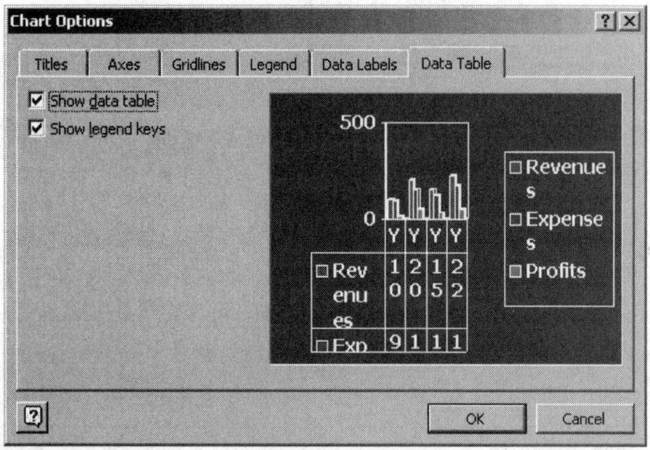

Figure C-11 The Data Table tab of the Chart Options dialog box.

11. (Optional for 3-D Charts) Right-click the chart object and choose the 3-D View command from the shortcut menu. When Graph displays the 3-D View dialog box, use its buttons to rotate the chart

object to better use its three dimensions (see Figure C-12). Click OK to close the 3-D View dialog box.

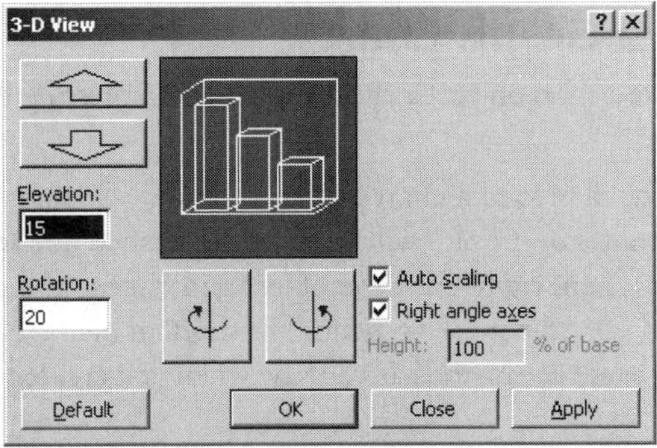

Figure C-12 The 3-D View dialog box.

12. To customize some element of the chart, right-click the chart part and choose the Format command from the shortcut menu. The exact name of the Format command will depend on which chart part you click. When Graph displays the Format dialog box, experiment with its tabs to change the appearance of the chart part (see Figure C-13).

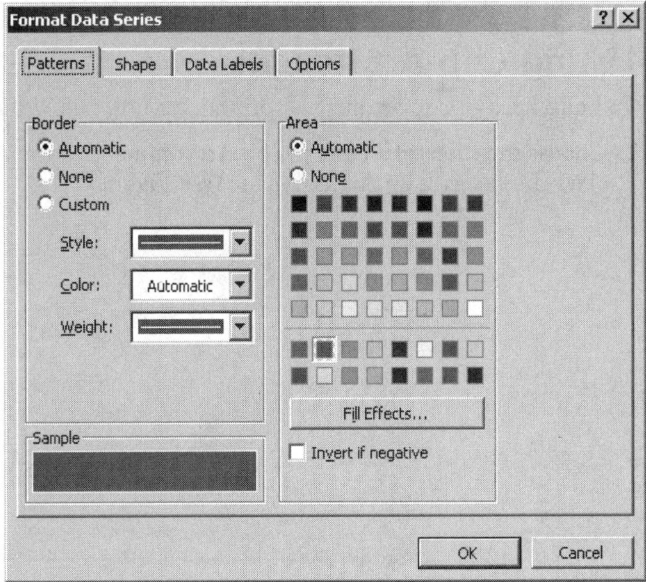

Figure C-13 The Format Data Series dialog box.

13. Close the chart object by clicking somewhere on the PowerPoint slide other than on the chart object.

Editing a Graph Chart

You can delete a chart object by clicking it and then pressing the Delete key.

You can make change to a chart object by double-clicking the chart object to open it. PowerPoint will draw a thick dashed line around the chart object. Then, right-click the object and choose the appropriate command from the shortcut menu. The shortcut menu that appears provides the same commands as you saw when you created the chart object.

SEE ALSO *Copying Objects*

Clip Art

You can add simple drawings and images, called clip art, to your PowerPoint presentation. PowerPoint supplies a rich set of clip art images through its clip art organizer. This organizer includes images that come with the Office suite of programs and images that you've collected in other ways, such as downloading them from the Internet.

Listing Clip Art Images

To build a list of clip art images you want to use, follow these steps:

1. Choose the Insert→Picture→Clip Art command. PowerPoint displays the Insert Clip Art task pane (see Figure C-14).

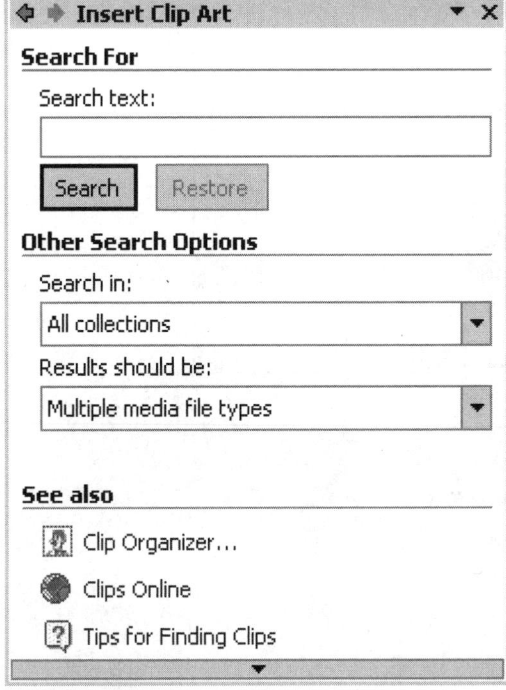

Figure C-14 The Insert Clip Art task pane.

2. Enter as much of the image's file name and extension as you know into the Search Text box. Use the ? wildcard in place of any characters you don't know and the * wildcard in place of any character sets you don't know.
3. Use the Search In box to specify where PowerPoint should look for clip art.
4. Use the Results Should Be box to restrict the search to only specified types of clip art.
5. Click the Search button to begin the search. When PowerPoint finishes, it displays a list of thumbnail images that match your search criteria (see Figure C-15).

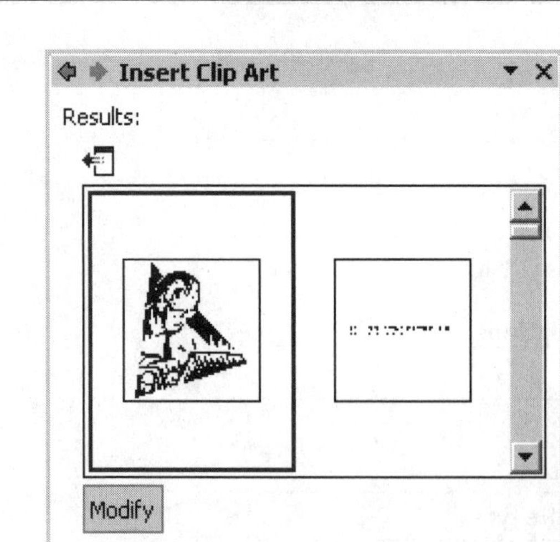

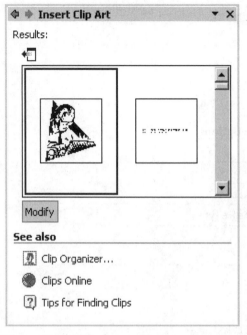

Figure C-15 The Insert Clip Art task pane showing thumbnail images.

Inserting a Clip Art Image

Once you build a list of the clip art images, you can easily insert an image. First, click in the PowerPoint presentation at the point where you want to insert the image. Then, click the image you want to insert. PowerPoint inserts the selected image at the location of the insertion point (see Figure C-16).

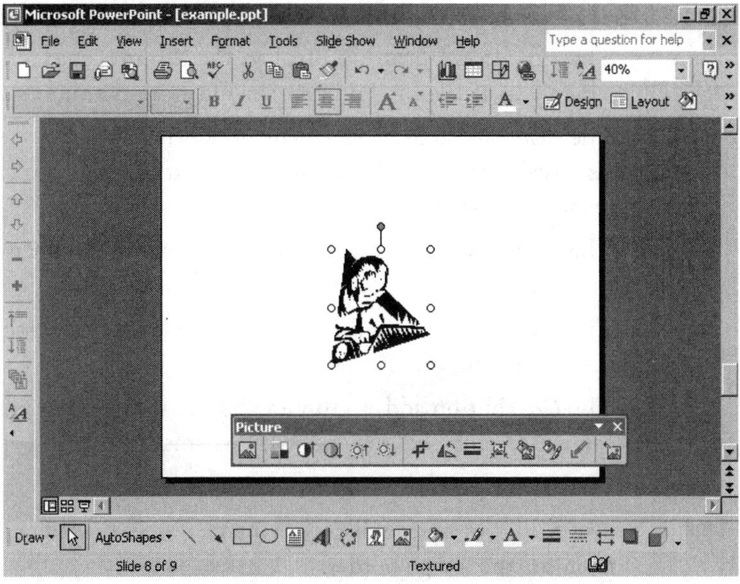

Figure C-16 A slide with a clip art image.

Editing a Clip Art Image

When you select a clip art image, PowerPoint adds the Picture toolbar to the window (see Figure C-17).

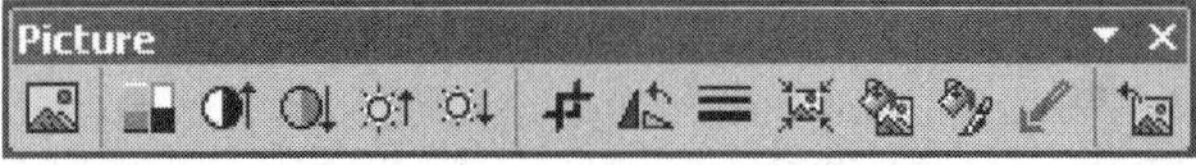

Figure C-17 The Picture toolbar.

You can use the Picture toolbar's buttons to make changes to the image:

- The *Insert Picture* button displays the Insert Picture dialog box, which you can use to add another image to the slide.
- The *Color* button displays a menu of coloring options—Automatic, Grayscale, Black & White, and Washout—which you can use to recolor the image.
- The *More Contrast* and *Less Contrast* buttons adjust the contrast of the image.
- The *More Brightness* and *Less Brightness* buttons adjust the brightness of the image.
- The *Crop* button adds a cropping border to the image, which you can use to crop the image down to a smaller size.
- The *Rotate Left* button turns the image 90 degrees to the left.
- The *Line Style* button displays a menu of lines that you can choose from for the image border.
- The *Compress Picture* button displays a dialog box that you can use to tell PowerPoint it should compress the images used in a presentation, delete cropped portions of images, reduce the image resolution, and use similar tricks.
- The *Recolor Picture* button lets you change the colors used in an image.
- The *Format Picture* button displays the Format Picture dialog box, which you can use to make changes to the picture's colors, size, position and so on.
- The *Set Transparent Color* button lets you remove a color from a picture, thereby making the picture transparent.
- The *Reset Picture* button undoes changes you've made using the Picture toolbar's buttons.

Using the Clip Organizer

The Clip Organizer works like a tailored version of the My Computer window or Windows Explorer tool just for working with clip art (see Figure C-18).

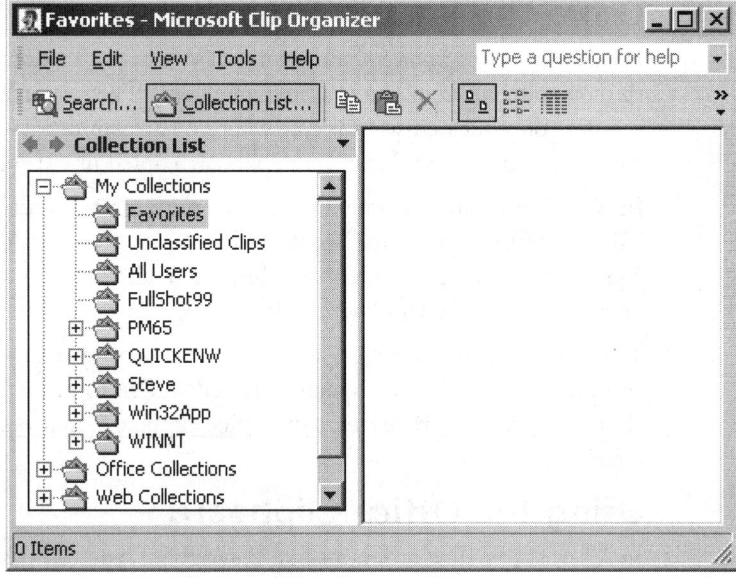

Figure C-18 The Clip Organizer window.

The Clip Organizer window organizes your images into three categories: My Collections, Office Collections, and Web Collections. To see the subcategories in any of these major categories, double-click the category folder icon. To see the images in a subcategory, double-click the subcategory folder icon. Clip Organizer displays a list of thumbnail images. You can right-click a thumbnail image to display a shortcut menu of commands useful for copying, moving and deleting clip art images.

NOTE *The Clip Organizer toolbar provides many of the same tools as the Windows Explorer or My Computer toolbar.*

Clipboard

When you're working with Microsoft Office applications like PowerPoint, the clipboard can actual refer to two different items: the system clipboard and the office clipboard. Both clipboards are temporary storage areas filled with items you cut and copy. However, the two clipboards work differently.

Using the System Clipboard

Whenever you copy or cut something in Windows, Windows stores the copied or cut item on the system clipboard. The system clipboard can store only one item as a time, so when you do copy or cut, the newly copied or cut item replaces the previously copied or cut item.

In Windows and in some Windows programs (although not in Microsoft Office programs like PowerPoint), when you paste an item, you actually copy the contents of the system clipboard to the active document or active window.

The system clipboard gets erased in two ways: when you turn off your computer and when you specifically tell Office to clear the office clipboard. When Office clears the office clipboard, it also clears the system clipboard.

Using the Office Clipboard

In Microsoft Office programs like PowerPoint, you can paste either from the system clipboard or the Office clipboard. Unlike the system clipboard, the Office clipboard can store up to twenty-four items. When you copy the twenty-fifth item, Office discards the first, or oldest, item.

To paste from the Office clipboard, first choose the Edit→Office Clipboard command so that the task pane lists the contents of the Office clipboard (see Figure C-19). Then, right-click the item you want and chose the Paste command from the shortcut menu.

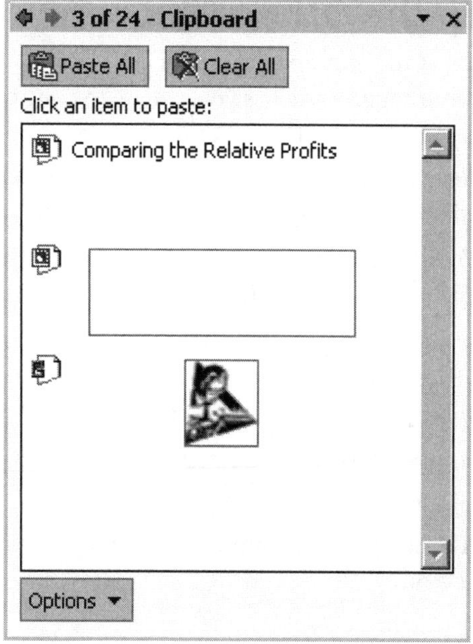

Figure C-19 The Clipboard task pane.

NOTE *To paste from the system clipboard, you choose the Edit→Paste command, click the Paste toolbar button, or use the Ctrl+V shortcut.*

The Office clipboard lets you copy items between Office documents and programs. For example, you can use the Office clipboard to copy an Excel chart to a PowerPoint presentation.

The Office clipboard gets erased when you close the last Office program. You can also erase the Office clipboard by clicking the Clear All button in the Clipboard task pane. (This also clears the system clipboard.) You can erase individual items in the Office clipboard by right-clicking the item and choosing the Delete command.

Customizing the Office Clipboard

The Options button at the bottom of the Clipboard task pane displays a pop-up menu of four toggle switches you can use to control how the Office clipboard appears in the PowerPoint program window:

- The *Show Office Clipboard Automatically* toggle switch tells PowerPoint to display the Clipboard task pane when copying.
- The *Collect Without Showing Office Clipboard* switch tells PowerPoint to collect copied items on the Office clipboard.
- The *Show Office Clipboard Icon On Taskbar* switch tells PowerPoint to display an Office Clipboard icon on the Taskbar. You can click this icon to display the Clipboard task pane.
- The *Show Status Near Taskbar* switch tells PowerPoint to display a message when copying to the Office clipboard.

PowerPoint puts a check mark in front of the menu command when the switch is turned on.

SEE ALSO *Copying Formatting, Copying Objects, Copying Tables, Copying Text*

Closing Presentations

To close a presentation, choose the File→Close command. Alternatively, click the presentation window's Close box.

NOTE *The document window's Close box is in the upper right corner of the program window just beneath the program window's Close box. The program window's Close box is in the corner of the program window. Close boxes are marked with an "X."*

To close all the open presentations, hold down the Shift key and choose the File→Close All command.

Closing Programs

To close, or exit, a program like PowerPoint, choose the File→Exit command. Alternatively, click the program window's Close box.

NOTE *The program window's Close box is in the upper right corner of the program window and is marked with an "X."*

Coloring

You can add color or change the color of most parts of a PowerPoint slide.

Coloring Text

To color text, select the text. Then click the Font Color toolbar button's arrow to display a pop-up menu of colors. Click the color you want for the selected text.

Alternatively, you can choose the Format→Font command to display the Font dialog box and then use the Color list box to select a color (see Figure C-20).

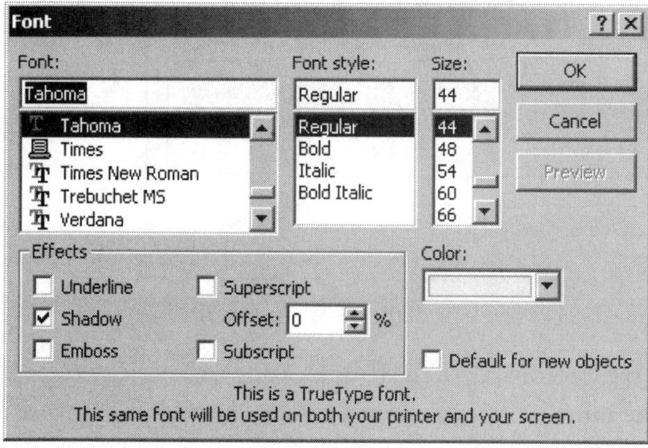

Figure C-20 The Font dialog box.

Both the Font Color button's pop-up menu and the Font dialog box's Color list box provide a More Colors option. If you select this option, PowerPoint displays the Colors dialog box. Use the Standard tab of the Colors dialog box to pick a color by clicking a color hexagon (see Figure C-21).

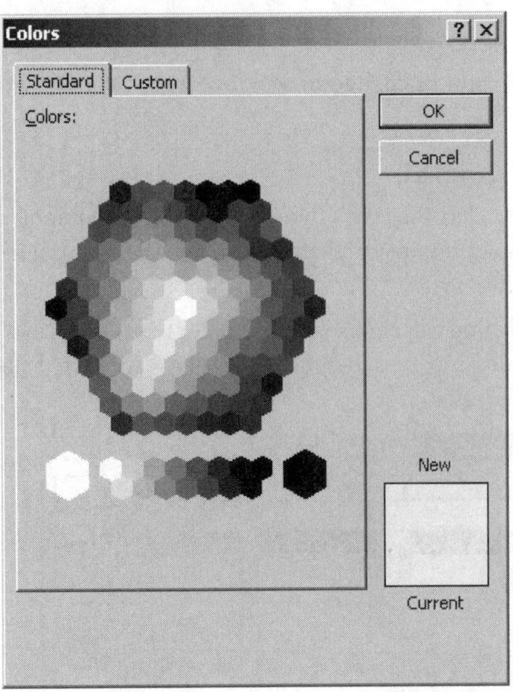

Figure C-21 The Standard tab of the Colors dialog box.

Use the Custom tab of the Colors dialog box to pick a color by clicking in the rainbow or by mixing a color as parts of red, green, or blue in an RGB color model or by mixing quantities of hue, saturation, and luminance in an HSL color model (see Figure C-22).

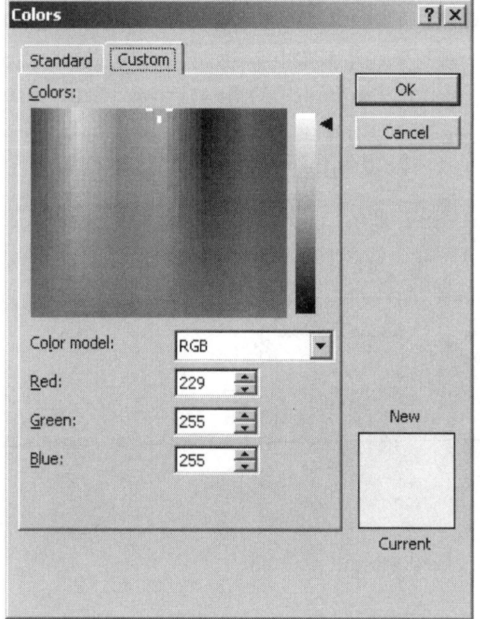

Figure C-22 The Custom tab of the Colors dialog box.

TIP *When you choose a color using the More Colors option, you may end up choosing a color that's not compatible (aesthetically) with the other colors in your presentation.*

NOTE *The advantage of using the Standard tab instead of the pop-up menu of colors or the font color list box's list of colors is that the Standard tab shows you both the current and new color.*

Coloring the Slide Background

To change the background color used for slides, choose the Format→Background command. When PowerPoint displays the Background dialog box (see Figure C-23), choose the background color you want from the drop-down list box.

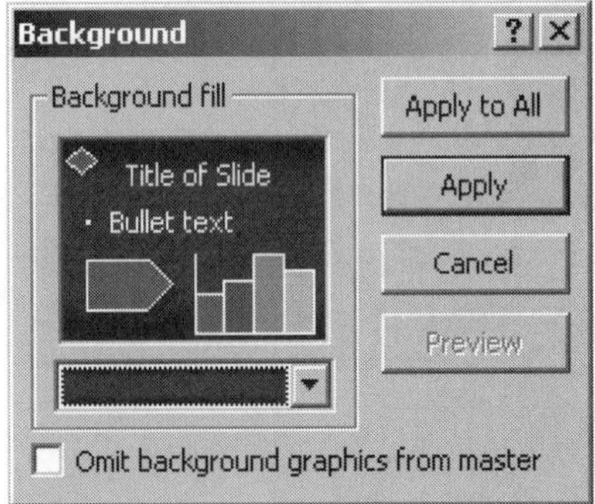

Figure C-23 The Background dialog box.

Coloring an Object

To color an object or some part of an object, right-click the object so that PowerPoint displays the shortcut menu. Choose the Format command so that PowerPoint displays the Format dialog box—the exact name of the command and dialog box will depend on the object you select—click the Colors And Lines tab (see Figure C-24). Then, use the Fill Color and Line Color boxes to pick the color you want.

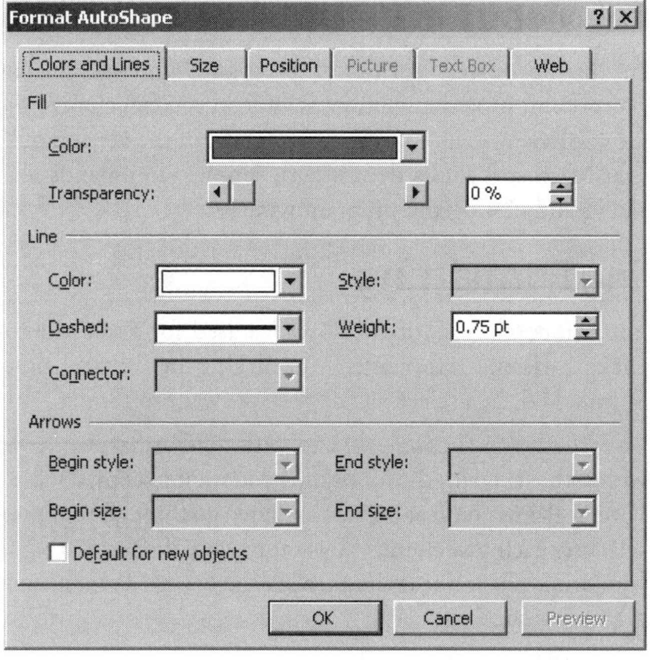

Figure C-24 The Colors And Lines tab of the Format AutoShape dialog box.

Comments see Speakers Notes

Computer Viruses

PowerPoint presentations can contain computer viruses because presentation documents can contain macros. All someone has to do is write a mischievous or destructive macro and then get you to open the presentation and run the program. For this reason, you'll want to be careful about opening strange presentation files. One way you can be careful is by disabling any macros in strange presentations you open. PowerPoint, fortunately, will ask if you want to do this when you open a presentation.

SEE ALSO *Macro Security*

Control Menu

In the upper left corner of program windows, including the PowerPoint program window, is an icon you can click to display the Control menu. The control menu, a relic of the version of Windows that Microsoft sold a decade ago, supplies commands for moving, sizing and closing the program window.

Copying Formatting

You can copy the formatting you've used for a selection of text by clicking within the formatted text, clicking the Format Painter toolbar button, and then selecting the text you want to format.

To format several chunks of text with the Format Painter tool, click within the text with the formatting you want to copy, double-click the Format Painter toolbar button, and then go through your presentation selecting each text chunk you want to copy the formatting to. When you format the last text chunk, click the Format Painter again to turn off format copying.

Copying Tables

To copy a table, first select the table and by right-clicking the table and then choosing the Select Table command. Then, click the Copy toolbar button. Finally, position the insert point at the location where the table should be copied and click the Paste toolbar button.

SEE ALSO *Tables*

Copying Text and Objects

PowerPoint provides several ways to copy text and other slide objects: To copy text or an object and the formatting, use any of the following methods:

- **Drag-and-drop.** Select text or object you want to copy by dragging the mouse. Then while holding down the Ctrl key, drag the selected text or object to a new location.
- **Edit→Copy and Edit→Paste commands.** Select the text or object, choose the Edit→Copy command, position the insertion point at the new location, and choose the Edit→Paste command.

- **Copy and Paste toolbar buttons.** Select the text or object, click the Copy button, position the insertion point at the new location, and choose the Paste toolbar button.
- **Office Clipboard task pane.** Select the text or object, click the Copy button or choose the Edit→Copy command, position the insertion point at the new location, and click the text or object you want to copy in the Clipboard task pane. If the Office Clipboard doesn't show, choose the Edit→Office Clipboard command.

NOTE *You aren't limited to copying text and objects just within a presentation. You can copy items between PowerPoint presentations and between different programs' documents—such as from your word processor program to PowerPoint. The only trick is that after you copy the item, you need to open the document into which you want to paste the item.*

If you don't want to copy the formatting, choose the Edit→Paste Special command in place of the Paste toolbar button or the Edit→Paste command. When PowerPoint displays the Paste Special dialog box, choose the Unformatted Text entry from the As list box (see Figure C-25).

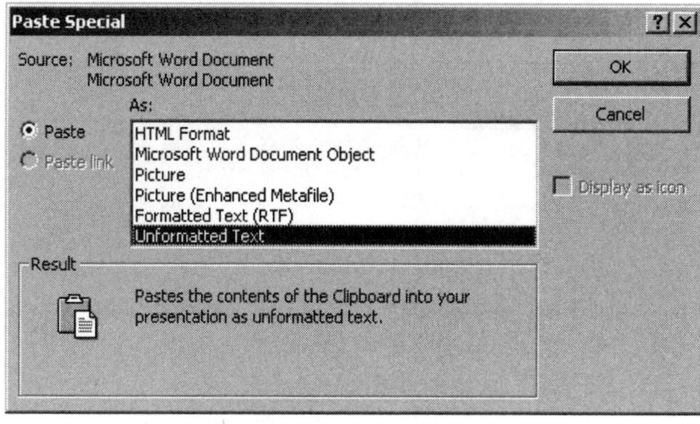

Figure C-25 The Paste Special dialog box.

SEE ALSO *Clipboard, Moving Text and Objects*

Custom Slide Show

A custom slide show is just a list, or subset, of slides you want to display as a separate, customized presentation.

Creating a Custom Slide Show

To create a custom slide show, choose the Slide Show→Custom Shows command. PowerPoint displays the Custom Shows dialog box (see Figure C-26).

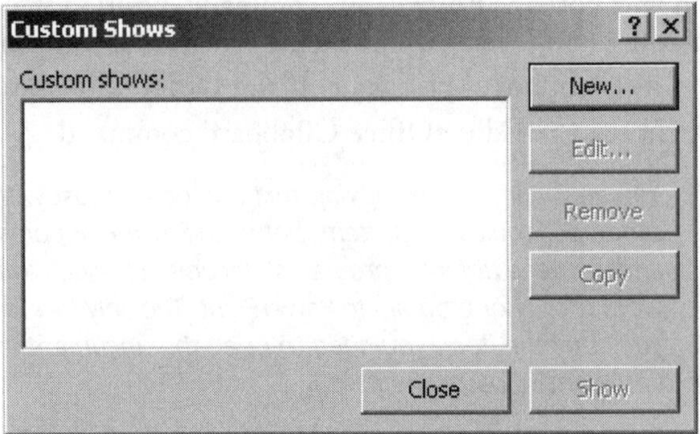

Figure C-26 The Custom Shows dialog box.

When PowerPoint displays the Custom Shows dialog box, click the New button. PowerPoint then displays the Define Custom Show dialog box (see Figure C-27). This dialog box lists the slides that make up your presentation using the Slides In Presentation box.

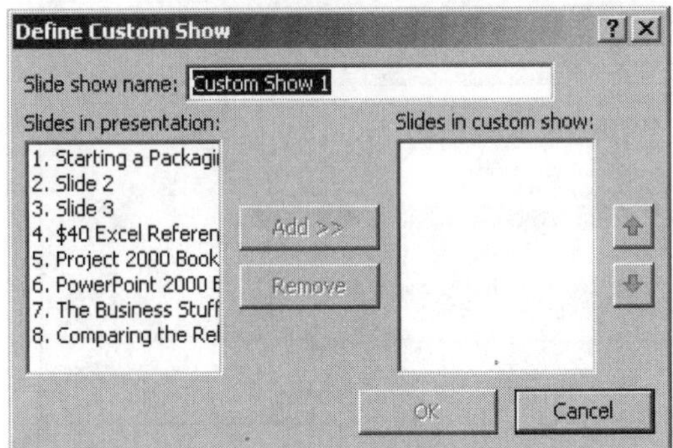

Figure C-27 The Define Custom Show dialog box.

To create a custom presentation or a custom show using some subset of these slides, click the first slide you want to add to the custom show, and then click the Add button. PowerPoint adds the slide to the Slides In Custom Show list box. This shows you that the slide you just added is the first one in your custom show. To add slides, click them and then click the Add button. Add slides to the custom show in the same order you want them to appear. After you've defined or identified all the slides you want to appear, click OK.

NOTE *You can move a slide shown in the Slides In Custom Show list box to a new position. To do this, click the slide to select it. Then click either the up-arrow or down-arrow button to the right of the Slides In Custom Show list box. When you do, PowerPoint moves the slide either up or down in the list.*

Showing a Custom Slide Show

To show a custom slide show, choose the Slide Show→Custom Shows command. When PowerPoint displays the Custom Shows dialog box, click the custom slide show you want and then the Show button (see Figure C-28).

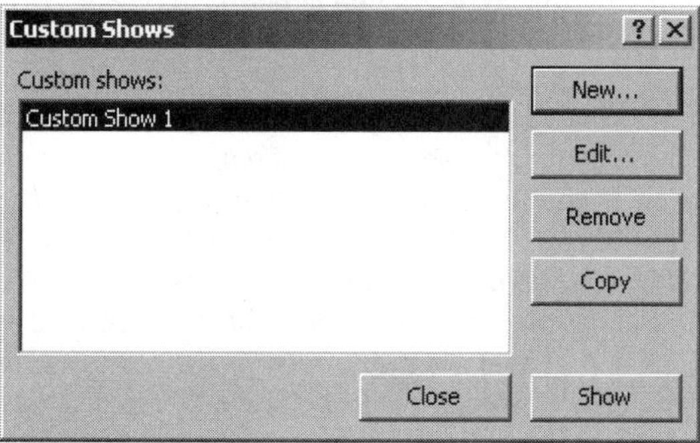

Figure C-28 The Custom Shows dialog box.

Cutting

You use the Cut toolbar button and the Edit→Cut command to move text, tables, and objects within and between documents.

SEE ALSO *Clipboard, Moving Text and Objects*

Datasheets

Microsoft Graph, which you can use to create charts for your PowerPoint presentations, stores the to-be-plotted values in datasheets (see Figure D-1). To enter a value into the datasheet, click a cell and type the value. To describe the data series being plotted, click the text labels in the first, unlabeled column and replace the default series labels

(East, West and North) with your series names. The series names are used on the chart legend.

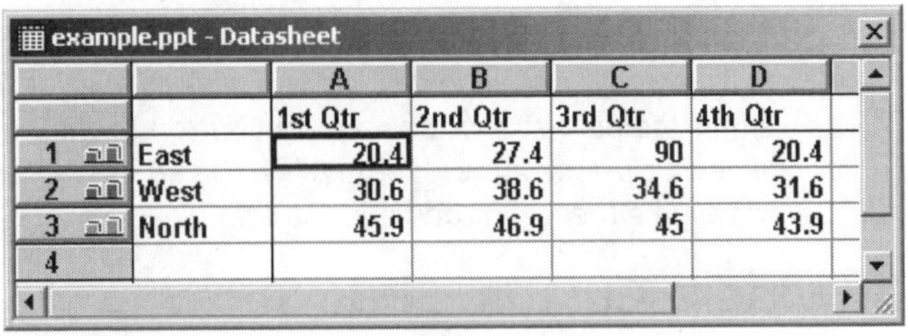

		A	B	C	D
		1st Qtr	2nd Qtr	3rd Qtr	4th Qtr
1	East	20.4	27.4	90	20.4
2	West	30.6	38.6	34.6	31.6
3	North	45.9	46.9	45	43.9
4					

Figure D-1 A Graph datasheet.

To provide data category names, click on the first, unlabeled row and replace the default category labels (1st Qtr, 2nd Qtr, 3rd Qtr, and 4th Qtr) with your category names. The category names label the chart axis.

TIP *Differentiating between a data series and a data category can be confusing. But you can often use a simple test to identify the data series. If you ask yourself the question, "What does a chart show?" Every one-word answer identifies a data series. On most real charts, the question and its answers are easy. A chart that shows sales over last decade, for example, uses sales as the data series. (What does the chart show? Sales.) One other quick identifier is this. In any chart that shows how something changes over time, time is the data category.*

SEE ALSO *Charts*

Dates

To add a date field code to a slide or slide handout, choose the Insert→Date And Time command. When PowerPoint displays the Header And Footer dialog box, click the tab—either Slide or Notes And Handouts—that corresponds to what you want to add a date or time to (see Figure D-2). Then, check the Date And Time box, select either the Update Automatically button (if you want to have the date or time updated using your computer's system clock) or the Fixed button (if you want to enter the date manually). If you do choose the Update Automatically option, select the date format you want from the list box, your language from the Language list box, and the calendar from the Calendar Type box.

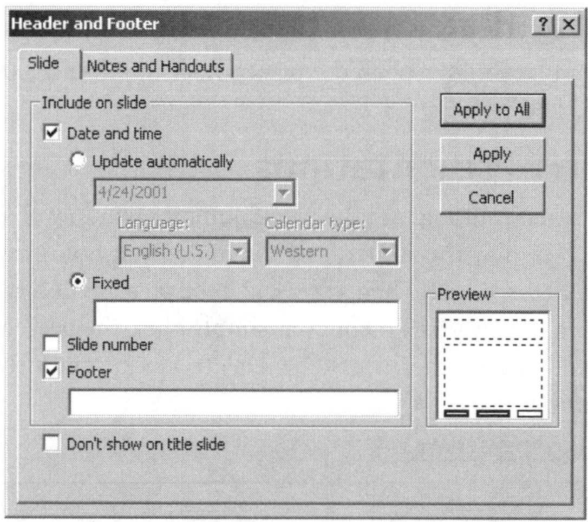

Figure D-2 The Slide tab of the Header And Footer dialog box.

SEE ALSO *Headers and Footers*

Delete Key

The Delete key erases the character or object that's just in front of the insertion point. In comparison, the Backspace key erases the character or object that's just in back of the insertion point.

Deleting

You can delete anything in a PowerPoint presentation and PowerPoint presentations themselves. In general, you delete everything in the same way: You click the item you want to delete and then press the Delete key. If you need more instruction than that, refer to the more detailed instructions that follow.

NOTE *PowerPoint supplies a command equivalent Delete key, the Edit→Clear command.*

Deleting Objects

To delete an object like a chart, picture or piece of WordArt, click the object to select it and then press the Delete key.

Deleting Placeholders

To delete a placeholder, click the placeholder to select it. Then press the Delete key.

Deleting Presentations

To delete a presentation, use the My Computer window or Windows Explorer to display the contents of the folder that holds the presentation (see Figure D-3). Then, right-click the presentation and choose Delete from the shortcut menu. Or, simply click the presentation to select it and then either press the Delete key or click the Delete toolbar button.

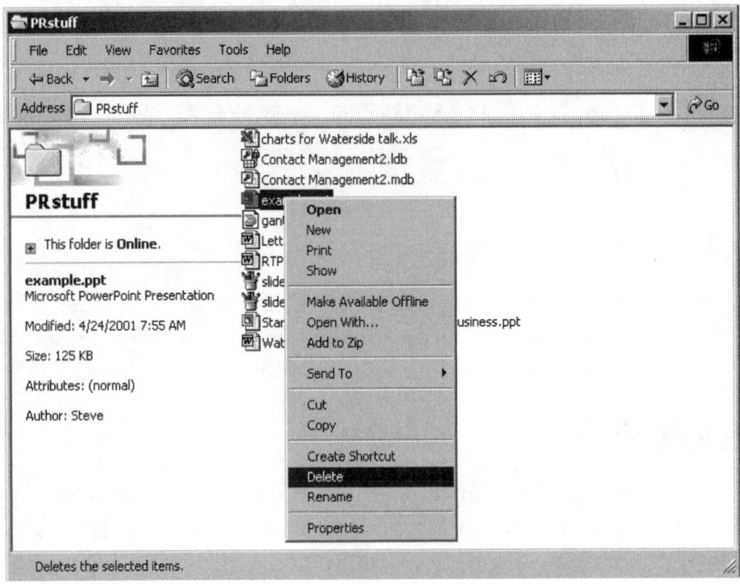

Figure D-3 The My Computer window.

NOTE *Both the My Computer window and Windows Explorer use an "X" to mark the Delete toolbar button on their toolbars.*

Deleting Speakers Notes

To delete speaker notes, select the notes in the notes pane and then press Delete.

Deleting Tables and Table Rows

To delete a table, click the table to select it and then press Delete.

To delete a row within a table, right-click the row and choose the Delete Rows command from the shortcut menu.

Deleting Columns

PowerPoint doesn't provide a command for deleting columns. If you have Microsoft Word, you may want to copy the table from PowerPoint to Word and use Word's Delete Columns command. (To use Word's Delete Columns command, right-click the column and choose Delete Columns from the shortcut menu.) After deleting the column, you could then move the table back to PowerPoint.

TIP *If you want to delete a table but save its information and you use Microsoft Word, consider moving the table to Word and then converting the table to paragraphs of text using Word's Table→Convert→Table To Text command. You could them move the text back to your PowerPoint presentation.*

Deleting Text

To delete text, select the text using the mouse or the keyboard and then press the Delete key.

Design Templates

A *design template* provides a color scheme that is used for all the presentation's slides: the *title master slide,* which shows how your title slide looks; and a *slide master slide,* which shows how the nontitle slides in your presentation look.

You can choose a design template in two ways. Which way you choose the design template depends on whether you're just starting to create your presentation or have already created the presentation.

Selecting a design template as you start

The most common way to select a design template is to select a design template before you begin creating your presentation. When you start PowerPoint, it displays the New Presentation task pane (see Figure D-4). This New Presentation task pane lets you indicate whether you want to create a new presentation using the AutoContent Wizard, a design template, or a blank presentation. You can also indicate that you are not creating a new presentation and will instead open an existing presentation.

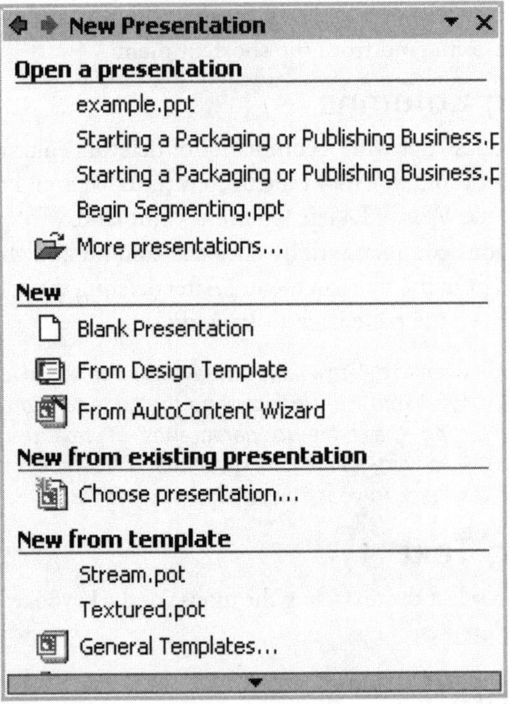

Figure D-4 The New Presentation task pane.

If you do indicate that you want to create a new presentation using a design template, PowerPoint replaces the New Presentation task pane with the Slide Design task pane (see Figure D-5). You can select one of the design templates from the list by clicking it.

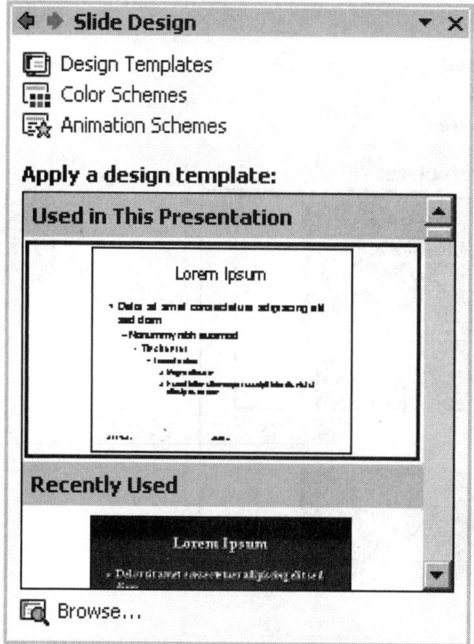

Figure D-5 The PowerPoint window showing the Slide Design task pane.

Selecting a design template after you start

To change the design template for an existing presentation, display the Slide Design – Design Templates task pane (see Figure D-6). Then, right-click the design template you want and choose either the Apply To All Slides command or the Apply To Selected Slides command.

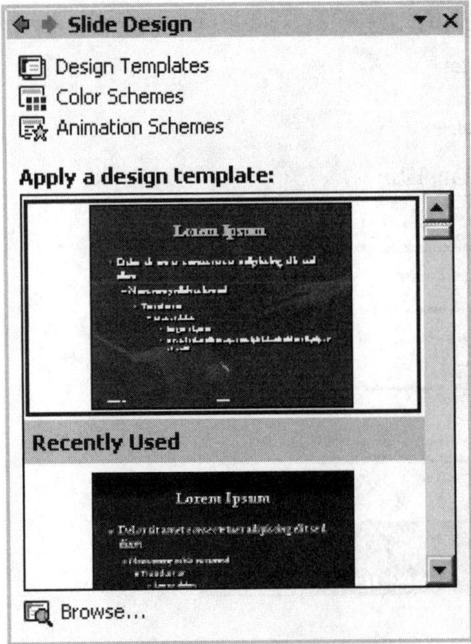

Figure D-6 The Slide Design – Design Templates task pane.

TIP *To display the Slide Design – Design Templates task pane, click the down arrow button at the top of the task pane and choose the Slide Design – Design Templates option.*

NOTE *PowerPoint stores its design templates in a folder named Presentation Designs. The Presentation Designs folder is a subfolder in the Templates folder. The Templates folder is a folder in whatever folder you chose to install Microsoft Office. Presentation design templates, by the way, use the file type specification .pot.*

Creating your own design templates

When you do have a presentation that looks exactly the way you want future presentations to look, you can turn this presentation's formatting and design information into a design template. To do this, choose the File→Save As command. When PowerPoint displays the Save As dialog box, first use the Look In box to select the folder you've used to store the design templates (see Figure D-7). As noted, design templates are typically stored in the Presentation Designs subfolder, a folder in the Templates folder, which is in turn a subfolder in the Microsoft Office folder. Next, use the Save As Type list box to indicate that what you want to save is a design template. You can do this by opening the Files Of Type box and then choosing the Design Template entry. After you provide this information, you can click the Save button.

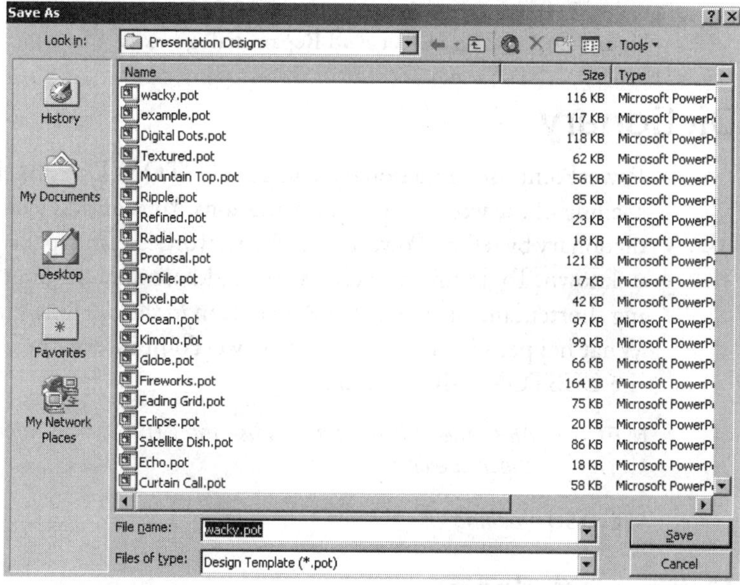

Figure D-7 The Save As dialog box.

After you have created a design template, you can use it in the future by choosing it from the Slide Design – Design Templates task pane.

Detect and Repair

The Help→Detect And Repair command finds and fixes errors in the Office program files. To use this command, first find your Office or PowerPoint installation CD. Then choose the command. PowerPoint displays the Detect And Repair dialog box (see Figure D-8). Use the two check boxes on the Detect And Repair dialog box to specify whether you want your shortcuts to Office restored as part of the repair and whether you want your customized settings saved or want to revert to the default settings. Then click Start.

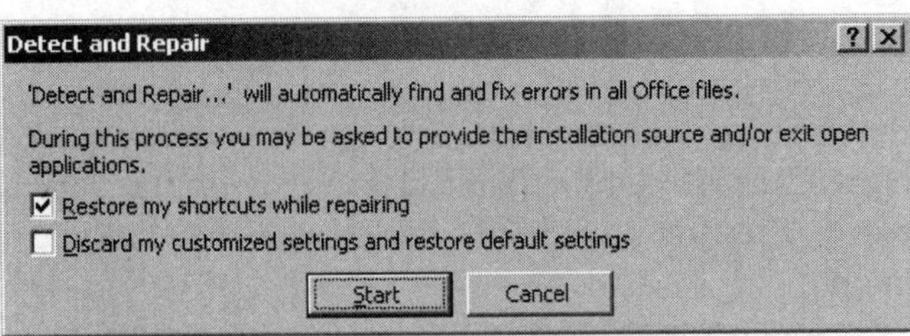

Figure D-8 The Detect And Repair dialog box.

Dictionary

PowerPoint uses a dictionary, named CUSTOM.DIC, to check the spelling of the words in your presentations. You can add words to this dictionary by telling PowerPoint when a word isn't misspelled but just unknown. To do this, you choose the Add command from the spelling shortcut menu or click the Add button in the Spelling dialog box. What happens in this case is that PowerPoint inserts the word into the CUSTOM.DIC dictionary.

NOTE *All of the Office programs use the CUSTOM.DIC dictionary to check spelling.*

SEE ALSO *Spelling*

Drag-and-drop

Drag-and-drop refers to copying or moving items with your mouse. For example, if you select text or an object, you can move the selection by dragging it to a new location. And if you select text or an object and hold down the Ctrl key, you can copy the selection by dragging it to a new location.

SEE ALSO *Copying Text and Objects*

Drawing

PowerPoint includes a drawing tool which you can use to add lines, arrows, shapes and images to your presentations. To begin drawing, display the Drawing toolbar by choosing the View→Toolbars→Drawing command (see Figure D-9).

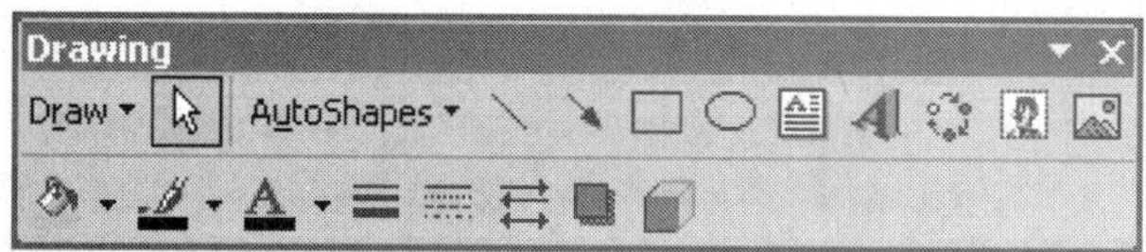

Figure D-9 The Drawing toolbar.

NOTE *The Drawing toolbar can either be free-floating, as shown in Figure D-9, or it can be docked. Typically, the Drawing toolbar is docked and located along the bottom edge of the PowerPoint program window.*

Drawing Lines, Arrows, Rectangles and Ovals

The Drawing toolbar includes buttons for drawing lines, arrows, rectangles (including squares) and ovals (including circles):

- To draw a line or arrow, click the *Line* or *Arrow* button, click at the point where your line or arrow should begin and drag the mouse to the point where the line or arrow should end.
- To draw a rectangle, click the *Rectangle* button, click at the point where the rectangle's top left corner should be and drag the mouse to the point where the rectangle's bottom right corner should be.
- To draw an oval, click the *Oval* button, click at the point where the oval's top left corner should be and drag the mouse to the point where the oval's bottom right corner should be.

TIP *To make your rectangle a square or your oval a circle, hold down the Shift key as you drag the mouse.*

Drawing Text Boxes

A text box is a box into which you can enter text. To add a text box to a document, click the Drawing toolbar's Text Box button, then draw the text box by dragging the mouse. To make your text box square, hold down the Shift key while you drag the mouse. After you draw your text box, type the text you want the box to hold (see Figure D-10).

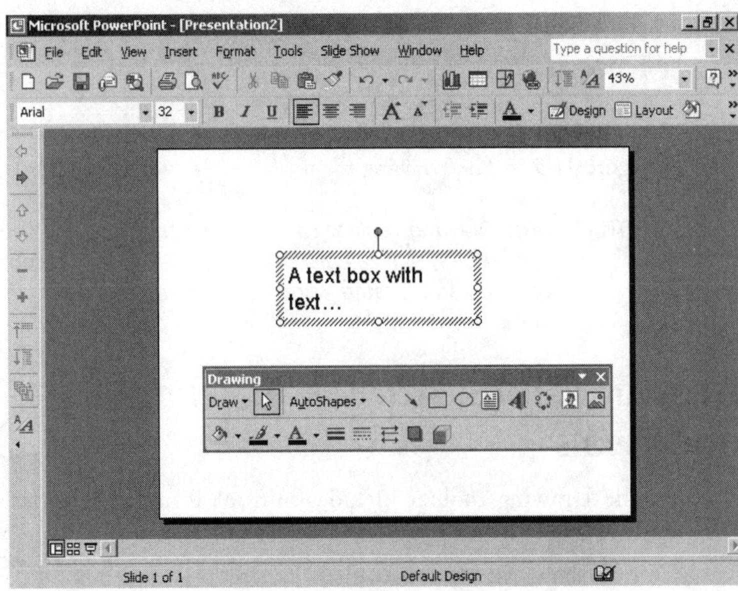

Figure D-10 A text box with text.

NOTE *Text box text doesn't appear in the outline.*

Drawing AutoShapes

The Drawing toolbar includes an AutoShapes tool which lets you draw dozens of common shapes such as hearts, stars, polygons, and flow chart symbols. To draw an autoshape, click the AutoShapes tool and then select one of the AutoShapes menu commands: Lines, Connectors (which are shapes that connect lines), Basic Shapes, Block Arrows, Stars And Banners, Callouts or More Shapes. When PowerPoint displays a list of the autoshapes within the selected category, click the one you want to add (see Figure D-11). Then, drag the mouse to size and position the autoshape (see Figure D-12).

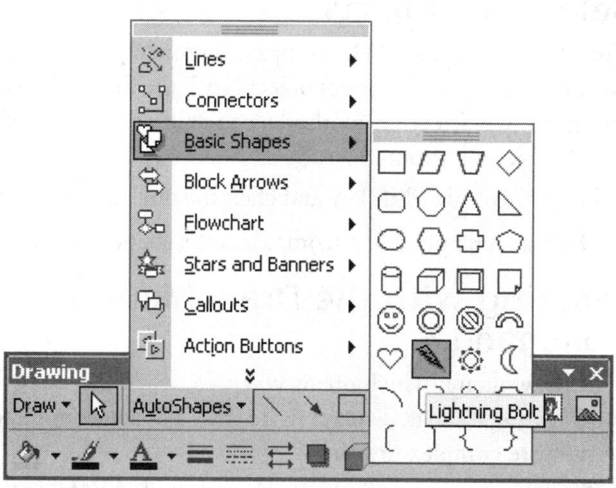

Figure D-11 A menu of autoshapes.

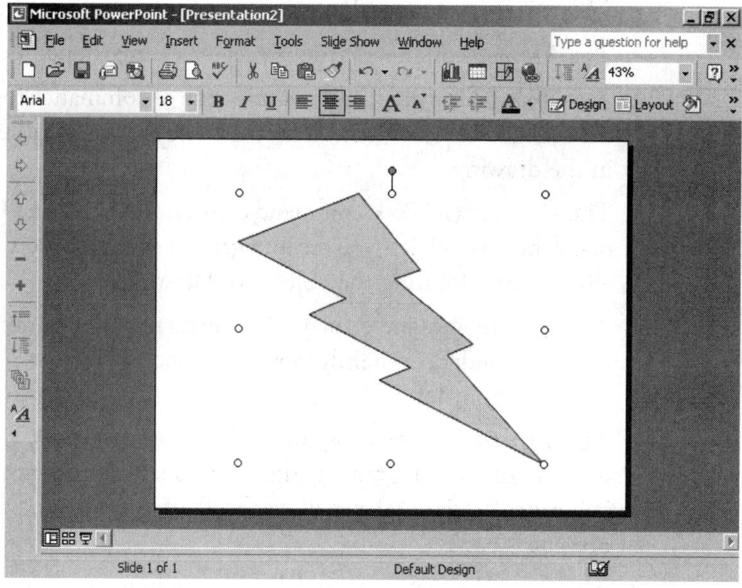

Figure D-12 An autoshape.

Selecting Objects

The Drawing toolbar's Select Objects button lets you select more than one drawing object. To select objects with the Select Objects button, you have two selection methods available once you've clicked the Select Objects button:

- Hold down the Shift key and click the objects you want to select.
- Draw a rectangle that encompasses the shapes you want to select.

Working with the Draw Menu's Commands

The Draw menu, which opens when you click the Draw button on the Drawing toolbar, displays more than a dozen commands for creating more complex drawings.

- The *Group* command groups the selected objects so they can be moved, sized, and formatted as a group.
- The *Ungroup* command ungroups previously grouped items.
- The *Regroup* command groups previously ungrouped items.
- The *Order* command displays a submenu of commands for moving the selected object or objects to the front or back of other objects in the drawing.
- The *Grid and Gridlines* command displays the Grid And Gridlines dialog box, which lets you create a grid on slides for more precisely aligning and locating the objects you draw.
- The *Nudge* command displays a submenu menu of commands you can use to nudge, or slightly move, the selected object or objects up, down, right or left.
- The *Align Or Distribute* command displays a submenu of commands for changing the alignment (right versus left, for example) or distribution (horizontal versus vertical) of the selected object or objects.
- The *Rotate Or Flip* command displays a submenu of commands for rotating objects.
- The *Reroute Connectors* command lets you change where connectors connect.

- The *Edit Points* command lets you change the line used in a curve, a freeform shape or a scribble.
- The *Change AutoShape* command lets you change the autoshape of the selected autoshape object.
- The *Change AutoShape Default* command lets you pick the default autoshape used within each autoshape category.

Formatting Drawing Objects

You can usually change the appearance or format of a drawing object by right-clicking the object, choosing the Format AutoShape command from the shortcut menu, and then using the dialog box that PowerPoint displays to color the shape and its border, change the lines used to draw the shape, and add or remove patterns (see Figure D-13).

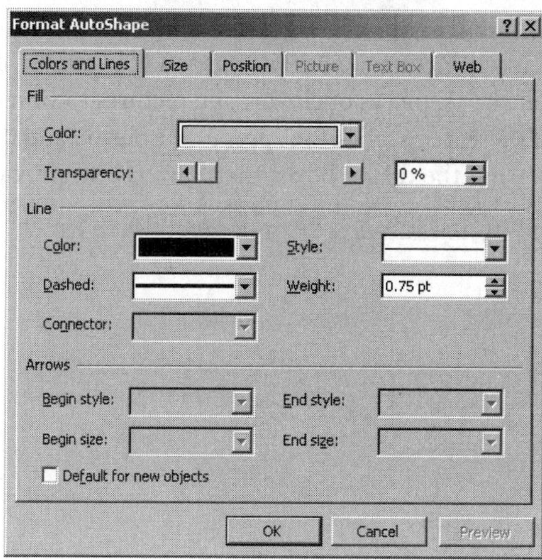

Figure D-13 The Format AutoShape dialog box.

The Drawing toolbar also provides toolbar buttons for making common formatting changes to drawing objects:

- To change the color of the selected item, click the *Fill Color* button's arrow and then choose the color you want from the pop-up menu of colors.
- To change the color of the selected line or arrow, click the *Line Color* button's arrow and choose the color from the pop-up menu of colors. Click the color you want for the line.

- To change the color of the selected text, click the *Font Color* button's arrow and then select a line style from the pop-up menu of line weights.
- To change the weight of the selected line or arrow, click the *Line Style* button's arrow to display a pop-up menu of line weights. Click the line weight you want.
- To change the selected solid line or arrow into a dashed line or arrow—or vice versa—click the *Dashed* button's arrow and then select a dash style from the pop-up menu of dashed line options.

Inserting WordArt, Diagrams, Organizational Charts, and Pictures

Use the Insert WordArt, Insert Diagram Or Organization Chart, Insert Clip Art, and Insert Picture toolbar buttons to add WordArt, diagrams, organizational charts, pieces of clip art and pictures to your drawing. To add any of these items, click the appropriate button and then identify the item using the dialog boxes that PowerPoint provides.

SEE ALSO *Clip Art, Organization Chart, Pictures, WordArt*

Editing Text

To edit text on a slide, in the outline, or in the notes pane, select the text and then type the replacement text.

SEE ALSO *Backspace Key, Delete Key*

E-Mail

You can e-mail the open PowerPoint presentation by choosing the File→Send To→Mail Recipient (As Attachment) command. PowerPoint opens your default e-mail client (this may be Microsoft Outlook or Microsoft Outlook Express), creates a new blank message and attaches the PowerPoint presentation to the message (see Figure E-1). To send the presentation, address the e-mail message, provide a subject and message text, and click Send.

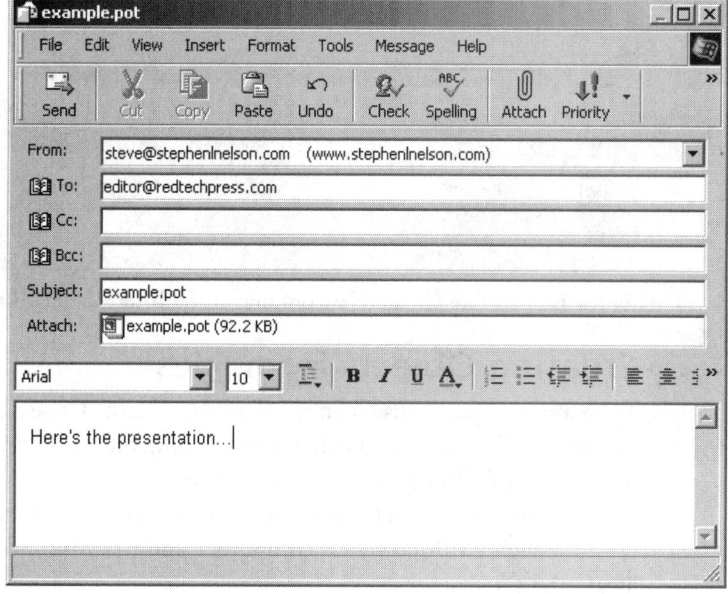

Figure E-1 An e-mail message window that includes a presentation attachment.

TIP *You can also e-mail PowerPoint presentations starting from your e-mail client. When you do this, you e-mail the presentation in the same way as you e-mail any file—typically by clicking the Attachment button and then using a dialog box to find and identify the to-be-attached file.*

Embedding Objects

To embed an object, such as a picture or some item created by another program, choose the Insert→Object command so that PowerPoint displays the Insert Object dialog box.

Creating New Objects

To create a new object, click the Create New button and then select the type of object you want to create from the Object Type list box (see Figure E-2). When you click OK, Windows opens the program that creates the selected object type so you can create the object. When you exit the creating program, Windows returns you to PowerPoint and places the new object in your presentation.

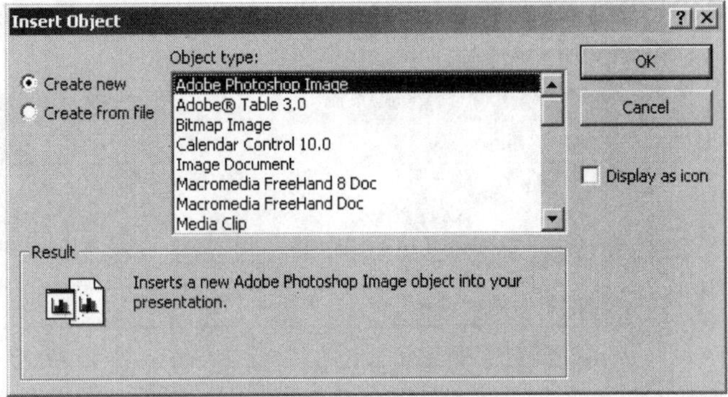

Figure E-2 The Create New options of the Insert Object dialog box.

Creating Objects from Files

To create an object by using an existing file, click the Create From File button (see Figure E-3). Then enter the complete path name for the file into the File Name box. If you don't know the complete path name, click the Browse button to display the Browse window, which you can use to navigate through your computer's and network's folders and locate the file.

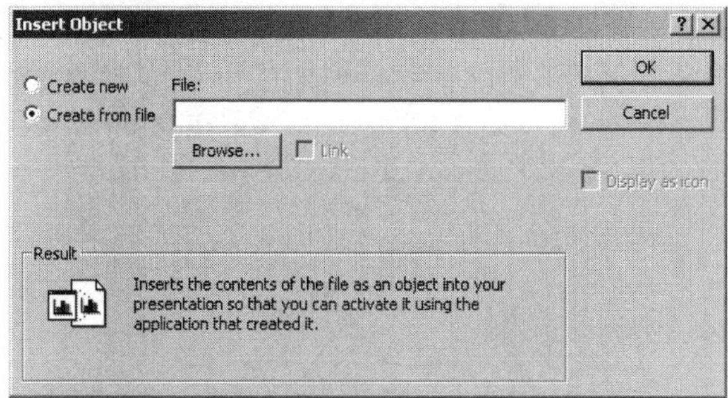

Figure E-3 The Create From File options of the Insert Object dialog box.

SEE ALSO *Pathname*

Ending Lines

You can end a line of text either by pressing the Enter key or the Shift and Enter key in combination. If you end a line by pressing the Enter key, you end both the line and the paragraph, which you may not want to do. Some formatting applies to paragraphs (like alignment and line spacing), and by moving to a new line you also create a new bullet point.

If you enter a line by pressing the Shift key and the Enter key, PowerPoint moves to the next line without starting a new paragraph or bullet point—even though to your eyes it may look as if one paragraph or bullet point has ended and new one started.

SEE ALSO *Insertion Point*

Enter key

In PowerPoint, the Enter key serves several purposes. When you're working with text in a presentation, pressing the Enter key tells PowerPoint that it should enter an end-of-paragraph marker, and move to the next line of the slide or outline.

When you have a PowerPoint dialog box open, pressing the Enter key tells PowerPoint to accept the dialog box's current settings.

If you're showing a PowerPoint presentation slide show, pressing the Enter key tells PowerPoint to display the next slide.

SEE ALSO *Ending Lines*

Exiting PowerPoint

To exit PowerPoint, choose the File→Exit command or click the PowerPoint program window's Close box.

SEE ALSO *Closing Presentations, Closing Programs*

Exporting

You can export text and objects from PowerPoint so they can be used in other programs and other documents. Probably the easiest way to export text or an object is to select the text or object, choose the Edit→Copy command to copy the text or object to the clipboard, open the new document or program into which you want to export the text or object, and then choose the Edit→Paste command.

You can also export text by saving a presentation file in a format that can be imported by the program to which you want to move the document. To do this, choose the File→Save As command. Save the document in the usual way—except use the Files of Type list box to choose a file format the importing program will recognize.

SEE ALSO *Clipboard, Copying Text and Objects, Presentations*

Fast Saves

If you choose the Tools→Options command, click the Save tab, and check the Allow Fast Saves box, PowerPoint will save your documents more quickly (see Figure F-1). In essence, when you do this, you tell PowerPoint you don't care if the files that get saved are a little big, you just want them saved more quickly. With a fast save, PowerPoint doesn't go the work of first cleaning up a file before saving. Normally, it does do this.

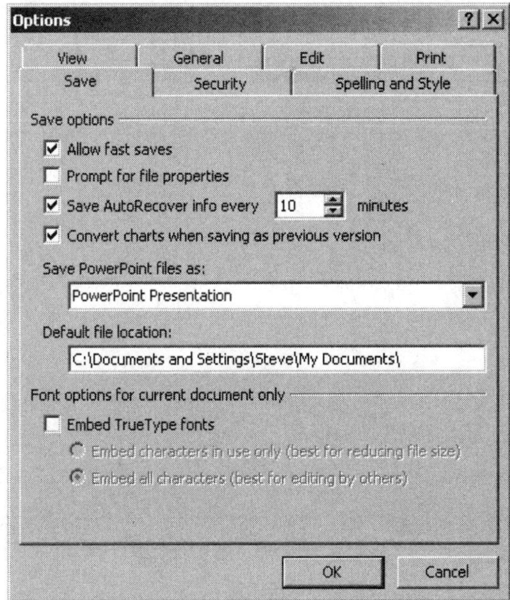

Figure F-1 The Save tab of the Options dialog box.

File Format

Different programs use different formats, or structures, for their document files. The presentations you create in PowerPoint, for example, use a different format than the workbooks you create in Excel (the spreadsheet program that comes with Microsoft Office) and the documents you create in Word (the word processing program that comes with Microsoft Office).

By default, PowerPoint 2002 and the two previous versions of PowerPoint, PowerPoint 2000 and PowerPoint 97, use the same presentation format, but other presentation programs and earlier versions of PowerPoint use other formats.

You can choose which format PowerPoint should use for a presentation when you save the presentation file. To do so, select the file format from the Files Of Type list box, which appears on the Save As dialog box (see Figure F-2).

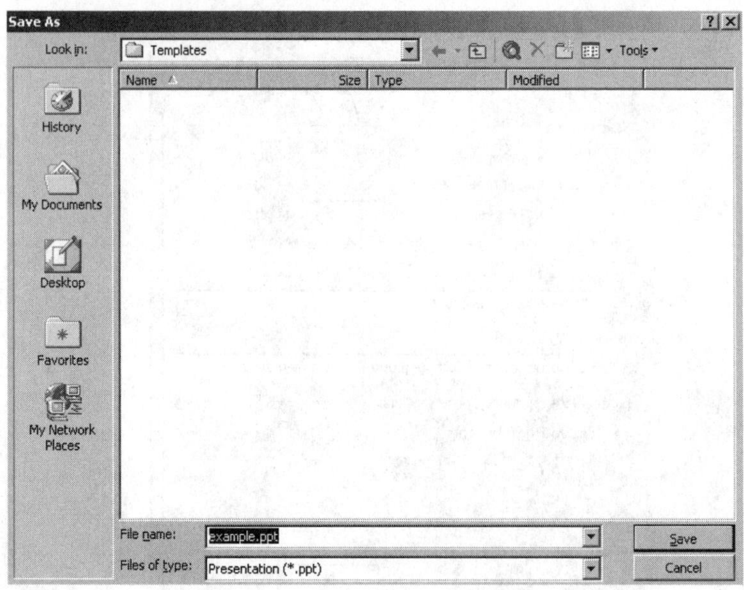

Figure F-2 The Save As dialog box.

SEE ALSO *Exporting, Presentations*

File Extensions

Windows appends a three-character file extension to your file name to identify the type of file. PowerPoint presentations, for example, use the file extension PPT. PowerPoint design templates use the file extension POT. The dictionaries that Microsoft Office applications such as PowerPoint use to check your spelling use the file extension DIC. Word documents use the file extension DOC.

Typically, you don't enter the file extension for a file. A program such as PowerPoint adds this automatically, based on the type of file you're creating or saving. Sometimes you can specify the file extension with the file name—and when you can your file extension may determine the type of file the application program creates.

SEE ALSO *File Names*

File Names

You name your presentation by entering a name into the File Name box when you use the Save As dialog box. (To get to the Save As dialog box, you choose the File→Save As command.)

Your document name can be any valid file name, which means your file name can up to 215 characters including spaces. Letters and numbers can used in file names. Some symbols can, but not the symbols that follow:

\ / : * ? " < > |

SEE ALSO *Presentations*

File Properties

PowerPoint and other Office programs collect information about the files you create. You can view this information by choosing the File→Properties command. PowerPoint displays the presentation's properties dialog box (see Figure F-3). The properties dialog box provides five tabs of information:

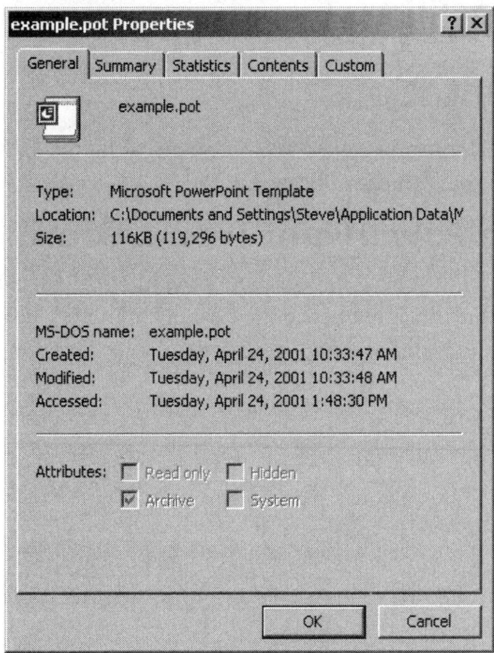

Figure F-3 The General tab of the document properties dialog box.

- The *General* tab provides document name, type, location, size, and file attributes information.
- The *Summary* tab provides spaces to collect and store information about the document title, subject, author, and so forth.
- The *Statistics* tab reports on the number of slides, paragraphs, words, bytes, notes and media clips in the presentation.
- The *Contents* tab identifies the fonts, design template, OLE objects, and slide titles used in the presentation.
- The *Custom* tab lets you collect and store other pieces of information about the presentation, such as when the presentation was complete, where it's been routed, and who the editor was.

TIP *You can get file properties information using the My Computer window or Windows Explorer. To do this, display the folder with the file, right-click the file to display the shortcut menu, and then choose the Properties command.*

Files see Presentations

Film see 35mm Slides

Finding Presentations

You can locate lost or misplaced presentations using the PowerPoint Search tool or the Windows Search tool.

Using the PowerPoint Search Tool

To use the PowerPoint Search tool, choose the File→Open command, click the Tools button, and choose the Search command. PowerPoint displays the Search dialog box (see Figure F-4).

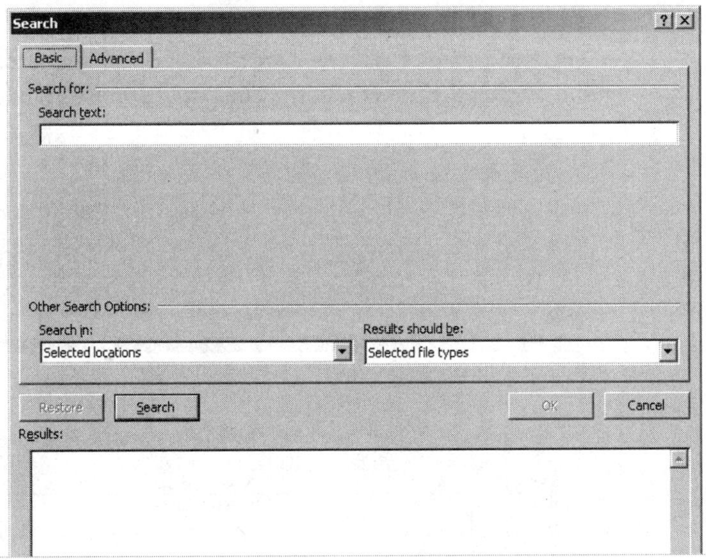

Figure F-4 The Basic tab of the Search dialog box.

If you know the file name, click the Basic tab and then follow these steps:

1. Enter the file name into the Search Text box. If you know a portion of the name, use that portion and the ? and * wildcards.

TIP *The ? character represents any single character (h?t finds any three letter filename that starts with an "h" and ends with a "t"). The * character represents any set of characters (June* finds any filename that starts with the word "June").*

2. Use the Search In box to specify where PowerPoint should look.
3. Use the Results Should Be list box to select which types of files you're looking for.
4. Click the Search button. PowerPoint begins searching for files (presumably presentations) that match your search criteria. As PowerPoint finds matching presentations, it lists them.
5. To open a presentation in the Results list, double-click it.

If you don't know the file name but know something about the presentation's characteristics—such as what the presentation contains or who created the presentation—click the Advanced tab (see Figure F-5).

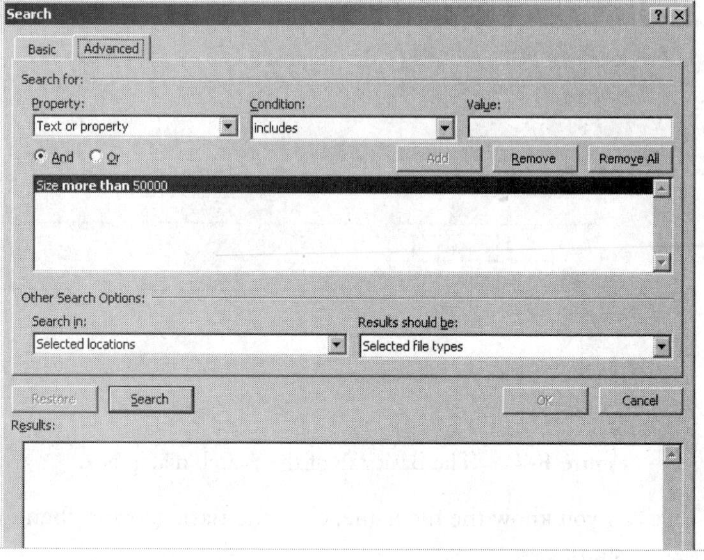

Figure F-5 The Advanced tab of the Search dialog box.

1. Use the Property list box, Condition list box, and Value list box to identify a file characteristic you can describe. For example, select Text Or Property from the Property list if you know some the text contained in the presentation, and then select Includes from the Condition box and enter the search text into the Value box. As another example, select Size from the Property list box if you know something about the size of the presentation, then select one of the comparison operators (Equal To, Not Equal To, More Than, Less Than, At Least, At Most) from the Condition list box, and then enter the file size in bytes (not kilobytes) into the Value box.
2. Use the Search In box to specify where PowerPoint should look.
3. Use the Results Should Be list box to select which types of files (probably presentations) you're looking for.

4. Click the Search button. PowerPoint begins searching for presentations that match your search criteria. As PowerPoint finds matching presentations, it lists them.
5. To open a presentation in the Results list, double-click it.

Using the Windows Search Tool

The Windows operating system also provides a search tool that can be useful for locating lost or misplaced PowerPoint presentations. Unfortunately, the confusing number of Windows operating systems makes it difficult to provide a "one-size-fits-all" set of instructions. Nevertheless, the steps that follow provide general instructions for finding files using Windows 2000 and Windows XP. With both of these operating systems, you can take the following steps to search for and locate presentations:

1. Click the Start button and choose the Search→For Files Or Folders command. Windows displays the Search Results window (see Figure F-6).

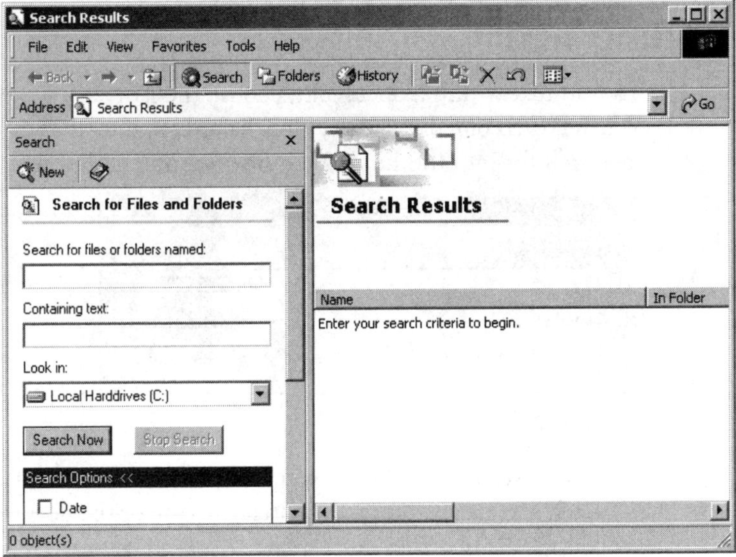

Figure F-6 The Search Results window.

2. If you know the file name, enter it into the Search For Files Or Folders Named box. If you know a portion of the name, use that portion and the ? and * wildcards.

3. To find files that use a word, phrase, or string of text, enter that word, phrase, or text string into the Containing Text box.
4. Use the Look In list box to specify on which drives Windows should look.
5. Optionally, use the Date, Type, Size and Advanced Options boxes to further refine the search. (Only the Date box shows in Figure F-6.) If you check one of these boxes, Windows displays other boxes and buttons you use to describe the criteria in detail.
6. Click the Search Now button. Windows begin searching for files that match your search criteria. As Windows finds matching files, it lists them.
7. To open a file in the Search Results window, double-click it.

TIP *You can do and will probably want to do other work with your computer while the search goes on. Complex searches, such as those that look inside presentations for matching text, can take a long time.*

Finding Text

To find text within a document, choose the Edit→Find command. When PowerPoint displays the Find dialog box, enter the text you want to search for into the Find What box (see Figure F-7).

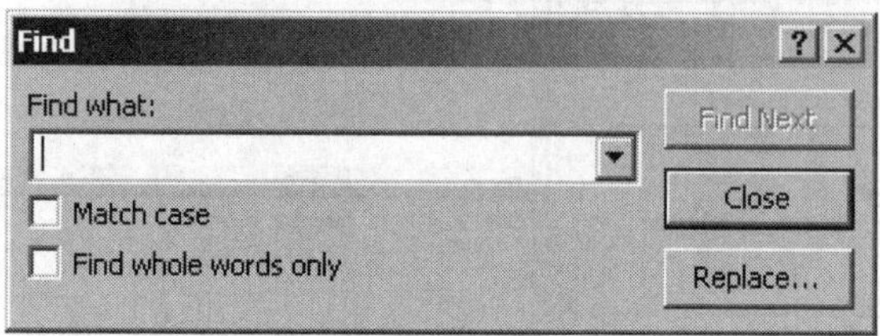

Figure F-7 The Find dialog box.

- Use the *Match Case* checkbox to indicate whether the case of your search text needs to exactly match the case of the document text.
- Use the *Find Whole Words Only* checkbox to indicate whether PowerPoint should only find whole word occurrences of the search text. For example, if you check this box and use "war" as your search text, PowerPoint will not find text such as "hardware," "warrant," and "thwart."

Click the Find Next button to start PowerPoint searching the presentation. If PowerPoint finds the text, it highlights the text but leaves the Find dialog box open but inactive. You can work in the presentation, including making changes the selected text. To continue searching, click the Find Next button again.

Fonts

You can change the font, style, point size and font effects used for presentation text using either the Formatting toolbar's buttons and boxes or the Format→Font command.

To use the Formatting toolbar buttons and boxes, first select the text. Then use the Font and Font Size boxes or the Bold, Italic and Underline buttons to make your changes.

To use the Format→Font command, select the text and then choose the command (see Figure F-8).

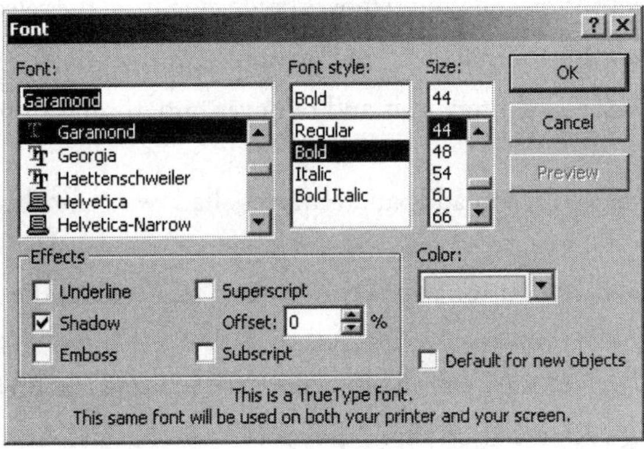

Figure F-8 The Font dialog box.

- Use the *Font* list box to select a font for the text.
- Use the *Font Style* list box to italicize or bold the text.
- Use the *Size* list box to select a point size for the text.
- Use the *Effects* check boxes to add effects like superscripting, subscripting, and shadowing.
- Use the *Color* box to pick a color for the selected text.

SEE ALSO *WordArt*

Format Painter see Copying Formatting

Formatting Fonts see Fonts

Formatting Toolbar

The Formatting toolbar provides buttons and boxes for making almost two-dozen common formatting changes, as shown in the list below. Note, though, that not all of these tools will appear on your Formatting toolbar. If you're using a personalized toolbar, only the formatting toolbar buttons that you use most frequently will appear. If you're working with the default Formatting toolbar, only the first seventeen tools listed will appear.

- The *Font* box lets you pick a font for the selected text.
- The *Font Size* box lets you a point size for the selected text.
- The *Bold* button adds and removes boldfacing from the selected text.
- The *Italic* button italicizes and un-italicizes the selected text.
- The *Underline* button adds and removes underlining from the selected text.
- The *Shadow* button adds and removes shadowing for the selected text.
- The *Align Left* button aligns the selected text against the left edge of the slide.
- The *Center* button horizontally centers the selected text on the slide.
- The *Align Right* button aligns the selected text against the right edge of the slide.
- The *Numbering* button turns the selected paragraphs of text into a numbered list.
- The *Bullets* button turns the selected paragraphs of text into a bulleted list.
- The *Increase Font Size* button increases the size of the selected text to the next larger font size.

- The *Decrease Font Size* button decreases the size of the selected text to the next smaller font size.
- The *Decrease Indent* button un-indents the selected text.
- The *Increase Indent* button indents the selected text.
- The *Font Color* button colors the selected text.
- The *Slide Design* button displays the Slide Design task pane.
- The *New Slide* button displays the New Slide task pane.
- The *Slide Layout* button displays the Slide Layout task pane.
- The *Background* button displays the Background dialog box so the slide background can be recolored.
- The *Increase Paragraph Spacing* button increases the spacing between the selected paragraphs (probably bulleted or numbered points).
- The *Decrease Paragraph Spacing* button decreases the spacing between the selected paragraphs (probably bulleted or numbered points).
- The *Move Up* button moves the selected text up one line in the outline.
- The *Move Down* button moves the selected text down one line in the outline.
- The *Reset Toolbar* button lets you return to the default Formatting toolbar configuration.

TIP *To add a tool to the Formatting toolbar, click the down arrow at the right end of the toolbar. When PowerPoint displays a list of the additional toolbar boxes and buttons, click the tools you want.*

SEE ALSO *Personalized Menus and Toolbars*

Genigraphics see 35mm Slides

Graph

Graph is a small program that comes with Microsoft PowerPoint and other Microsoft Office programs. You use Graph to create charts for your PowerPoint presentations.

SEE ALSO *Charts*

Graphic Objects see Pictures

Grids and Guidelines

PowerPoint includes a grid you can add to slides to move precisely locate objects and text. To add the grid, choose the View→Grid And Guides command. When PowerPoint displays the Grid And Guides dialog box, use its boxes to specific how the grid works and looks (see Figure G-1).

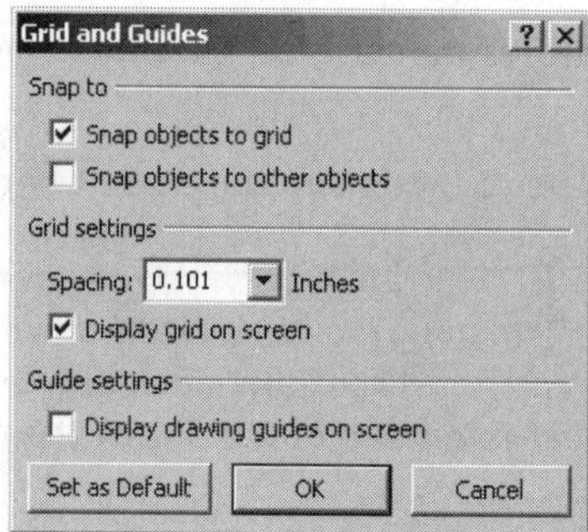

Figure G-1 The Grid And Guides dialog box.

- Use the *Snap To* boxes to specify whether objects should be moved by PowerPoint so they align against the grid. (PowerPoint only moves, or snaps, an object if it's close to the grid or object.)
- Use the *Grid Settings* boxes to describe the grid and indicate whether it should appear in the PowerPoint window (see Figure G-2).
- Use the *Guide Settings* box to add guides to the PowerPoint window which you can then use to move precisely align objects (see Figure G-3).

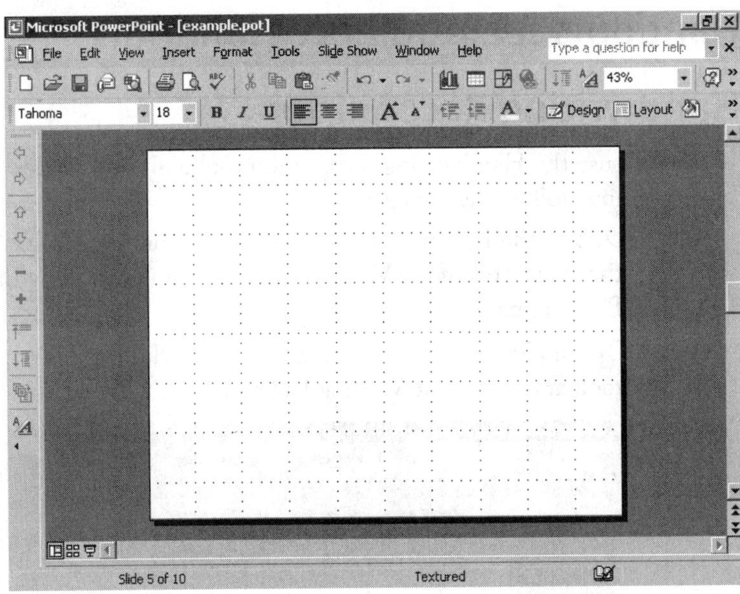

Figure G-2 A slide with a grid.

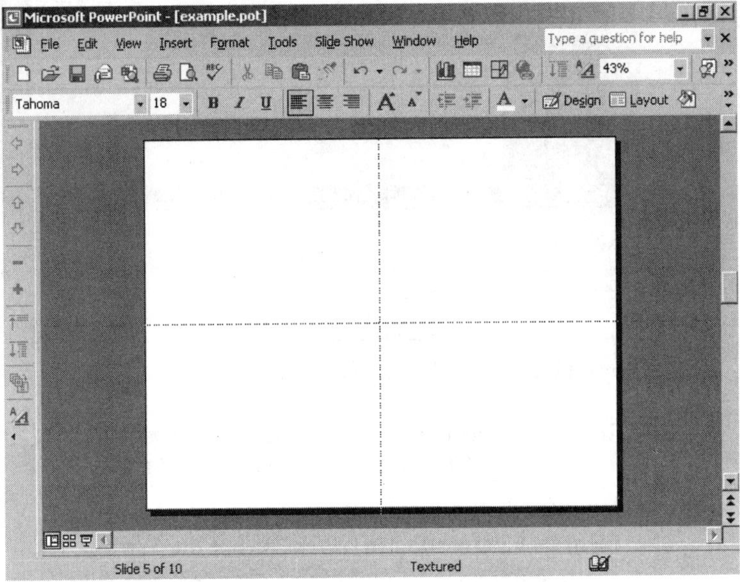

Figure G-3 A slide with guides.

Handouts see Audience Handouts

Handwriting Recognition

To use the Handwriting recognition tool built into Office XP programs, follow these steps:

1. Display the Language toolbar by clicking on the EN indicator in the status area of the Windows and choosing the Show Language Bar command.

2. Optionally, open the Writing Pad by clicking the Writing Pad toolbar button. The Writing Pad window opens (see Figure H-1).

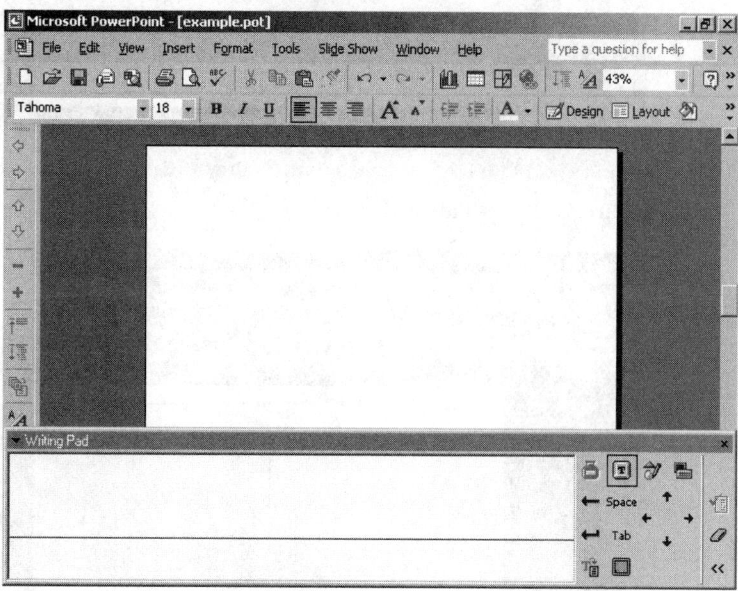

Figure H-1 The Writing Pad window.

NOTE *To write directly into the active document window, choose the Write Anywhere command from the Handwriting menu.*

3. Indicate whether you want your handwriting entered into the document as handwriting or as text. Click the Writing Pad's Ink button to enter your handwriting as handwriting. Click the Writing Pad's Text button to enter your handwriting as Text.

4. Place the insertion point at the location where you want your text inserted. Then, using your mouse or handwriting input device, neatly write or print text inside the Writing Pad window. Don't pause as you write. Do leave a space between words. As you write, Handwriting Recognition interprets your words, entering them at the insertion point. If you write something you want to erase, click the Writing Pad's Clear button.

TIP *The Writing Pad window includes buttons you can click to represent common keys such as the Backspace, Space, Enter and Tab keys. If you click the Expand button, the Writing Pad window expands to include buttons you can click to move the cursor one character up, down, right or left, to open the Drawing toolbar, and to display an onscreen keyboard you can use by clicking its buttons.*

5. To correct text you've entered with Handwriting Recognition, select the text and then either type the replacement text or handwrite the replacement text and click the Writing Pad's Correction button.

SEE ALSO *Drawing*

Headers and Footers

To add a header or footer to your slides, speakers notes or audience handouts, choose the View→Header and Footer command. When PowerPoint displays the Header and Footer dialog box, use its Slide and Notes And Handouts tabs to specify how your footer should look (see Figures H-2 and H-3).

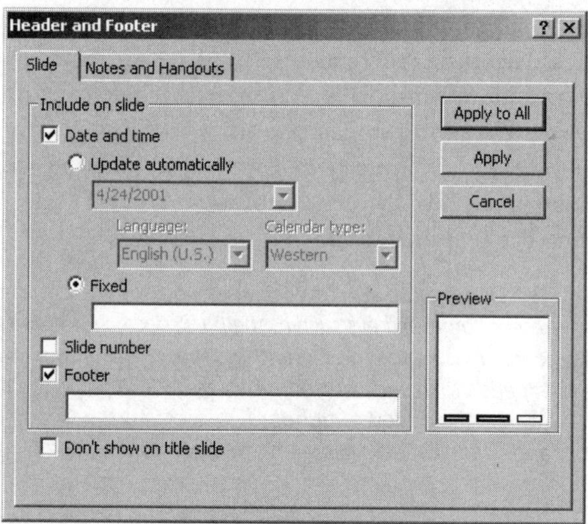

Figure H-2 The Slide tab of the Header And Footer dialog box.

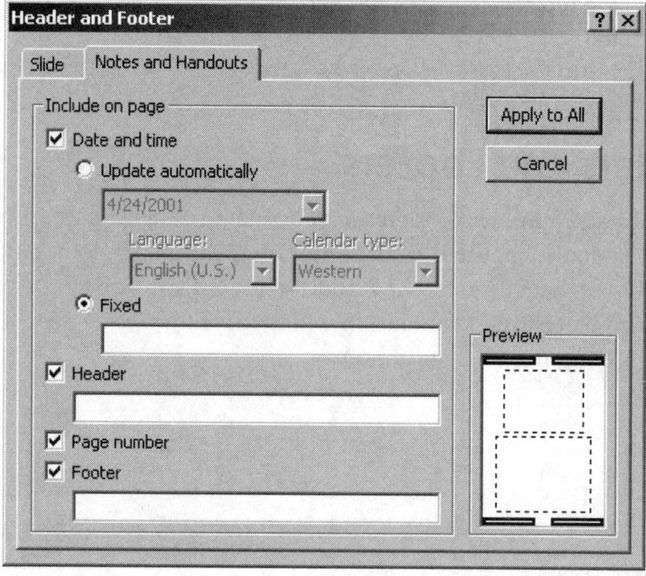

Figure H-3 The Notes And Handouts tab of the Header And Footer dialog box.

- Check the *Date And Time* box to include the date and, optionally, the time on your slides, notes, and handouts.
- Use the *Update Automatically* and *Fixed* buttons to specify whether or not you want PowerPoint to automatically update the date and time (using the system clock). Then use either the *Fixed* text box to provide the date and the *Update Automatically* text box to select a date format.
- Check the *Header* box (available on the Notes And Handouts tab) to add a header to the notes and handout pages—and then enter the header text into the *Header* text box.
- Check the *Slide Number* box (available on the Slide tab) to add the slide number to the footer.
- Check the *Page Number* box (available on the Notes And Handouts tab) to add the page number to the footer.
- Check the *Footer* box (available on the Notes And Handouts tab) to add a footer to the notes and handout pages—and then enter the header text into the Footer text box.
- Check the *Don't Show On Title Slide* box to leave the footer and header information off of the title slide.

SEE ALSO *Presentations, Slide Shows*

Help see Office Assistant, Troubleshooting

Hidden Slides

To hide a slide so that it doesn't show in a slide show, display the Slide Sorter view by choosing the View→Slide Sorter command (see Figure H-4). Then, right-click the slide you want to hide and choose Hide Slide from the shortcut menu.

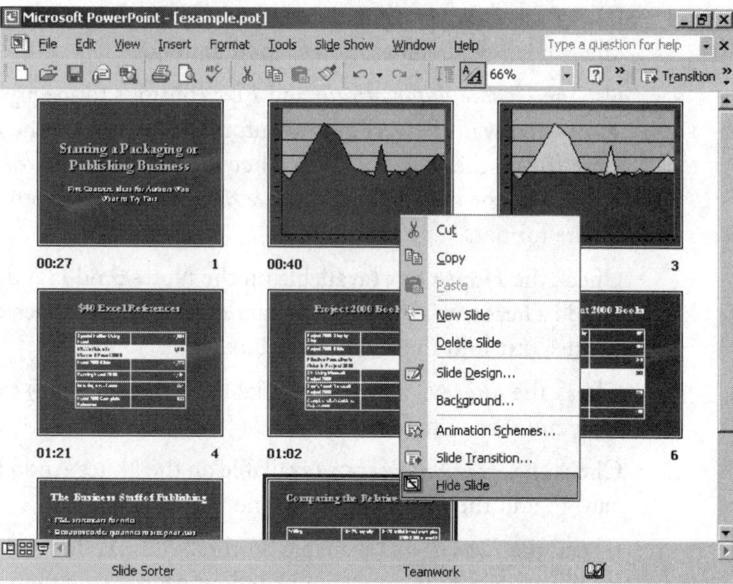

Figure H-4 The Slide Sorter view with the shortcut menu displayed and the Hide Slide command selected.

TIP *To select more than one slide, hold down the Ctrl key as you click the slides you want to select.*

Horizontal Page Orientation see Page Orientation

HTML

HTML is the file format used in Web pages. PowerPoint opens and saves HTML documents, which means you can use PowerPoint to create Web pages. To create an HTML, or Web, page in PowerPoint, choose the File→Save As command. Use the Save In and File Name boxes to specify where the Web Page should be saved and what it should be named. Select the Web Page entry from the Save As Type box. Click OK.

TIP *In some cases, you may just want to post a PowerPoint presentation to a web site rather than handing out paper copies of the presentation. A Web-available presentation may make it easier for your audience to later look back at your presentation, save paper, and give you the option of easily updating the presentation for changes or edits.*

SEE ALSO *Hyperlinks, URLs, Web Options, Web Pages*

Hyperlinks

Hyperlinks are clickable pictures and words that you can use to open a network or Internet resource—such as a Web page. To use a hyperlink, you simply click it. PowerPoint then opens the network resource (this might be another PowerPoint presentation) or an Internet resource (probably a Web page).

Linking to an Existing File or Web Page

To create a hyperlink to another file or Web page, follow these steps:

1. Select the text or picture you want to turn into a hyperlink.
2. Choose the Insert→Hyperlink command. When PowerPoint displays the Insert Hyperlink dialog box, click the Existing File Or Web Page button (see Figure H-5).

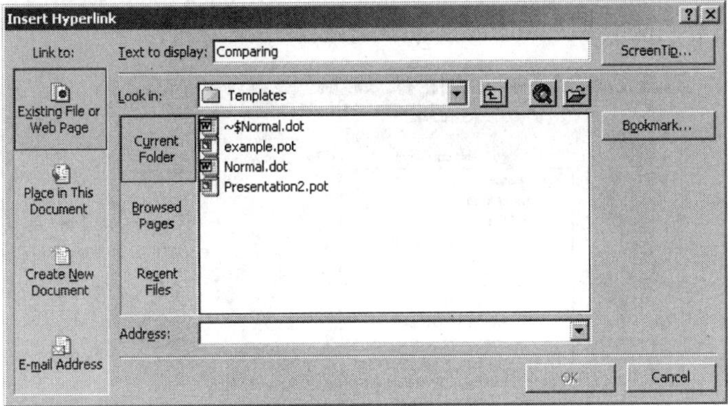

Figure H-5 The Insert Hyperlink dialog box with the Existing File Or Web Page options displayed.

3. Enter the Internet URL or network pathname that the hyperlink should point to in the Address box.

TIP *If you don't know the URL or network pathname, you may be able to find the document or web page by clicking the Current Folder, Browsed Pages and Recent Files buttons and then choosing the document or web page from the list box. You can also use the Look In box and the Up One Folder button to display the contents of other folders on your local network and the Browse The Web button to open a web browser window you can use to find the page you want to link to.*

4. Use the Text To Display box to provide text the web browser should display in its status bar when someone points to the link.

5. Optionally, use the ScreenTip button to provide text the web browser will display in a pop-up box when someone points to the link.

Linking to a Place in the Open Document

To create a hyperlink to another location in the open document, follow these steps:

1. Select the text or picture you want to turn into a hyperlink.

2. Choose the Insert→Hyperlink command. When PowerPoint displays the Insert Hyperlink dialog box, click the Place In This Document button (see Figure H-6).

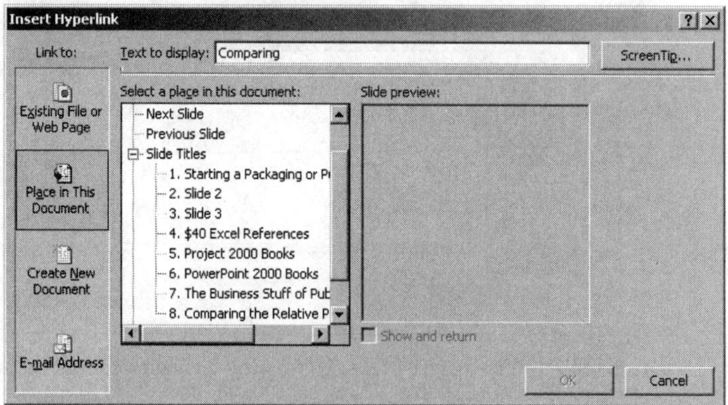

Figure H-6 The Insert Hyperlink dialog with the Place In This Document options displayed.

3. Use the Select A Place In This Document box to select whether you want to link to headings or bookmarks and, if so, which heading or bookmark you want.
4. Use the Text To Display box to provide text the web browser should display in its status bar when someone points to the link.
5. Optionally, use the ScreenTip button to provide text the web browser will display in a pop-up box when someone points to the link.

Linking to a New Document

To create a hyperlink to a new document, follow these steps:

1. Select the text or picture you want to turn into a hyperlink.
2. Choose the Insert→Hyperlink command. When PowerPoint displays the Insert Hyperlink dialog box, click the Create New Document button (see Figure H-7).

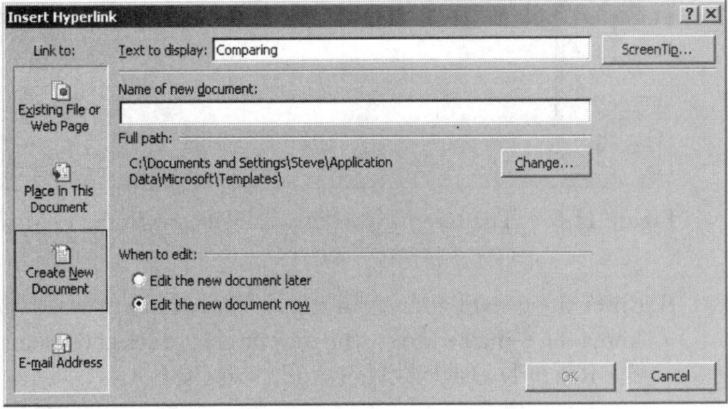

Figure H-7 The Insert Hyperlink dialog box with the Create New Document options displayed.

3. Enter the pathname of the new document in the Name Of New Document text box.
4. Use the Text To Display box to provide text the web browser should display in its status bar when someone points to the link.
5. Optionally, use the ScreenTip button to provide text the web browser will display in a pop-up box when someone points to the link.

6. To create the document now, click the Edit The New Document Now button. To postpone creating the document, click the Edit The New Document Later button.

Linking to an E-Mail Address

To create a hyperlink to an e-mail address, follow these steps:

1. Select the text or picture you want to turn into a hyperlink.
2. Choose the Insert→Hyperlink command. When PowerPoint displays the Insert Hyperlink dialog box, click the E-Mail Address button (see Figure H-8).

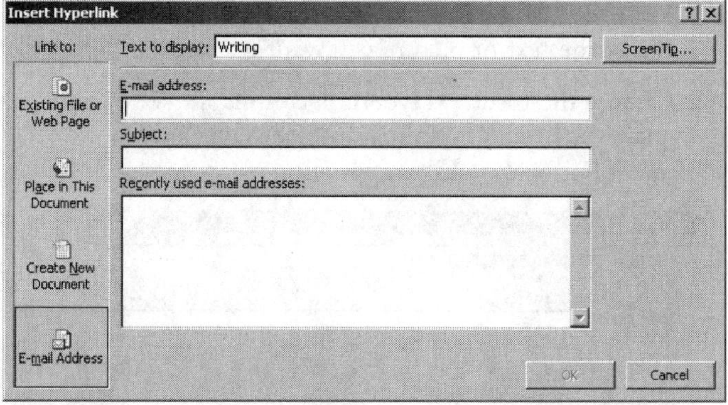

Figure H-8 The Insert Hyperlink dialog box with the E-Mail Address options displayed.

3. Enter the e-mail address in the E-Mail Address box. If you don't know the e-mail address, you may be able to select the address from the Recently Used E-Mail Addresses list box.
4. Optionally, enter a suggested message subject in the Subject box.
5. Use the Text To Display box to provide text the web browser should display in its status bar when someone points to the link.
6. Optionally, use the ScreenTip button to provide text the web browser will display in a pop-up box when someone points to the link.

Editing and Removing a Hyperlink

To change a hyperlink, right-click the hyperlink and choose the Edit Hyperlink command from the shortcut menu. PowerPoint displays a dialog box like the one you originally used to create the hyperlink. Use it to make your changes.

To remove a hyperlink, right-click the hyperlink and choose the Remove Hyperlink command from the shortcut menu.

SEE ALSO *HTML, Web Page Wizard*

Importing see Presentations

Indenting Paragraphs

To indent the selected paragraph, bulleted point, or numbered point, click the Increase Indent toolbar button. To un-indent the selected paragraph, bulleted point, or numbered point, click the Decrease Indent toolbar button.

NOTE *When you indent, you demote the text in the outline. When you un-indent text, you promote the text in the outline.*

SEE ALSO *Paragraphs*

Insertion Point

The insertion point is the flashing vertical line that shows where what you type is placed in a presentation or document. You can move the insertion point by clicking the mouse (the insertion point moves to where you click) or by using the arrow keys (the insertion point moves one character in the direction of the arrow).

Insert Key

The Insert key turns on and off PowerPoint's overtype feature. If overtype is turned on, what you type replaces the existing text in your outline or on a slide. If overtype is turned off, what you type is inserted in your outline or on your slide.

SEE ALSO *Editing Text, Insertion Point*

Italic Characters

You can italicize the selected text by clicking the Italic toolbar button or by pressing the Ctrl+I key combination. Press the Ctrl and I keys simultaneously.

You can un-italicize italic text in the same way. If you select italic text and then click the Italic toolbar button or press Ctrl+I, PowerPoint removes the italics.

NOTE *You can also use the Format→Font command to italicize and un-italicize text.*

SEE ALSO *Fonts*

Kiosk see Setting up a Presentation

Justifying Text see Alignment

Landscape Orientation see Page Orientation

Layouts see Slide Layouts

Line Spacing

To specify how lines in the selected paragraphs should be spaced, choose Format→Line Spacing and then use the Line Spacing dialog box to specify how PowerPoint should space lines of text (see Figure L-1):

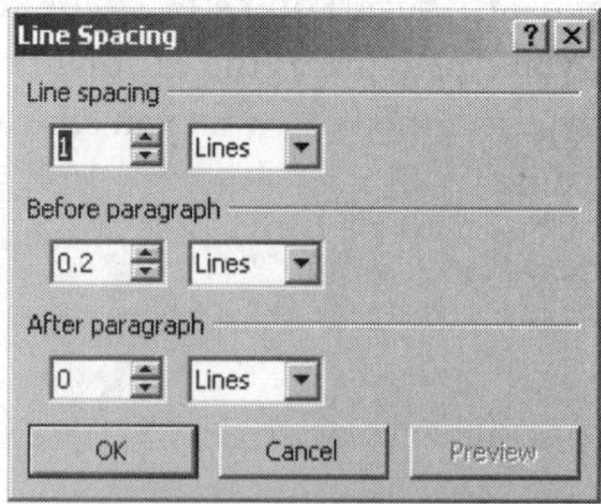

Figure L-1 The Line Spacing dialog box.

- Use the *Line Spacing* box to specify how much spacing you want between lines.
- Use the *Before Paragraph* box to specify how much spacing should come before a paragraph.
- Use the *After Paragraph* box to specify how much spacing should come after a paragraph.

SEE ALSO *Paragraphs*

Linking Objects see Embedding Objects

Lists see Bulleted Lists, Numbered Lists

Looping Slide Shows see Setting Up a Presentation

Lost Presentations see Finding Presentations, Program Errors

Macros

Macros are sequences of keystrokes or commands. You use macros within PowerPoint to automate repetitive actions.

Creating a Macro

To create a macro, follow these steps:

1. Choose the Tools→Macro→Record New Macro command. PowerPoint displays the Record Macro dialog box (see Figure M-1).

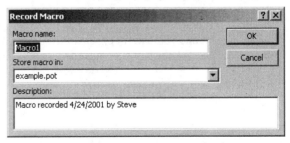

Figure M-1 The Record Macro dialog box.

2. Enter a name for the macro into the Macro Name box. You can use up to 80 characters but no spaces or symbols in the name.
3. Type the keystrokes and choose the commands that you want your macro to type and choose.
4. Choose the Tools→Macro→Stop Recording command.

Running a Macro

- To run your macro, choose the Tools→Macro→Macros command to display the Macro dialog box and then double-click the macro you want to run (see Figure M-2).

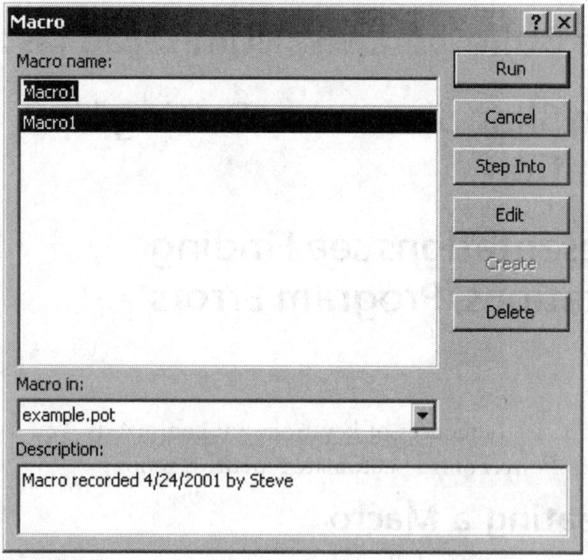

Figure M-2 The Macro dialog box.

NOTE *Editing and debugging PowerPoint macros, which are written in the Visual Basic for Applications programming language, is beyond the scope of this book. If you're interested in Visual Basic programming and you haven't programmed before, you'll find it useful to have a book that describes and discusses Visual Basic.*

Macro Security

To adjust PowerPoint's macro security, choose Tools→Macro→Security command. PowerPoint displays the Security dialog box (see Figure M-3). Use the Security Level tab's buttons to tell PowerPoint which macros it can safely run. Use the Trusted Sources tab to list the macro authors you've said you trust or to remove a macro author from a trusted source.

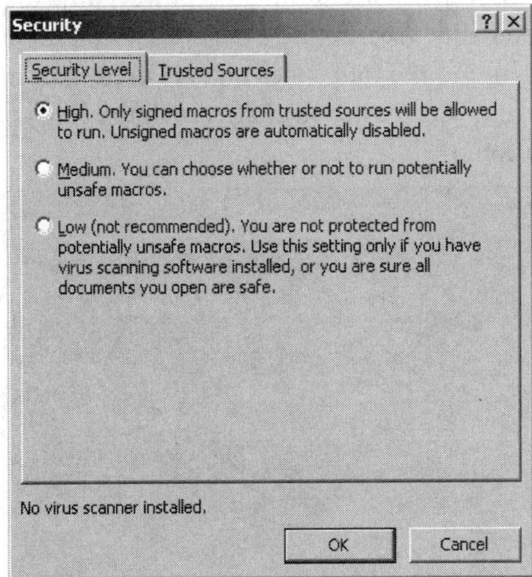

Figure M-3 The Security Level tab of the Security dialog box.

SEE ALSO *Password Protecting a Presentation, Privacy Options*

Magnification see Zoom

Master Slides

A master slide supplies a blueprint for creating individual slides. You can make a variety of changes to a master slide, and thereby to all the slides in your presentation. First, however, you need to display the master slide.

To display a master slide, choose the View→Master command. PowerPoint displays the Master submenu, which lists the three types of master slides: Slide Master, Handout Master, and Notes Master. When you are changing the appearance of your presentation, you work with the Slide Master (which specifies how the individual slides in your presentation look).

After you choose the appropriate Master submenu command—most commonly the Slide Master command—PowerPoint displays the appropriate master slide (see Figure M-4). This slide master shows object placeholders and the font styles that are used. Any formatting changes you make to the master slide affects all the rest of the slides in your presentation.

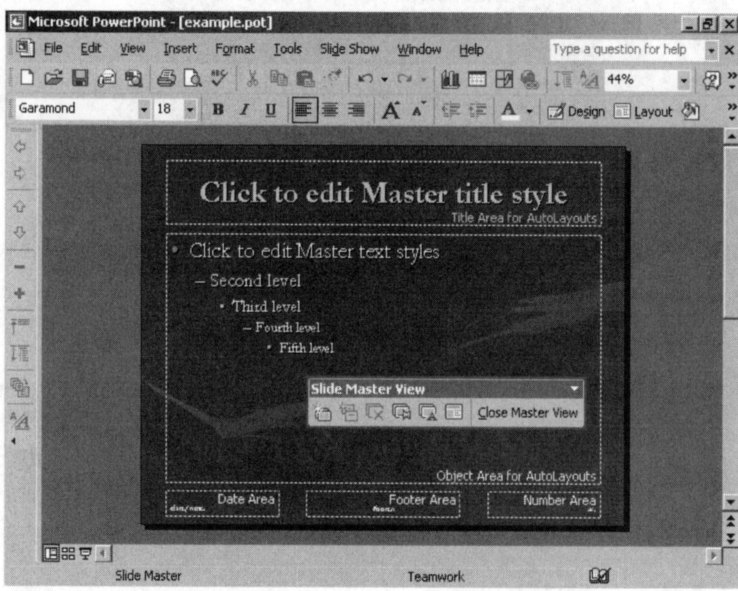

Figure M-4 Slide Master view.

Changing the Slide Master Background

To change the slide master background, choose the Format→Background command. When PowerPoint displays the Background dialog box choose a background fill for the slide master (see Figure M-5).

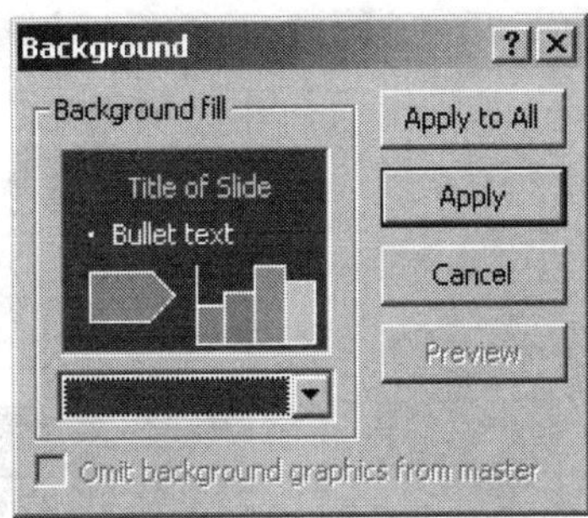

Figure M-5 The Background dialog box.

NOTE *You can use the Format→Background command to change only the background of a single slide or the background of a selected group of slides. To do this, you don't make changes to the slide master background but rather to the slide itself. When you're working with individual slides or sets of slides that are part of a large presentation, you can click the Background dialog box's Apply button. By clicking Apply, PowerPoint applies the background fill change to only the selected slide or slides.*

Changing the color scheme

You can change the color scheme used for a presentation via the slide master. To do this, display the Slide Design task pane. Then choose the Color Schemes hyperlink. When PowerPoint displays the color schemes in the Slide Design task pane, right-click the color scheme and choose either the Apply To All Masters or Apply To Selected Masters command (see Figure M-6).

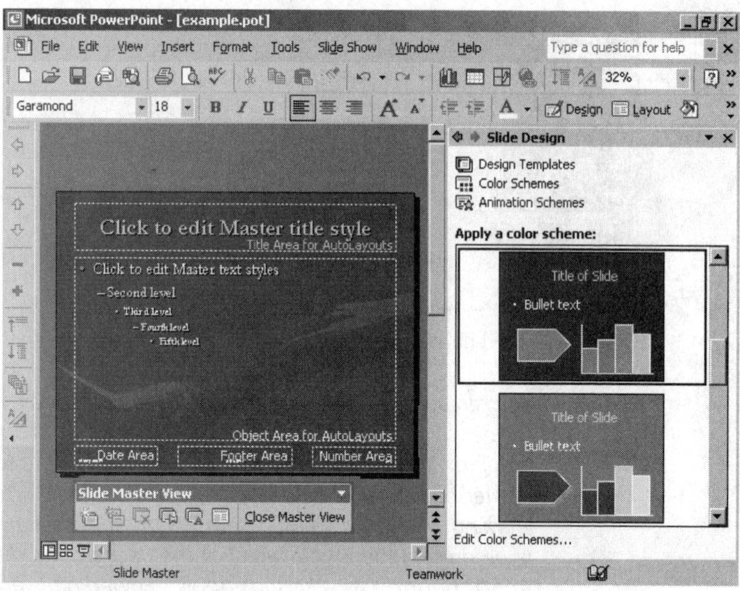

Figure M-6 The Slide Design task pane showing color schemes.

NOTE *A color scheme is made up of eight colors: a background color, a text and lines color, a shadows color, a title text color, a fills color, an accent color, an accent and hyperlink color, and an accent and followed hyperlink color.*

Changing text formatting

You can change the font, font style, point size, and other font specifications for the slides in your presentation by using the Format→Font command. To use this command, first display the slide master and then click the text object you want to change. After you've done this, choose the command and make your changes.

Meeting Minder

Meeting Minder lets you keep minutes or notes of a presentation meeting. To use the Meeting Minder, you right-click a slide during a slide show and choose the Meeting Minder command. PowerPoint displays the Meeting Minder dialog box (see Figures M-7 and M-8).

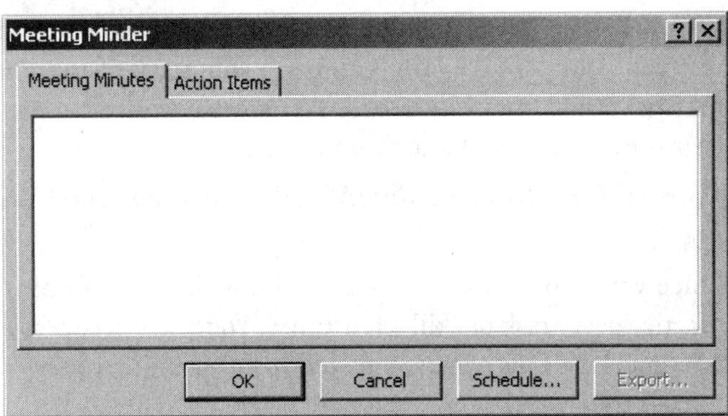

Figure M-7 The Meeting Minutes tab of the Meeting Minder dialog box.

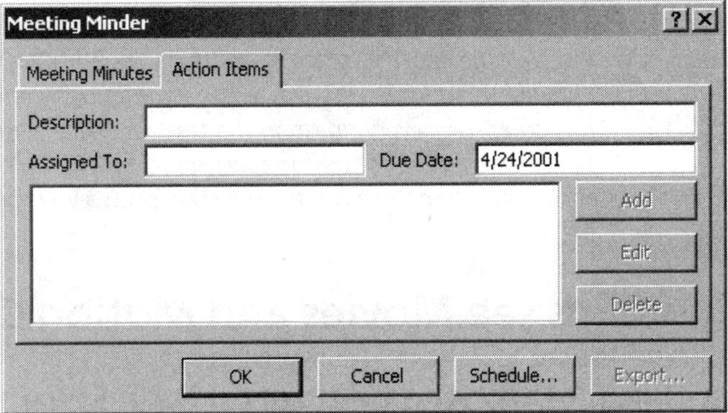

Figure M-8 The Action Items tab of the Meeting Minder dialog box.

You use the Meeting Minutes tab to record the minutes and the Action Items tab to record action items or to-do list items that stem from the presentation and meeting.

Microsoft Office User Specialist

Microsoft Corporation certifies PowerPoint users who can pass a test as Microsoft Office User Specialists. In the parlance of Microsoft, these users then become "MOUS certified." You don't learn anything new by becoming a MOUS certificate holder, but if you're in a career or an organization where certification delivers benefits, know that these tests are straightforward to prepare for and pass.

Your first step is to learn what material you need to know to pass the test you want to take. You can get a summary of the PowerPoint material tested from Microsoft's Web site at www.microsoft.com. Just visit the web site and search on the term:

Microsoft Office User Specialist (MOUS) PowerPoint 2002 Exam Objectives

Once you know what you need to know in order to pass the test, practice every task or skill a few times. You don't need a special study test or a class. This book should tell you everything you need to know to pass the test.

Once you've prepared, take the test at a local testing center. You can learn about any local testing centers from the local telephone directory or from the Microsoft Web site.

TIP *Perhaps the most important skill for passing a MOUS test is knowing how to use the Office Assistant. You can't rely on this tool to answer every question the test asks—there isn't time—but as long as you're comfortable using the Office Assistant, you should have time to ask it the question or two you can't answer on your own.*

Motion Clips see Movies and Motion Clips

MOUS see Microsoft Office User Specialist

Movies and Motion Clips

You can add motion clips or video clips to your slides.

Using Motion Clips from the Clip Gallery

To add a motion clip to your slide using the Movie Clip Gallery, take the following steps:

1. Choose the Insert→Movies And Sounds→Movie From Media Gallery command. PowerPoint displays the Insert Clip Art task pane (see Figure M-9).

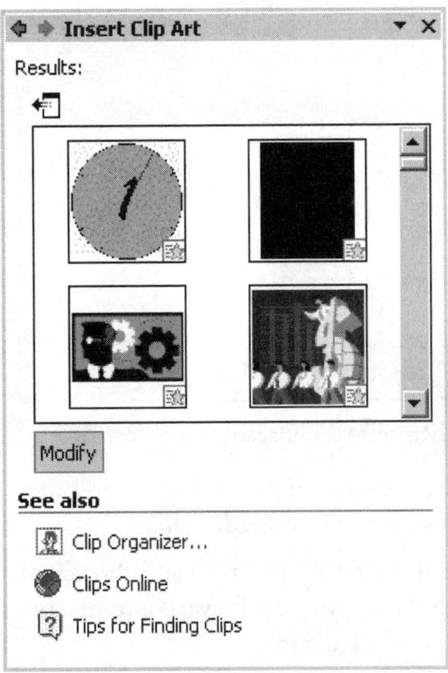

Figure M-9 The Insert Clip Art task pane.

2. Use the list box in the Insert Clip Art task pane to locate the motion clip you want to use on a PowerPoint slide. Or, you can click the Clip Organizer hyperlink and then use the clip organizer window to locate the motion clip you want (see Figure M-10).

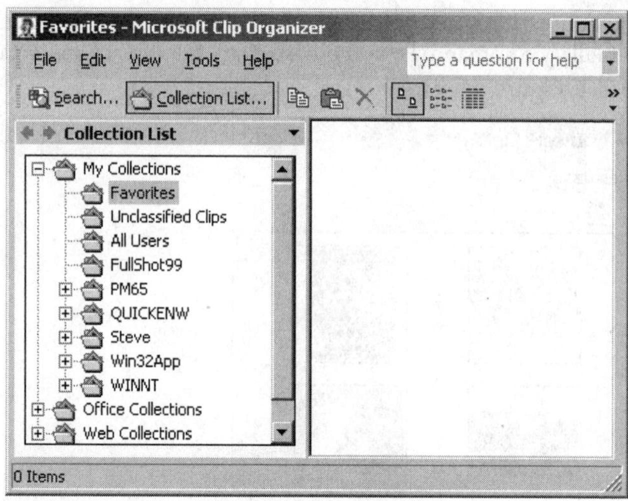

Figure M-10 The Microsoft Clip Organizer window.

3. Optionally, check the clip by right-clicking it and then choosing Preview/Properties from the shortcut menu.
4. Insert the motion clip by right-clicking it and choosing Insert from the shortcut menu. When you do, PowerPoint inserts the motion clip on the open or selected slide.

Using Motion Clip Files

To insert a motion or video clip stored as a file on your computer, take the following steps:

1. Choose the Insert→Movies And Sounds→Movies From File command. PowerPoint displays the Insert Movie dialog box (see Figure M-11).

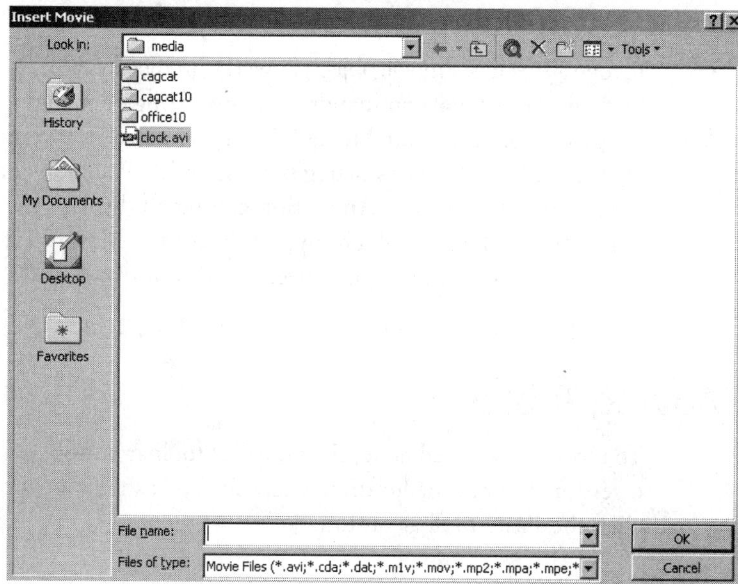

Figure M-11 The Insert Movie dialog box.

2. Use the Look In box to select the folder that holds the movie file. If the movie is really in a subfolder or a sub-subfolder, you might need to first select and open the parent folder.
3. Find the motion clip or video clip you want to use. After you've found the folder with the movie, double-click the movie file to insert the movie onto your slide. When PowerPoint asks whether you want your movie to play automatically when the slide is displayed, click the Yes or No button to answer.

Customizing a Movie Object

If you right-click a movie object, PowerPoint displays a shortcut menu that supplies several commands for customizing or changing the way a movie plays. The Edit Movie Object command, for example, displays the Movie Options dialog box which lets you loop and rewind the movie. The Custom Animation command displays the Custom Animation task pane, which supplies boxes and buttons for specifying start and stop times, play speeds, and so forth.

SEE ALSO *Customizing Multimedia Effects, Music, Sounds*

Moving Tables

To move the selected table, click the Cut toolbar button, position the insertion point at the location where the table should be moved, and click the Paste toolbar button.

SEE ALSO *Tables*

Moving Text and Objects

PowerPoint provides several ways to move slide text and objects:

- **Drag-and-drop.** Select text or object you want to move by dragging the mouse. Then drag the selected text or object to a new location.
- **Edit→Cut and Edit→Paste commands.** Select the text or object, choose the Edit→Cut command, position the insertion point at the new location, and choose the Edit→Paste command.
- **Cut and Paste toolbar buttons.** Select the text, click the Cut button, position the insertion point at the new location, and choose the Paste toolbar button.
- **Office Clipboard task pane.** Select the item, click the Cut button or choose the Edit→Cut command, position the insertion point at the new location, and click the item you want to copy in the Clipboard task pane. (If the Office Clipboard doesn't show, choose the Edit→Office Clipboard command.)

NOTE *You aren't limited to moving items just within a presentation or the PowerPoint program. You can move items between PowerPoint presentations and even between different programs' documents—such as from Microsoft Word to PowerPoint. The only trick is that after you cut or copy the item, you need to open the presentation or document into which you want to paste the item.*

SEE ALSO *Clipboard, Copying Text and Objects*

Music

You can also play a music CD track during a presentation. To do this, you need, predictably, the CD in your computer's CD drive or DVD drive.

To play a sound or track from a CD, choose the Insert→Movies And Sounds→Play CD Audio Track command so that PowerPoint displays the Movie And Sound Options dialog box. Use the Play CD Audio Track Start boxes to enter the track number of the first track you want to play and the Play CD Audio Track End boxes to enter the track number of the last track you want to play (see Figure M-12). To play only one track, enter the same track number into both boxes.

Figure M-12 The Movie And Sound Options dialog box.

To play only a portion of the track, enter the starting times in the Start At box and the ending times in the End At boxes. Using the Start At and End At boxes means, of course, that you need to know the exact time the portion of the track you want to listen to starts and ends.

If you want to have the track continue to replay, you can check the Loop Until Stopped box. The Loop Until Stopped box appears near the top of the Movie And Sound Options dialog box in the Play Options area.

SEE ALSO *Sounds*

Net Show Server see Broadcasting Presentations

Normal View see Views

Notes see Speakers Notes

Numbered Lists

You can turn the selected paragraphs or bulleted points into a numbered list by clicking the Numbering toolbar button. You can also turn the selected paragraphs into a numbered list by choosing the Format→Bullets and Numbering command, clicking the Numbered tab, and clicking the box that shows the numbering you want (see Figure N-1).

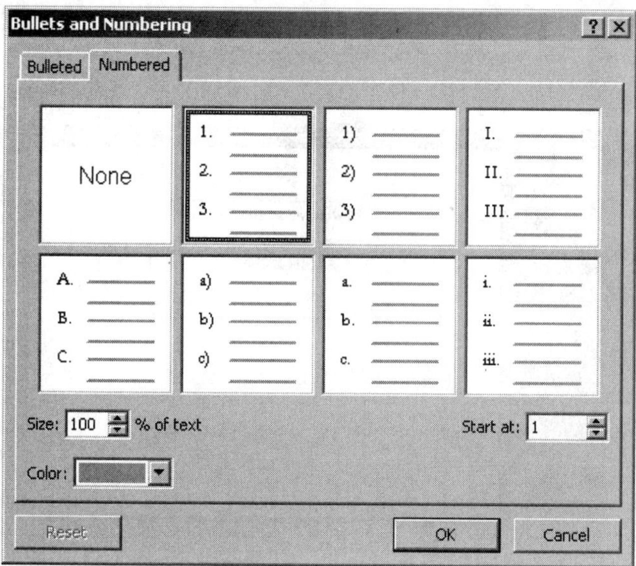

Figure N-1 The Numbered tab of the Bullets and Numbering dialog box.

If you're creating multiple numbered lists, you may need to use the Start At box to get PowerPoint to number the paragraphs correctly. PowerPoint guesses at how it should number paragraphs, but when you're working with long lists that take more than one slide, PowerPoint's guesses are less likely to be correct.

NOTE *If you customize numbering in some way you later realize doesn't make sense, you can use the Reset button, which appears on the Numbered tab, to remove your customization.*

Office Assistant

In Office programs, the Office Assistant supplies help. To use the Office Assistant, click the Office Assistant. (If the Office Assistant isn't already displayed, choose the Help→Show Office Assistant command.) Then type your question into the box provided and click Search. The Office Assistant displays a list of help topics that may answer your question (see Figure O-1).

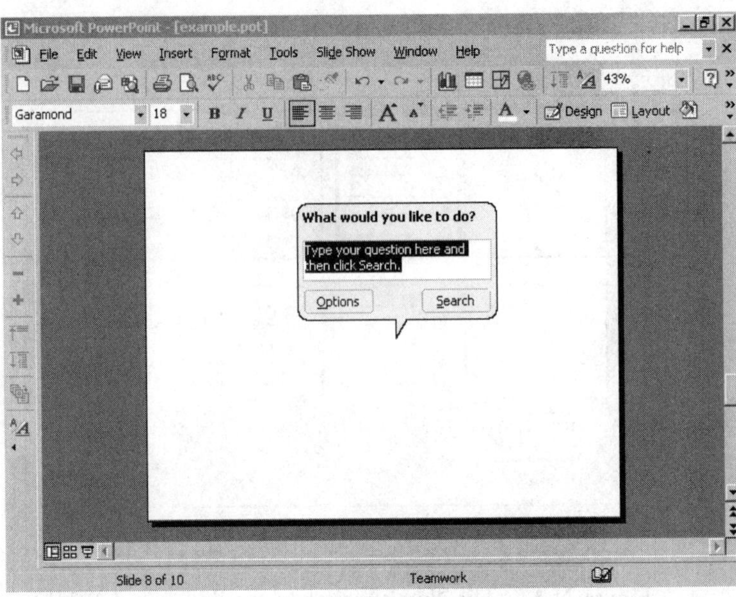

Figure O-1 The Office Assistant's help balloon.

Click the help topic you want to see (see Figure O-2). The Office Assistant opens the PowerPoint help file (see Figure O-3).

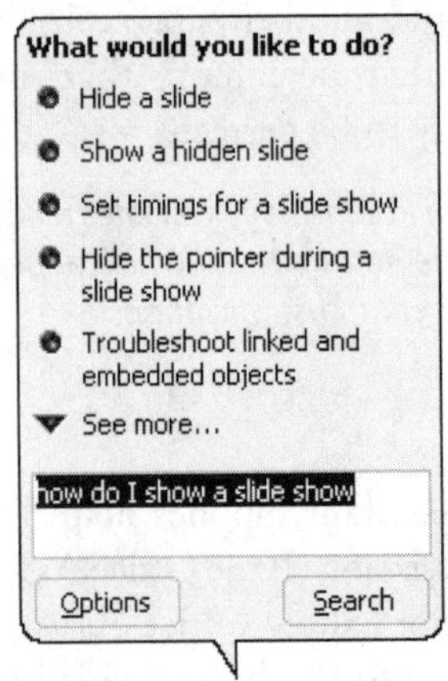

Figure O-2 The Office Assistant's list of help topics.

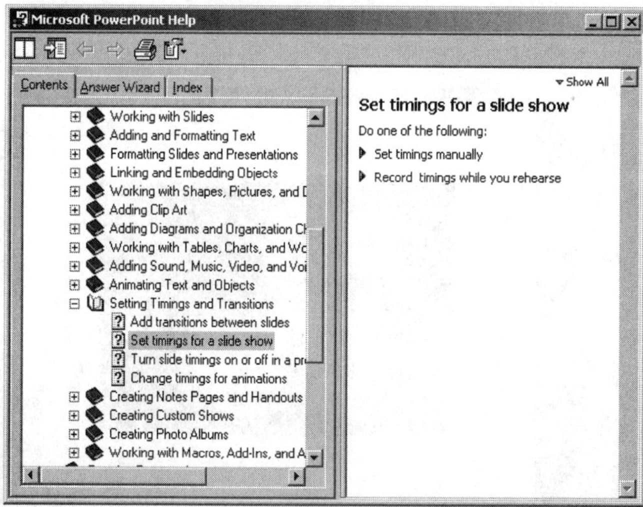

Figure O-3 The Help window.

TIP *You can also ask the Office Assistant a question by typing the question directly into the Ask A Question box, which is actually labeled, "Type your question here."*

SEE ALSO *Troubleshooting*

Object

In addition to text, you can place other items such as charts and a wide variety of other objects on a slide (see Figure O-4). PowerPoint calls these items *objects*.

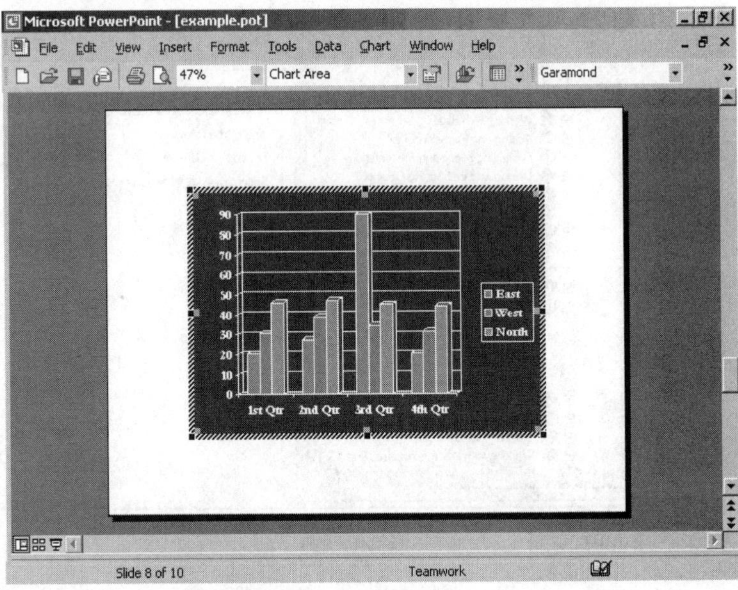

Figure O-4 A PowerPoint slide with a chart object.

Anything you can create or store on your computer can probably be turned into an object and then placed on a PowerPoint slide. Objects can be little images or pictures stored as files on your hard disk; or even things like charts, organization charts and drawings you create with PowerPoint's many applets.

NOTE *PowerPoint supplies several small programs, called applets. The applets are essentially miniature programs that are built into the larger PowerPoint program. PowerPoint includes the Microsoft Graph applet, for example, which lets you create charts and graphs. The Microsoft Organization Chart applet, also available from within the PowerPoint program, lets you create organization charts.*

Organization Chart

PowerPoint also lets you add organization chart objects to slides.

Adding an organization chart

To add an organization chart to a slide, follow these steps:

1. Select the slide.

2. Choose the Insert→Picture→Organization Chart command. PowerPoint adds an organization chart object to the slide and displays the Organization Chart and Drawing toolbars (see Figure O-5).

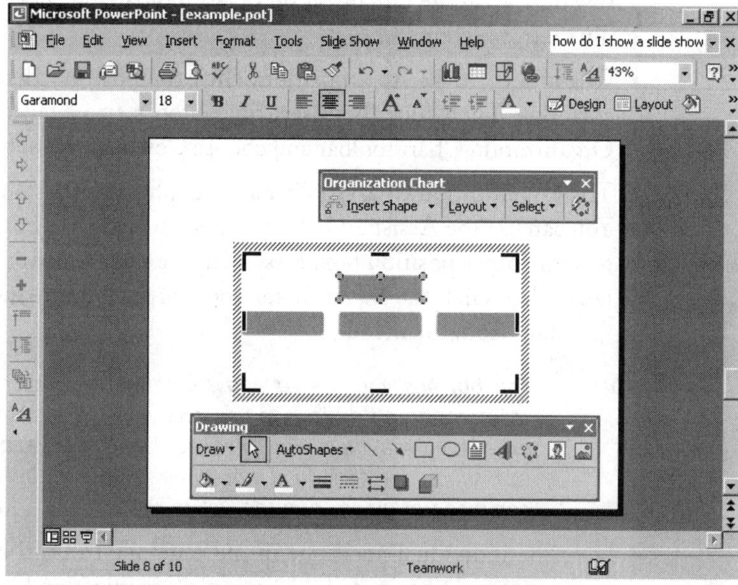

Figure O-5 The PowerPoint window showing an organization chart object.

3. Describe the organization's structure using boxes and lines. Each of the boxes on the organization chart represents a position. Some positions are manager positions, and some positions are subordinate positions. Although the Organization Chart program initially creates a rough guess of your organizational structure (a manager with three subordinates), you need to update this organizational structure to reflect reality. You do this by removing any unneeded boxes and then adding any new, necessary boxes.

- To add a subordinate position, click the box that represents the subordinate's manager. For example, if you want to add a fourth subordinate to the Manager box, you click the Subordinate button and then the Manager box. Then click the Insert Shape tool's arrow button on the Organization Chart toolbar and choose Subordinate from the menu.
- To add a coworker to a position, click the position that has the coworker. Then click the Insert Shape tool's arrow button on the Organization Chart toolbar and choose Coworker from the menu.
- The Organization Chart toolbar also supplies an Assistant button. You can use the Assistant button to add an Assistant Position box to some other position box. First click the position with an assistant. Then click the Insert Shape tool's arrow button and choose Assistant from the menu.

NOTE *The buttons you use to add subordinates, coworkers, and assistants aren't difficult to use, and your best bet is simply to experiment with them. You can remove any organization position box simply by clicking it and then choosing the Edit→Cut command or by pressing the Delete key.*

4. Describe individual positions in more detail. To do this, click a position box. When you do, Microsoft Organization Chart turns the box into a text box. Type the position information you want. Typically, you put the name of the person filling the position on the first line and put the person's title on the second line. If you want, you can also include a line or two of comment or general information. You can edit this position box text in the same way you edit text anywhere else. You then need to continue to describe the other positions until you construct the completed organization chart (see Figure O-6).

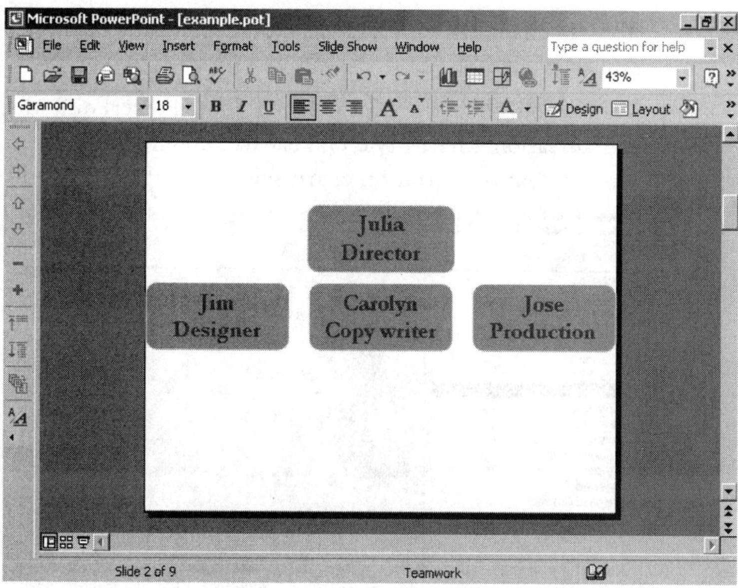

Figure O-6 A simple organization chart.

Customizing an organization chart

Organization Chart objects can be customized in a variety of ways:

The Layout menu displays a menu of pictures that show the various organization chart styles you can use. The Layout menu also includes four commands for resizing and rearranging the organization chart, its boxes, and its lines: Fit Organization Chart To Contents, Expand Organization Chart, Scale Organization Chart, and AutoLayout. Again, these commands show pictures that explain what they do. You choose the command that shows a picture of what you want.

To format text in an organization chart object, first select the position box or boxes you want to reformat. You can select one position box by clicking it. If you want to select all position boxes, or some group of them, choose the Select menu command that corresponds to the group of position boxes you want to arrange. After you've selected the position boxes you want to change, you can use the Format→Font command to change the font.

You can change the appearance of the organization chart by using the AutoFormat tool.

When you click the AutoFormat tool, PowerPoint displays the Organization Chart Style Gallery (see Figure O-7). To change the look of your organization chart, select one of the styles listed.

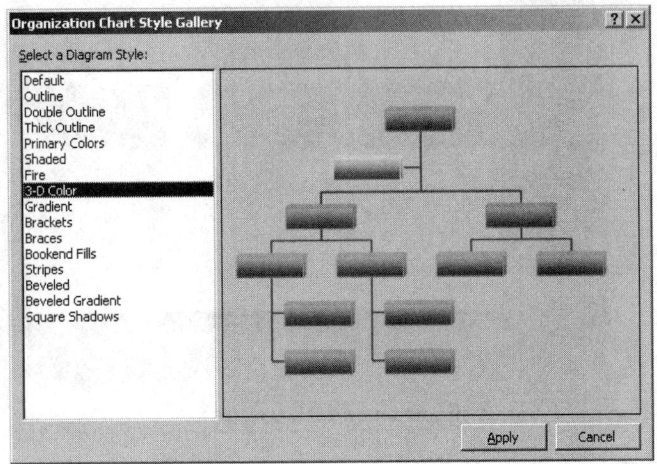

Figure O-7 The Organization Chart Style Gallery window.

OLE

OLE, the name of the Windows technology, lets you copy and paste objects between documents. It is OLE, for example, that lets you copy an Excel chart and then paste that chart into a PowerPoint presentation. You don't have to know anything special in order to use OLE. And that's part of the attractiveness of the technology. If you can copy, cut and paste, you can use OLE.

SEE ALSO *Copying Text and Objects, Embedding Objects, Moving Text and Objects*

Online Meeting see Broadcasting Presentations

Overtyping see Insert Key

Outlining a Presentation

An Outline lists the slides in a presentation, slide text, and each slide's bulleted points.

If you create a new presentation using the AutoContent Wizard, PowerPoint creates a rough-draft outline for you. If you create a new presentation based on a design template or a blank presentation, you must create your outline.

To create an outline from scratch or to modify an existing outline, you use the Outline pane (see Figure O-8).

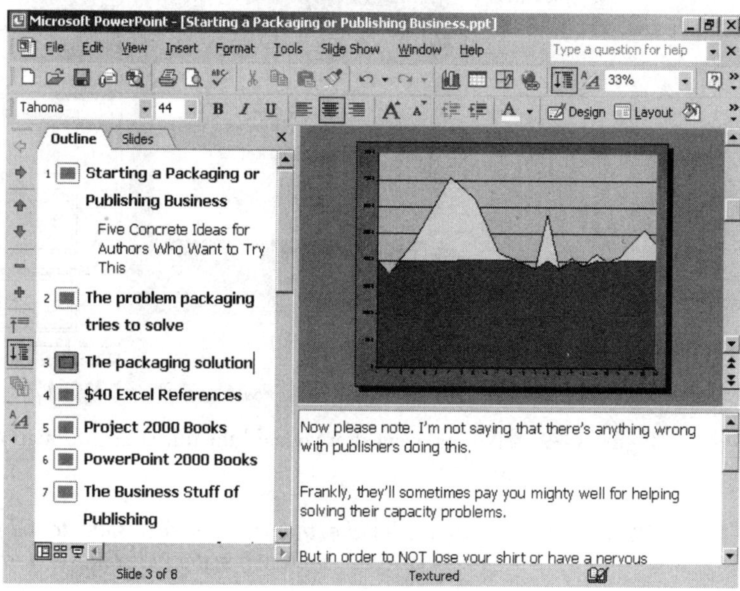

Figure O-8 The Outline pane.

Creating an outline from scratch

If you don't use the AutoContent Wizard to create an outline, you need to create your outline from scratch. The outline lists the slides you want in your presentation. The outline also includes bullet points for each slide, if appropriate.

To create an outline from scratch, follow these steps:

1. Click the outline tab in the Outline pane and then click the first slide listed in the Outline pane. This slide shows only a number 1 and a small slide icon. After you select the slide, type the text you want to title or label the first slide of your presentation (see Figure O-9).

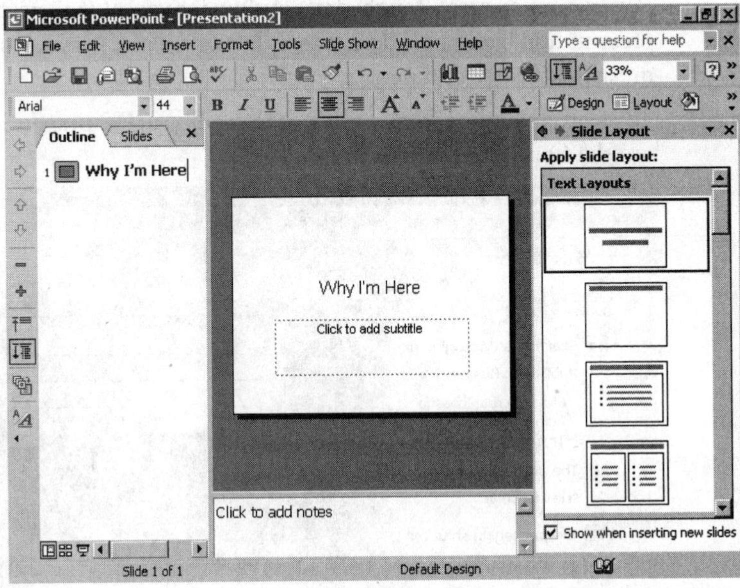

Figure O-9 Normal view after you add the title slide information to the outline.

NOTE *PowerPoint uses the title of your first slide to fill the title placeholder on the slide shown in the Slide pane in Normal view.*

2. To describe the next slides in your presentation, press the Enter key. PowerPoint adds a new, blank slide to the outline. To give this slide a title, select the slide by clicking; then type the slide title.

You need to describe each of the other slides you want in your presentation. To do this, you can just repeat the process described in the preceding paragraph.

TIP *You don't have to add slides to the outline by entering slide titles into the Outline pane. You can also insert a slide by choosing a slide layout from the Slide Layout task pane. To add a slide to your presentation, choose the slide layout that includes the correct set of object placeholders. You can use the Slide Layout task pane to add slides to the outline when you know what object placeholders you want on the slide. You don't need to do this, but you can.*

3. To add bulleted text to a slide and your outline, click the outline tab in the Outline pane and then select the slide by clicking its icon. Then press the End key to move the selection cursor to the end of the slide title. Next, press the Enter key. PowerPoint adds a new line to the outline for the new slide that it assumes you want to add. However, you don't want to add a new slide. You want to add bulleted text to the slide listed on the preceding line of the outline. So press the Tab key. PowerPoint indents the line selected in the outline. Now type the first line of bulleted text. After you've typed the first line, press Enter. PowerPoint inserts a line—only this time it knows that the line is another line of bulleted text. Type this next line of bulleted text. If you need to add additional lines of bulleted text, press Enter again and type again (see Figure O-10).

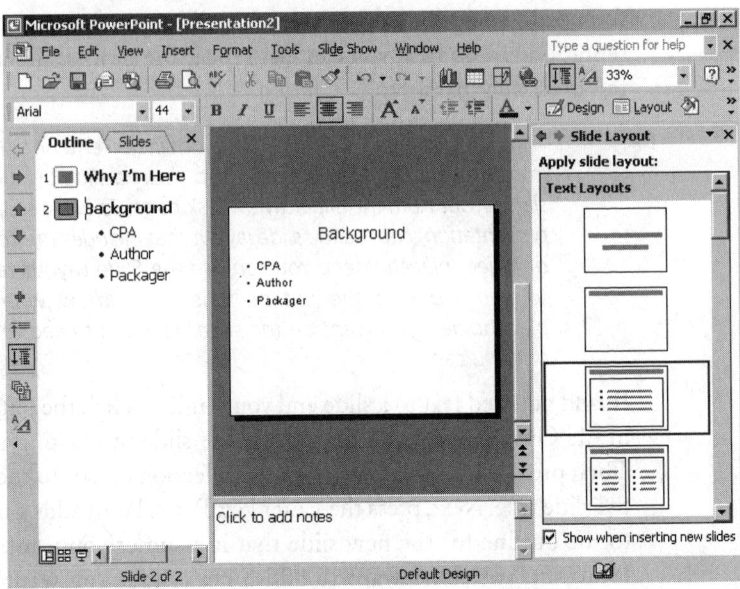

Figure O-10 Normal view after you add the bulleted text information to the outline.

To add bulleted text to other slides in your presentation, you follow the same process described in the preceding paragraph. First, you select the slide, and then you create bulleted text by adding lines to the outline—only at a lower, indented level.

TIP *Keep an eye on the slide shown in the Slide pane. You don't have that much space for text on your slides. Practically speaking, you often don't have room for more than a short, punchy title and three or four short bulleted text chunks.*

Importing an Outline

PowerPoint can often import an outline you've created in another program—such as an outline you've created using your word processing program. If PowerPoint can interpret your outline—because you've used tabs to indicate outline levels or Microsoft Word styles—simply by opening the outline file for PowerPoint, PowerPoint will use the imported outline as the basis for creating a PowerPoint outline.

TIP *When you import an outline, you are in effect starting with a blank presentation and then copying the outline text from the document that contains the outline. Although this method might seem to be a good way to create an outline, especially when you know another program well, it is probably not the best way to work. It's to your advantage to work within PowerPoint to create your presentation outlines because PowerPoint lets you see immediately how much slide text you are adding by using the Slide pane.*

To import an outline, follow these steps:

1. To tell PowerPoint that you want to open another document, choose the File→Open command. PowerPoint displays the Open dialog box (see Figure O-11). To tell PowerPoint that you want to look at other types of files (which will include those created by your outlining program), open the Files Of Type list box and select the All Outlines entry.

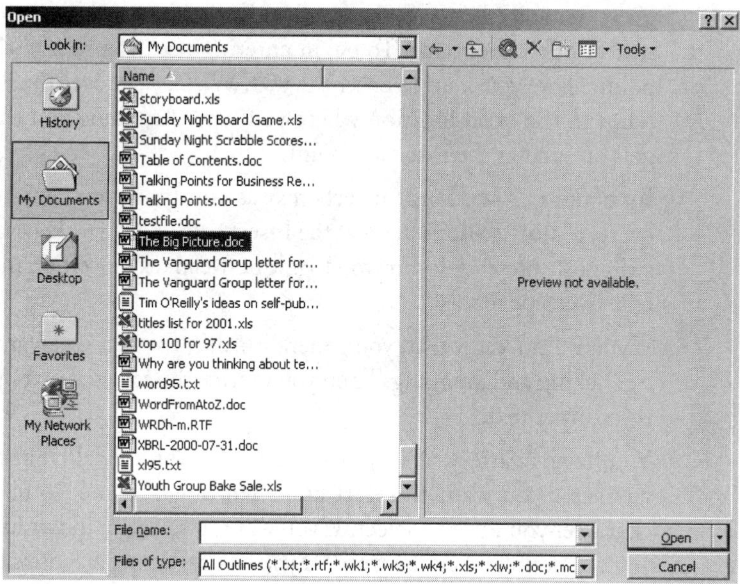

Figure O-11 The Open dialog box.

2. Locate the folder with the outline document by first opening the Look In drop-down list box and then selecting the disk and folder location. If your outline document is stored in a subfolder, you might need to select the subfolder from the list box that appears in the area beneath the Look In drop-down list box.

3. Open the outline document. PowerPoint will import the outline document into PowerPoint and then use its information to build a PowerPoint outline.

NOTE *In order for PowerPoint to import an outline document, it uses a converter tool. If PowerPoint doesn't have the right converter tool already installed and available for use, you might need to install the converter tool first. To do this, find the Microsoft Office XP or Microsoft PowerPoint 2002 CD and insert it into your CD drive. PowerPoint will install the needed converter tool automatically, simply as part of the outline import process.*

After you've imported the outline document, you can work with it in the exact same way as you work with an outline you've created using the AutoContent Wizard or an outline you've created by typing text into the Outline pane.

Editing Your Outline

You enter and edit text in the Outline pane in the same way as you enter text in other programs. To begin entering text, you first click at the point where you want to enter the text. Windows moves the insertion point to the exact location where you type. Anything you then type gets entered at the insertion point.

By default, PowerPoint inserts text as you type. You can, however, overtype text. To do this, press the Insert key. The Insert key is a toggle switch. By pressing Insert, you toggle between text-insertion mode and text-overtype mode.

If you want to edit text, you generally select the text you want to edit by clicking and dragging. Then you replace the selected text by typing the correct text.

You have a variety of ways to select text. You can click at the first character you want to select and then drag the mouse to the last character you want to select. If you want to select an individual word, you can double-click the word. If you want to select an entire line, you can click the area in front of the line, just in front of the bullet or the slide icon. But note that if you select a slide title line of text, you'll also select the bulleted text.

To delete text, select the text and then choose the Edit→Clear command. Or, select the text and then press the Delete key.

Using the Outlining toolbar

If you are going to do much work with a PowerPoint outline, use the Outlining toolbar (see Figure O-12). It provides several useful buttons you can click to make outlining easier. To display the Outlining toolbar, choose the View→Toolbar command. PowerPoint displays the Toolbar submenu. To tell PowerPoint that you want to use the Outlining toolbar, choose the Outlining command from the Toolbar submenu. When you do, PowerPoint places a check mark in front of the Outlining command.

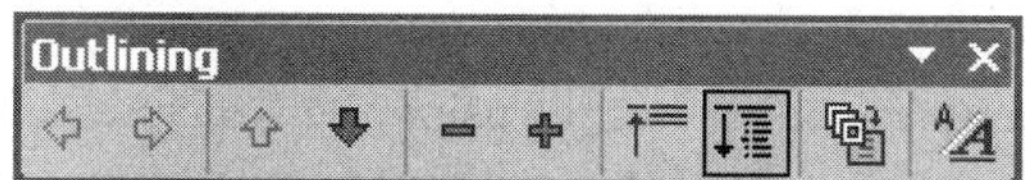

Figure O-12 The Outlining toolbar.

NOTE *The Outlining toolbar can be either docked or floating. Figure O-12 shows a floating Outlining toolbar, but the Outlining toolbar is usually docked against the left edge of the PowerPoint window.*

- The *Promote* and *Demote* buttons let you promote and demote outline text. You can use the Promote button, for example, to turn a bulleted point into a slide. And you can use the Demote button to turn a slide into a bulleted point.
- The *Move Up* and *Move Down* buttons let you move text up and down. To move a line of text up, first select the text and then click the Move Up button. The Move Up button is an arrow pointing upward. If you want to move text down, first select the text and then click the Move Down button. The Move Down button shows an arrow pointing downward. If you move bulleted text up or down, you simply rearrange the bulleted points. However, if you move slides up and down, you rearrange the order of the slides in the presentation.

NOTE *By moving outline text, you rearrange the order of slides and bullet points.*

- The Outlining toolbar provides *Collapse* and *Expand* buttons you can use to show more outlining detail and to hide outlining detail. To hide the lower levels of an outline—those levels below the slide title level—select the portion of the outline you want to hide. Then click the Collapse button. The Collapse button shows a minus sign. If you later want to expand the previously collapsed portion of the outline, select the previously collapsed lines of the outline. Then click the Expand button. The Expand button shows a plus symbol.
- If you click the *Collapse All* button, PowerPoint collapses the entire outline so that only the slide titles show.
- If you collapse the entire outline using the Collapse All toolbar button, you can click the *Expand All* button to later uncollapse the outline.
- The *Summary Slide* button creates a summary slide that lists some or all of the slides in your presentation.
- The *Show Formatting* button shows the outline text using the same character fomatting as the slides.

Pack And Go Wizard

You don't need the PowerPoint program in order to show a presentation. You can create a stand-alone version of a presentation that includes all the slides in your presentation and make a copy of the PowerPoint Viewer program, which lets you show those slides.

To create such a stand-alone presentation, first open the presentation and then choose the File→Pack And Go command. PowerPoint starts the Pack And Go Wizard (see Figure P-1). To use the wizard, just answer its questions by clicking buttons and filling in boxes.

Figure P-1 The first Pack And Go Wizard dialog box.

The Pack And Go Wizard assumes that you want to package the active presentation, but you can package any presentation you've already created (see Figure P-2).

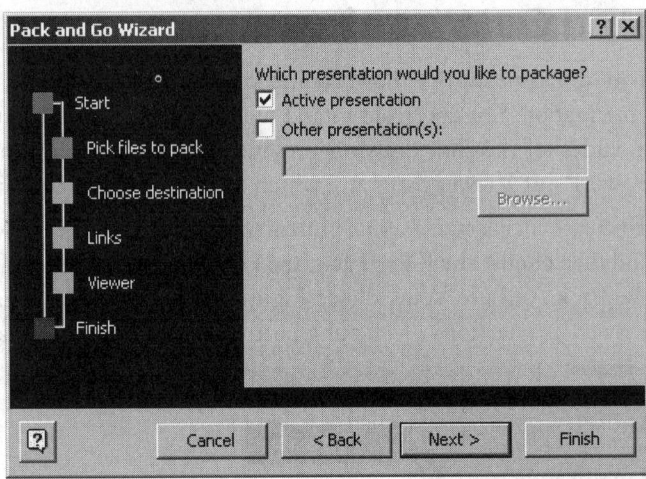

Figure P-2 The second Pack And Go Wizard dialog box.

The Pack And Go Wizard asks which removable disk you want to use to create the stand-alone presentation (see Figure P-3). The wizard's other dialog boxes ask you about which building blocks, such as linked files and fonts, you want to bundle with your presentation. (Your best bet is to simply accept the default or suggested settings if you have questions.)

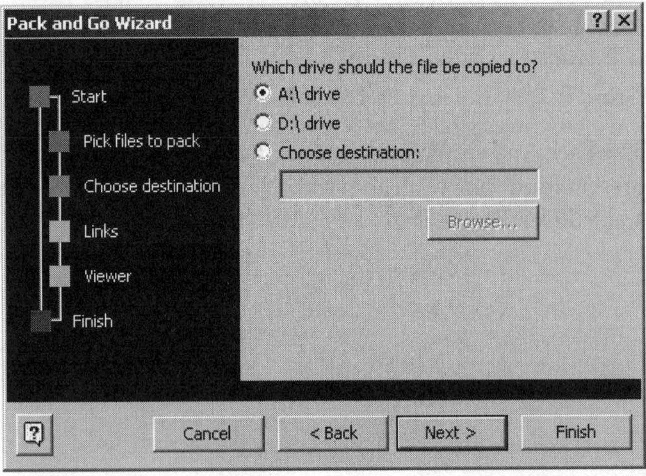

Figure P-3 The third Pack And Go Wizard dialog box.

After you've provided this information, you simply click Finish. PowerPoint then creates a stand-alone version of your presentation and copies this information to the removable disk you've indicated. PowerPoint will also copy the PowerPoint Viewer program you use to view this stand-alone program.

NOTE *The PowerPoint Viewer program, when it is installed, takes roughly 5 megabytes of disk space.*

Page Orientation

PowerPoint will print your presentation slides, handouts, note pages, and outlines in either a portrait orientation or a landscape orientation. To change the current orientation of the open document, choose the File→Page Setup command. Use the Slides Portrait and Landscape buttons to specify the page orientation of printed slides. Use the Notes, Handouts and Outline buttons to specify the page orientation of printed speakers notes, audience handouts, and outlines (see Figure P-4).

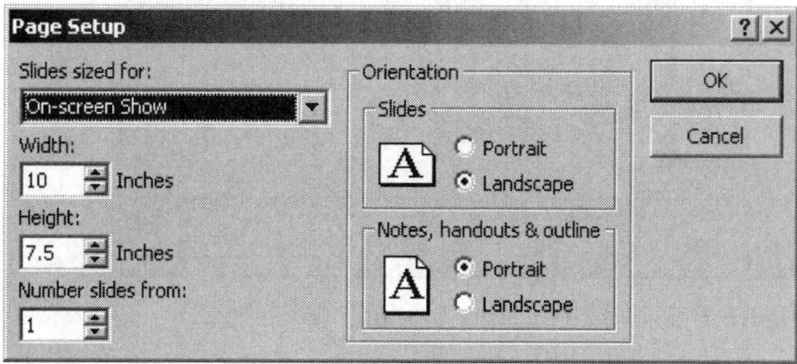

Figure P-4 The Page Setup dialog box.

SEE ALSO *Audience Handouts, Presentations, Outlines, Speakers Notes*

Paragraph

PowerPoint, like Microsoft Word, views as a paragraph any block of text that ends with you pressing the Enter key. Therefore, a paragraph in PowerPoint is any chunk of text that ends with the Enter key being pressed. The bulleted or numbered points on a slide, for example, are paragraphs.

NOTE *Interestingly, pressing the Enter key actually adds to the text a special, hidden symbol called the end-of-paragraph marker.*

Password Protecting a Presentation

To add password protection to a presentation, choose the File→Save As command, click the Tools button, and then choose the Security Options command. PowerPoint displays the Security Options dialog box, which you use to add and remove passwords (see Figure P-5).

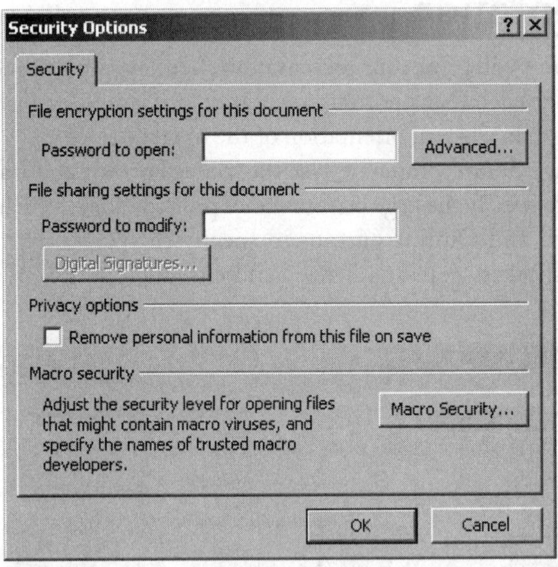

Figure P-5 The Security Options dialog box.

Adding Protection

To add a password which PowerPoint will require before it opens the presentation, enter the password into the Password To Open box. To add a password which PowerPoint will require before it saves the presentation using the same name and location, enter the password into the Password To Modify box. Your passwords may use any combination of letters, symbols and numbers, up to 15 characters. Capitalization counts.

Removing Protection

To remove a password from a previously protected document, delete the contents of the Password To Open and Password To Modify boxes.

Using Advanced Encryption

Click the Advanced button to display a list of encryption methods PowerPoint can use to protect your presentation (see Figure P-6). While PowerPoint's normal encryption is adequate in most settings, extremely sensitive data may warrant a more secure encryption.

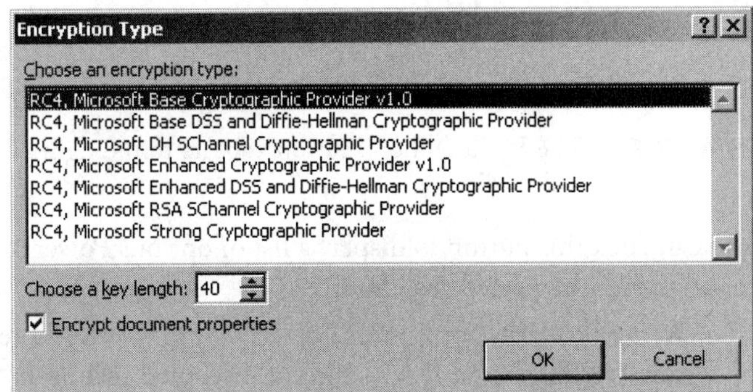

Figure P-6 The Encryption Type dialog box.

SEE ALSO *Macro Security, Privacy Options*

Pasting

When you copy or move some item, your last step is to paste the item from the clipboard. You typically paste using the Paste toolbar button, the Edit→Paste command, the Office Clipboard, or indirectly by dragging the mouse.

SEE ALSO *Clipboard, Copying Text and Objects, Moving Text and Objects, Paste Options button*

Paste Options button

When you paste a text selection in PowerPoint, PowerPoint displays a Paste Options button in your document (see Figure P-7).

Figure P-7 The Paste Options button appears to the right of the last bullet point.

You can click this button to display a list of options PowerPoint uses for adjusting the pasted selection:

- *Keep Source Formatting* tells PowerPoint to use the same format ting for the pasted text as the cut or copied text used.
- *Use Design Template Formatting* tells PowerPoint to format the pasted text so it matches the design template.
- *Keep Text Only* tells PowerPoint not to format the pasted text.

SEE ALSO *Clipboard, Copying Text and Objects, Moving Text and Objects*

Pathname

A pathname describes a file's location on your computer or network. Typically, a pathname includes three parts: the disk or network drive letter, folder and subfolder information, and the file name and extension. For example, look at the pathname shown below:

f:\atoz\powerpoint\proposal.ppt

The first portion of this pathname, *f:*, identifies the drive on which the folders and their files are stored. The second part of the pathname, *\atoz\powerpoint*, names the folder and subfolder where the file is stored. The *atoz* part of the pathname identifies the folder, and the *powerpoint* part of the pathname identifies the subfolder. The *proposal.ppt* identifies the exact file by giving its file name and the file extension.

NOTE *The back slashes separate the drive letter, folder and subfolder names, and the file name.*

SEE ALSO *File Extensions, File Names*

Personalized Menus and Toolbars

PowerPoint personalizes your menus and toolbars. Menu commands and toolbar buttons you're likely to use or that you've recently used appear. Menu commands and toolbar buttons that you're not likely to use or haven't used in a long time don't appear.

To change the way the PowerPoint's personalized menus and toolbars work, choose the Tools→Customize command and click Options tab (see Figure P-8). Then, use the Options tab to change the way the PowerPoint's personalized menus and toolbars work.

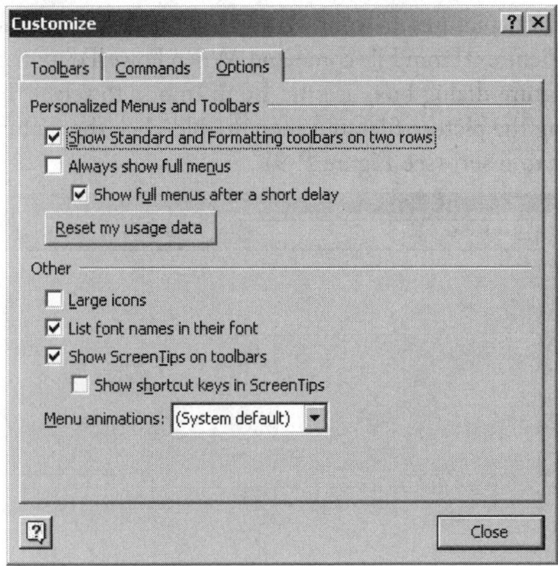

Figure P-8 The Options tab of the Customize dialog box.

- Check the Show Standard And Formatting Toolbars On Two Rows box to tell PowerPoint to use two separate toolbars for the Standard and Formatting toolbars rather than one personalized toolbar of just your most recently used tools.
- Check the Always Show Full Menus box to tell PowerPoint to display full menus rather than personalized menus.

- Check the Show Full Menus After A Short Delay check box if you're using personalized menus but want the full menu to appear if you hold the menu open for a few seconds.
- Click the Reset My Usage Data button to tell PowerPoint to start over in its analysis of which commands you've recently or are frequently using. This analysis is what PowerPoint uses to determine which commands and toolbar buttons go onto your personalized menus and toolbars.

SEE ALSO *Toolbars*

Pictures

You can add pictures to your PowerPoint slides by choosing the Insert→Picture→From File command. When PowerPoint displays the Insert Picture dialog box, use the Look In box to select the folder containing the picture files and then double-click the picture image you want to insert (see Figure P-9).

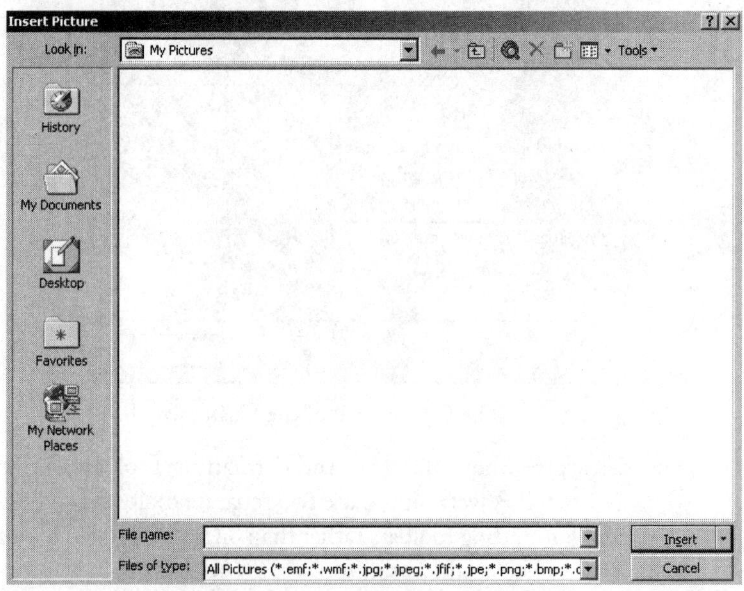

Figure P-9 The Insert Picture dialog box.

TIP *You can copy and move pictures in the same way that you copy and move other objects in a document. You resize a picture object by clicking the picture to select it and then dragging the selection handles. To delete a picture, click it and press Delete.*

SEE ALSO *Clip Art, Copying Text and Objects, Moving Text and Objects*

Placeholder

In PowerPoint, you enter text and any other items you use for slides into an area of a slide called a placeholder. A chunk of text, for example, goes into a placeholder. A picture, table, or chart also goes into a placeholder.

Placeholders amount to boxes, or areas, that you use to affix things to a slide (see Figure P-10). You can almost think of them as being like glue.

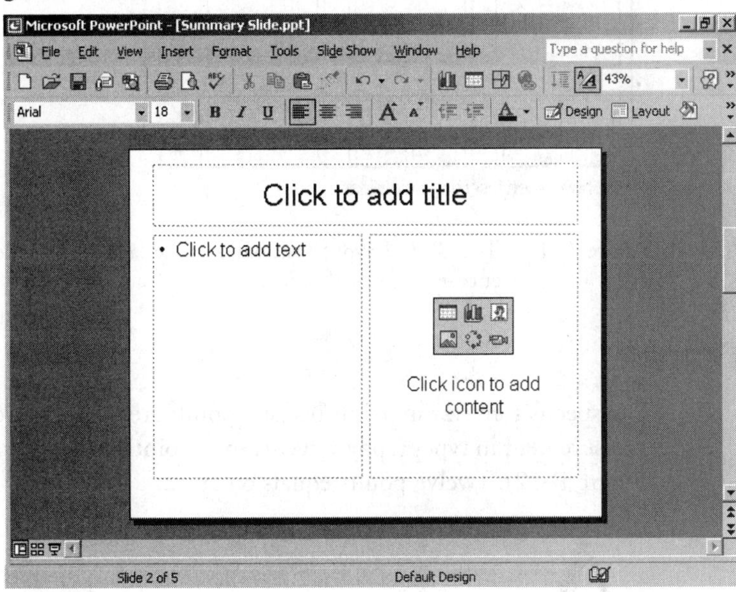

Figure P-10 A slide with placeholders.

Different slide layouts provide different sets of placeholders. For this reason when you use the Slide Layout task pane to choose a slide layout, you choose a slide layout for its placeholders (see Figure P-11).

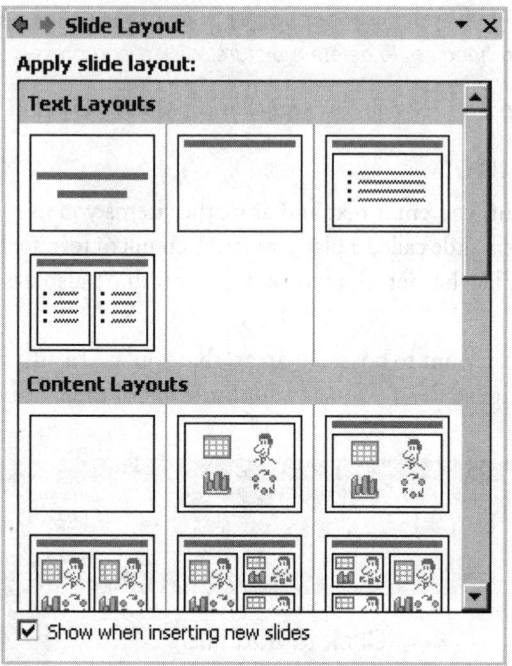

Figure P-11 The Slide Layout task pane's slide layouts provide different sets of placeholders.

Point

You specify font size in points because points are the standard unit of measurement in typography. Seventy-two points equal one inch (see Figure P-12). Twelve points equals one pica.

Figure P-12: An "A" in 72-point type.

SEE ALSO *Fonts*

Portrait Orientation see Page Orientation

Presentation

A presentation consists of the slides you've created. A presentation is also, from the PowerPoint perspective, a document file. What is stored on your hard disk or on a removable disk, like a floppy disk or zip disk, is actually the presentation file.

If you've worked with Microsoft Word or any other word processing program, you can think of the relationship between a presentation and a slide in the same way you think of a document and a page. A document, such as a report you create using Word, consists of individual pages that combine to make the complete document. The individual pages of the report are stored in the document. In the same way, PowerPoint slides combine to make the complete presentation, which is actually stored in a presentation file.

Creating a New Presentation

To create a new blank presentation to which you'll add slides, click the New toolbar button.

To create a new presention using the AutoContent Wizard or a design template, choose the File→New command. When PowerPoint opens the New Presentation task pane, click one of the hyperlinks listed in the New or New From Template areas (see Figure P-13).

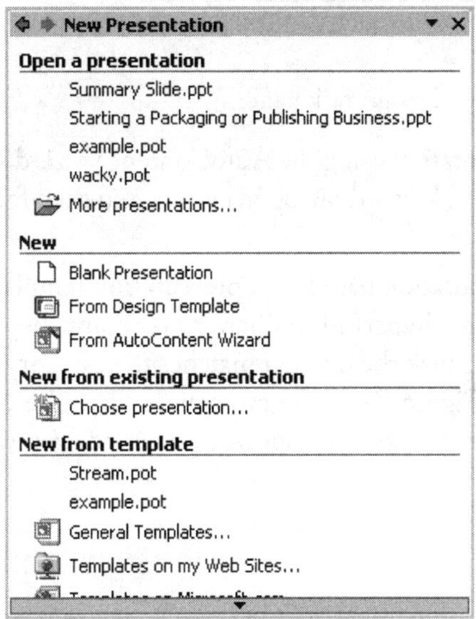

Figure P-13 The New Presentation task pane.

To create the new presentation based on a design template, click the From Design Template hyperlink to display the Slide Design task pane and then click the design template you want to use (see Figure P-14).

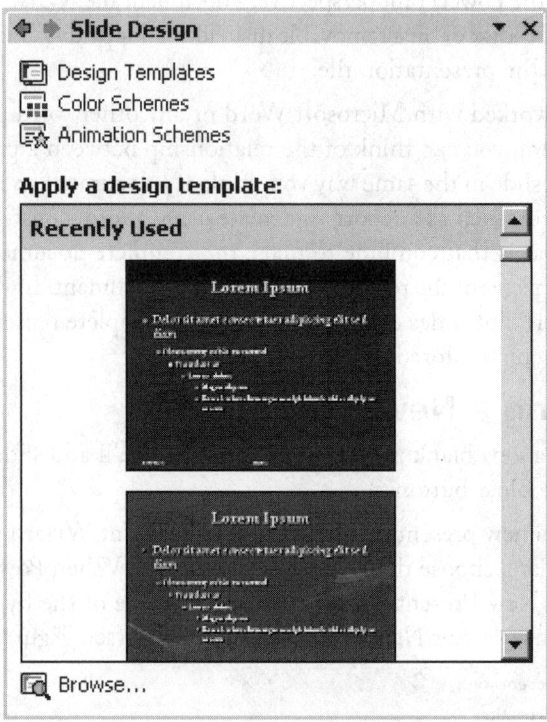

Figure P-14 The Slide Design task pane.

To create a new presentation using the AutoContent Wizard, click on the From AutoContent Wizard dialog hyperlink and then follow the wizard's instructions.

To create a new presentation based on a presentation template, click the General Templates hyperlink. When PowerPoint displays the Templates dialog box, click the tab that matches the category of template you want (see Figure P-15). Then, double-click the template icon that most closely matches the specific document you want.

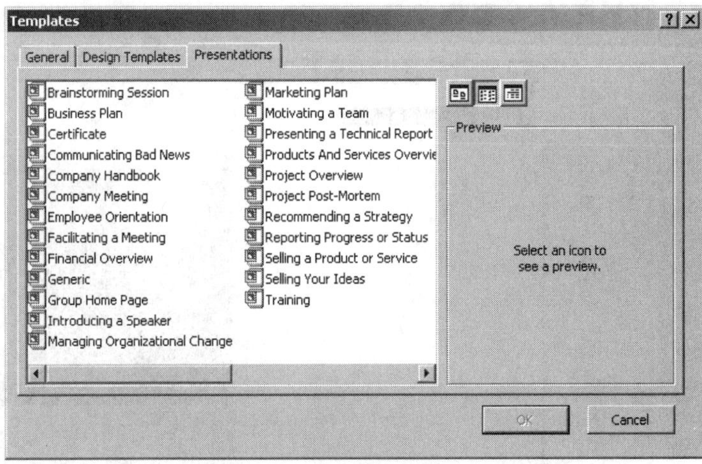

Figure P-15 The Templates dialog box.

NOTE *The Templates On My Web Sites and Templates On Microsoft.com hyperlinks, also available in the New Presentation task pane, let you retrieve PowerPoint templates over the Internet and Web.*

Opening a Presentation

You have several convenient choices for opening a presentation:

- **Documents menu.** If a presentation is listed under the Documents menu (displayed when you click the Start button and point to the Documents command) you can open the presentation by clicking it on the Documents menu.
- **New Presentation task pane.** If the New Presentation task pane shows a hyperlink to the presentation, you can open the presentation by clicking its hyperlink.
- **File menu list.** If a presentation is one you've recently opened using PowerPoint, the presentation may be listed at the bottom of the File menu. In this case, you can open the presentation by choosing it from the File menu.
- **File→Open command.** You can choose the File→Open command to display the Open dialog box (see Figure P-16). To use the Open dialog box, first select the folder containing your presentation from the Look In list box. Then, when PowerPoint lists the files in that folder, scroll through the list until you find the one you're looking for. When you see it, double-click it to open it.

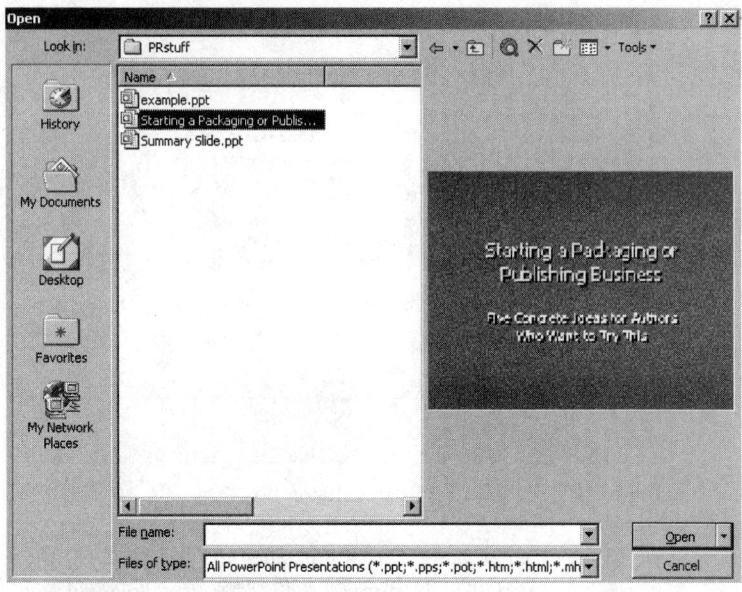

Figure P-16 The Open dialog box.

- **Open toolbar button.** You can also click the Open toolbar button to display the Open dialog box (see Figure P-16). Again, to use the Open dialog box, select the folder containing your presentation from the Look In list box, scroll through the list of presentation until you find the one you're looking for, and then double-click that document to open it.
- **My Computer or Windows Explorer.** If you use the My Computer window or Windows Explorer to display the folder containing your presentation, you can double-click the presentation to open it. When you open a PowerPoint presentation, Windows first starts PowerPoint and then instructs PowerPoint to open the presentation.

Closing a Presentation

To close a presentation, choose the File→Close command or click the document window's Close box.

NOTE *If you make changes to a presentation that hasn't been saved, PowerPoint asks if you want to save your presentation or lose your changes.*

TIP *You can close all the open presentations by holding down the Shift key and then choosing the File→Close All command.*

Saving a Presentation

To save a presentation, choose the File→Save command or click the Save toolbar button.

The first time you choose the File→Save command or click the Save toolbar button for new presentation, PowerPoint displays the Save As dialog box so you can name the file and specify where it should be saved (see Figure P-17). To use the Save As dialog box, follow these steps:

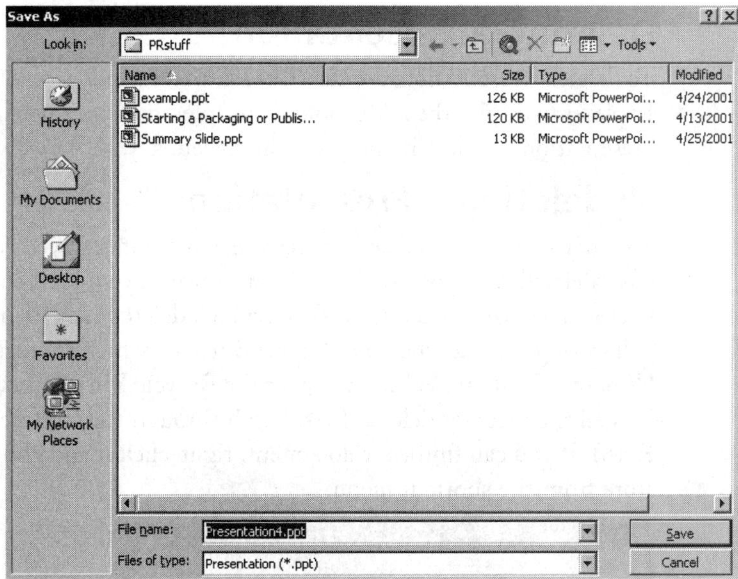

Figure P-17 The Save As dialog box.

1. Use the Look In box to pick the folder you want to save the presentation in.
2. Enter the name you want to use for the presentation into the File Name box.
3. (Optional) If you want to use this presentation with other programs or share the presentation with someone who doesn't have PowerPoint, open the Files Of Type list box and select a file format.

Re-Saving a Presentation

The subsequent times you save a presentation—the times after you've provided a name and specified a folder location—you also save the document using the File→Save command or the Save toolbar button.

When you re-save a presentation, PowerPoint doesn't display the Save As dialog box. It assumes you want to use the same file name and location.

Renaming and Relocating a Presentation

To name a presentation or relocate a presentation you've already saved, choose the File→Save As command, which again displays the Save As dialog box. Then, use the Save As dialog box to specify the new file name or location.

Deleting a Presentation

To delete a presentation, use the My Computer window or Windows Explorer to display the folder holding the presentation. Then click the presentation to select it and press the Delete key.

Undeleting a Presentation

You may be able to undelete, or restore, a presentation you've previously deleted. Windows sets aside a percentage of your hard disk space to store recently deleted files. To see which deleted files Windows is still storing, double-click the Recycle Bin icon, which appears on the Windows Desktop. Windows opens the Recycle Bin window, which lists all the recently deleted files. Scroll through the list (see Figure P-18). If you can find your document, right-click it and choose Restore from the shortcut menu.

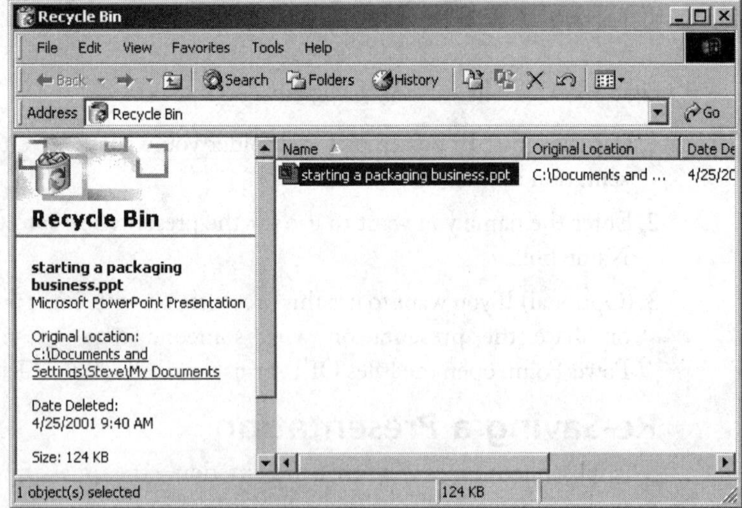

Figure P-18 The Recycle Bin window.

Importing a Presentation

To import a presentation into PowerPoint—say a presentation someone created using another presentation program—just open the presentation. PowerPoint comes with filters that let it open most popular presentation program's files.

NOTE *PowerPoint may prompt you for the installation CD if you didn't install the import filters when you originally installed PowerPoint.*

When PowerPoint can't successfully import a presentation, use the program that created the presentation—this might be the other presentation program, for example—to save the presentation in a common file format such as the Rich Text Format file format and open that presentation.

TIP *PowerPoint will open outlines you've created in Word and use those outlines as the basis of a presentation.*

Printing a Presentation

To print a presentation, click the Print toolbar button or choose the File→Print command. If you click the Print button, PowerPoint prints your presentation using the default, or usual, print settings. If you choose the Print command, PowerPoint displays the Print dialog box (see Figure P-19).

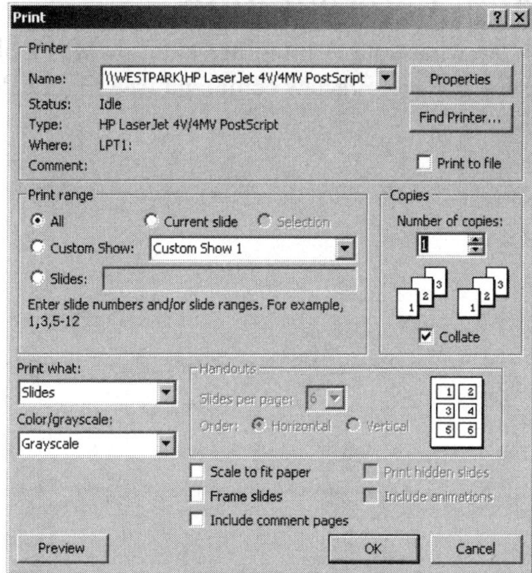

Figure P-19 The Print dialog box.

Use the Print dialog box's buttons and boxes to specify exactly how PowerPoint should print:

- Choose the printer from the Name list box, if the Name box doesn't already show the printer.
- Use the Print Range buttons to indicate whether you want to print all the slides in the presentation, just the current slide, a custom slide show (which is just a subset of the slides), or some set of slides.
- Use the Copies boxes to specify the number of copies you want printed and whether copies should be collated.
- Use the Print What list box to indicate whether you want to print presentation's slides, the speaker note pages, handouts, or an outline.
- Use the Color/Grayscale box to indicate whether you want to print in color, in grayscale tones, or in black and white.
- If you use the Print What list box to indicate that you want to print a handout for your audience, use the Handouts buttons and boxes to pick the number of slide images that should go on a handouts page and to specify how these images should be arranged.
- Use the check boxes at the bottom of the Print dialog box to further control how the presentation's slides are printed.

Previewing a Presentation

You can preview what your printed presentation will look like by choosing the File→Print Preview command (see Figure P-20).

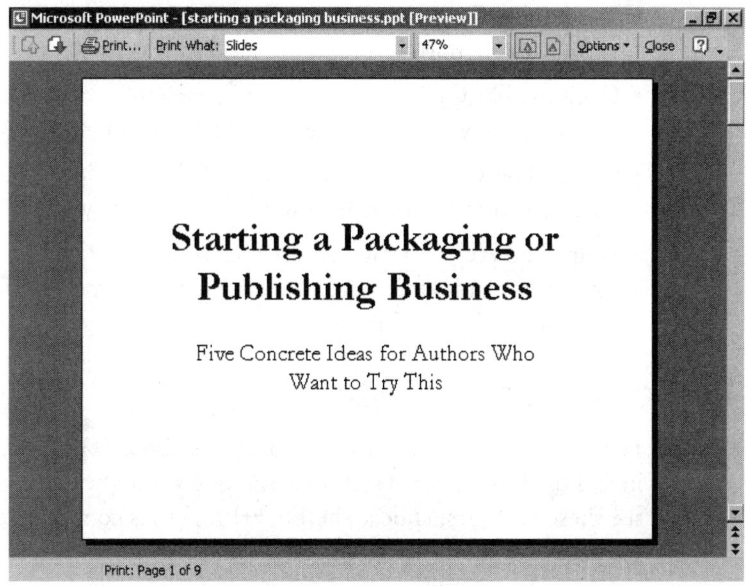

Figure P-20 The Print Preview window.

TIP *To preview a presentation, choose the Slide Show→View Show command or press the F5 key.*

The Print Preview window includes a toolbar with several handy tools for previewing your document:

- **Previous Page.** The Previous Page button tells PowerPoint to display the previous page in the Print Preview window.
- **Next Page.** The Next Page button tells PowerPoint to display the next page in the Print Preview window.
- **Print.** When you want to print the document, click the Print button. Or, choose the File→Print command.
- **Print What.** The Print What box lets you specify what PowerPoint will print—slides, handouts or speakers notes.
- **Zoom.** The Zoom box lets you adjust the size of the previewed document to the specified percentage of its actual size.
- **Landscape.** The Landscape button tells PowerPoint to print the PowerPoint slides using a landscape page orientation.

- **Portrait.** The Portrait button tells PowerPoint to print the PowerPoint slides using a portrait page orientation.
- **Options.** The Options button opens a menu of commands for fine-tuning the way PowerPoint will print the presentation information.
- **Close.** The Close button closes the Print Preview window and returns you to the regular PowerPoint program window.
- **Help.** The Help button lets you click some item, such as a button or menu command, and see relevant information from the PowerPoint help information file.

Presentation Statistics

PowerPoint collects a variety of statistics about your presentations including the number of slides, paragraphs, words, bytes and notes. To see these statistics, choose the File→Properties command and click the Statistics tab (see Figure P-21).

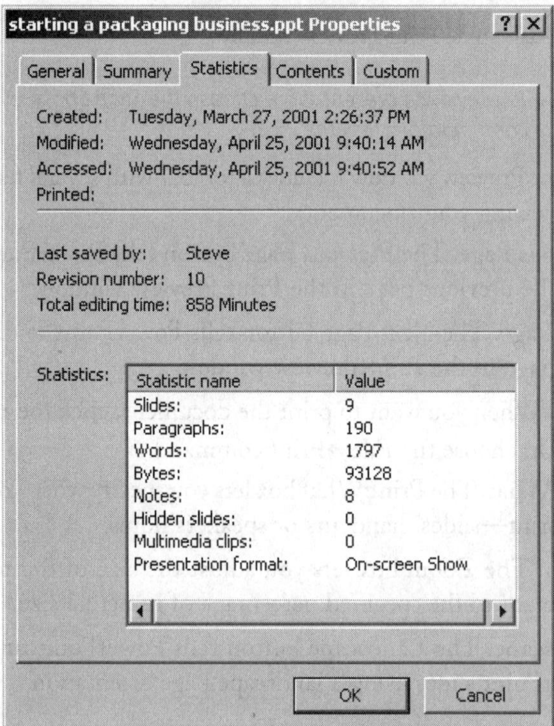

Figure P-21 The Statistics tab of Properties dialog box.

Previewing Presentations see Presentations, Slide Shows

Printer Setup

Normally, you set up and configure your printer using the Printers tool, available on the Windows Control Panel. You can also, however, configure your printer from within PowerPoint. To do so, choose the File→Print command and click the Properties command button. PowerPoint will open the printer's Properties dialog box (see Figure P-22). You can use its tabs to make changes to things such as the type of paper the printer uses, the quality at which the printer prints, and the page orientation.

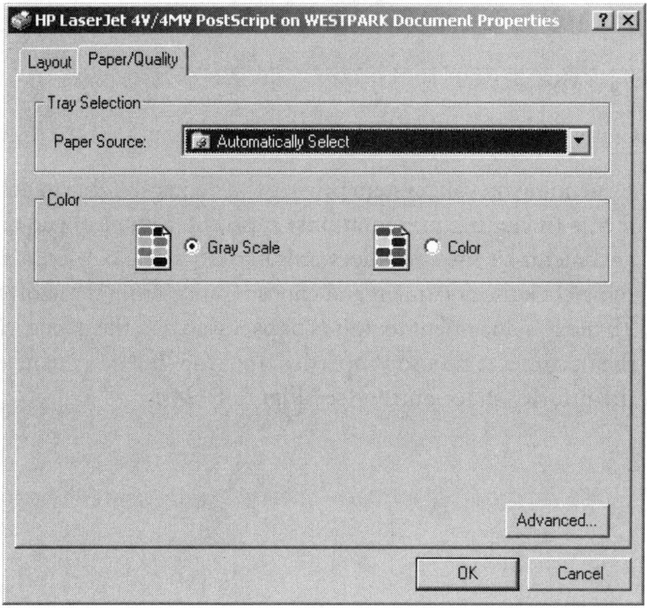

Figure P-22 An example printer properties dialog box.

NOTE *Different printers' properties dialog boxes look different.*

TIP *For information on working with your printer's properties dialog box, refer to the printer's documentation.*

Printing Presentations see Presentations

Print Queue

Windows shows a print queue, or line, of the documents, including presentations, waiting to print on a printer if you click the Start button, point to the Settings command, click the Printers command, and then double-click the printer (see Figure P-23).

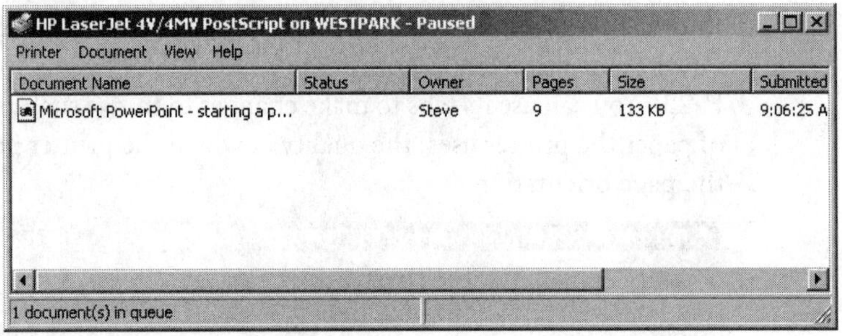

Figure P-23 A printer window.

Depending on your system privileges, you may be able to delete documents (including presentations) from the printer queue or to move documents backwards or forwards in the queue. To delete a document, right-click the document and choose Cancel from the shortcut menu. To move a document forwards or backwards in the queue, right-click the document, choose Properties from the shortcut menu and adjust the priority slider button (see Figure P-24).

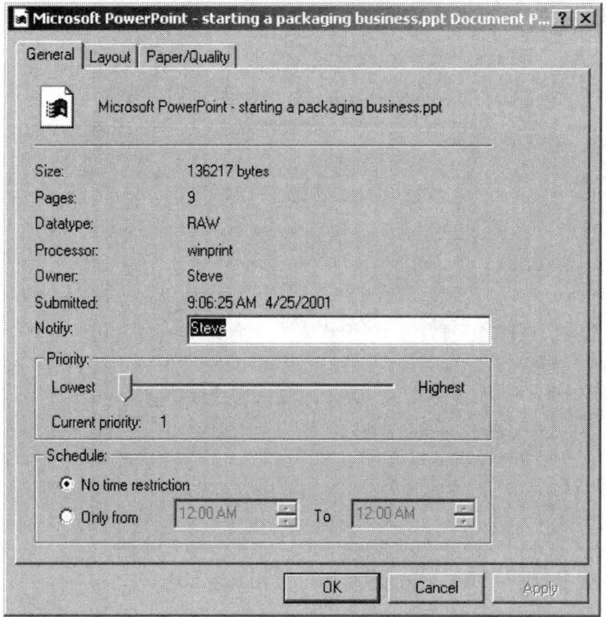

Figure P-24 The Printing document's properties dialog box.

SEE ALSO *Presentations, Printer Setup*

Privacy Options

You can limit the amount of secondary information stored with a presentation by adjusting PowerPoint's privacy options. To adjust PowerPoint's privacy options, choose the File→Save As command, click the Tools button, and then choose the Security Options command. PowerPoint displays the Security option dialog box (see Figure P-25). Check the Remove Personal Information From This File On Save to erase personal information (like your name) from the document before it's saved.

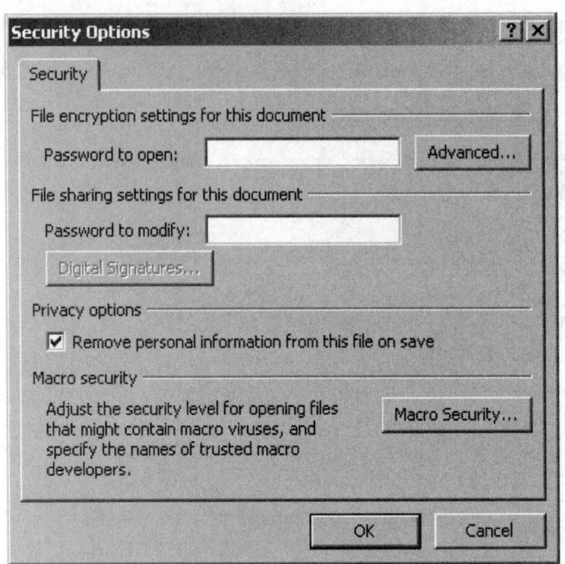

Figure P-25 The Security Options dialog box.

SEE ALSO *Macro Security, Password Protecting a Document*

Program Errors

PowerPoint program errors will occur. When this happens, either PowerPoint will stop responding, or hang, or PowerPoint will abort and stop. When these program errors occur, you may lose work.

Restarting PowerPoint

If PowerPoint aborts, you can restart the program in the same way that you start PowerPoint. For example, click the Start button, point to Programs, and then click on the Microsoft PowerPoint item.

When the PowerPoint program stops responding, you may be able to recover the application. To do this, click the Start button, point to Programs, Microsoft Office Tools, and then click the Microsoft Office Application Recovery item. When Windows displays the list of Office programs, select the PowerPoint program and click either the Recover Application or Restart Application button.

NOTE *If you just want to close the unresponsive program, and lose recent changes to the files, click the Start button, point to Pro-*

grams, Microsoft Office Tools, and click the Microsoft Office Application Recovery item, and then click End Application.

Recovering Presentations

When PowerPoint restarts or recovers after failing or stalling, you need to review the presentations listed in the Document Recovery pane. These are the presentations that were open when the PowerPoint program error occurred. You'll want to review the recovered presentations to find which are worth salvaging, and then save those.

NOTE *In the Document Recovery Pane, a file labeled as "recovered" includes more recent changes that the file labeled as "original."*

To open recovered presentations, point to the presentations in the Document Recovery pane, click the arrow button next to the presentations, and click Open.

To save presentations, point to the presentations, click the arrow button next to the presentations, and click Save As.

SEE ALSO *Presentations*

Recycle Bin

When you delete a PowerPoint presentation stored on one of your computer's local fixed disk drives, Windows doesn't immediately erase the presentation from the disk. Instead, Windows moves the file to the Recycle Bin folder. Eventually, Windows removes the "deleted" file from the Recycle Bin (to make room for other, more recently "deleted" files) but until that time you can recover the PowerPoint presentation by opening the Recycle Bin folder, selecting the file, and choosing the File→Restore command.

SEE ALSO *Presentations*

Redo see Undoing Mistakes

Rehearsing

PowerPoint includes a handy tool you can use to rehearse your presentation. To rehearse your presentation, including and perhaps especially the spoken part, open the presentation file you want to rehearse. Then choose the Slide Show→Rehearse Timings command. PowerPoint starts the slide show and also displays a Rehearsal timing toolbar you can use to time your presentation (see Figure R-1).

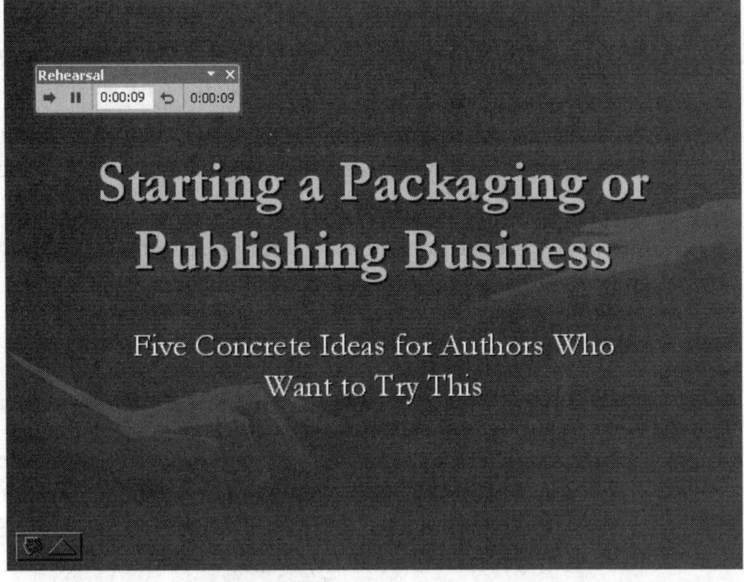

Figure R-1 The PowerPoint window with the Rehearsal timing toolbar.

The Rehearsal timing toolbar includes two timers—one that shows the time you've spent on that slide and one that shows the amount of time you've already spent on the presentation. The Rehearsal timing toolbar also includes a Pause button you can click to stop your rehearsal and the timer, a Next button you can use to move to the next slide, and a Repeat button you can use to restart the rehearsal timing.

To rehearse your presentation, simply say whatever you want to say about a slide using the same speaker's notes you'll use for your actual presentation. Then click the Next button and continue for the next slide. As you continue to move through the slides of your presentation, PowerPoint will track your time.

After you complete your presentation, PowerPoint displays a message box that shows the total time you spent for the slide show (see Figure R-2). You can also tell PowerPoint, simply by clicking the Yes button, that you want to record the time you spent on each slide and store this information with the slide. You might want to record your rehearsal timing information because you can later use these times to automate the display of the next slide.

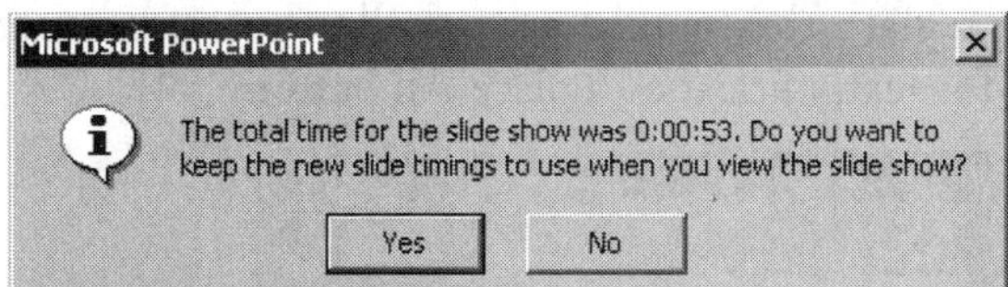

Figure R-2 The message box that reports on rehearsal timings.

NOTE *You can use rehearsal timings during a slide show to advance to the next slide.*

SEE ALSO *Setting Up a Presentation*

Replacing a Font

The Format→Replace Font command displays the Replace Font dialog box, which you can use to make wholesale changes in the fonts used in a presentation (see Figure R-3). Use the Replace box to identify the font you want to change. Use the With box to select the new font you want to use.

Figure R-3 The Replace Font dialog box.

SEE ALSO *Fonts*

Replacing Text

To replace text within a document, choose the Edit→Replace command. When PowerPoint displays the Replace dialog box, enter the text you want to search for into the Find What box and the replacement text in the Replace With box (see Figure R-4). Click the Find Next button to start PowerPoint searching the presentation. If PowerPoint finds the text, it highlights the text and makes your document window the active document window while leaving the Replace dialog box open but inactive. To replace the found text, click the Replace button. To continue searching, click the Find Next button again. To replace the found text and all other occurrences of the searched-for text, click the Replace All button.

Figure R-4 The Replace dialog box.

Use the Replace dialog box's check boxes to fine-tune your search criteria:

- Check the Match Case box to indicate whether the case of your search text needs to match exactly the case of the document text.
- Check the Find Whole Words Only box to indicate whether PowerPoint should only find whole word occurrences of the search text. For example, if you check this box and use "war" as your search text, PowerPoint will not find text such as "hardware," "warrant," and "thwart."

NOTE *PowerPoint's Find and Replace command do not allow the use of the ? wildcard or * wildcard characters.*

Resizing Objects see Sizing Objects

Resizing Text see Fonts

Resizing Windows see Sizing Windows

Rotating Objects

You can rotate, or spin, many of the objects you place on PowerPoint slides. To do so, click the object to select. Then, drag the green selection handle (see Figure R-5).

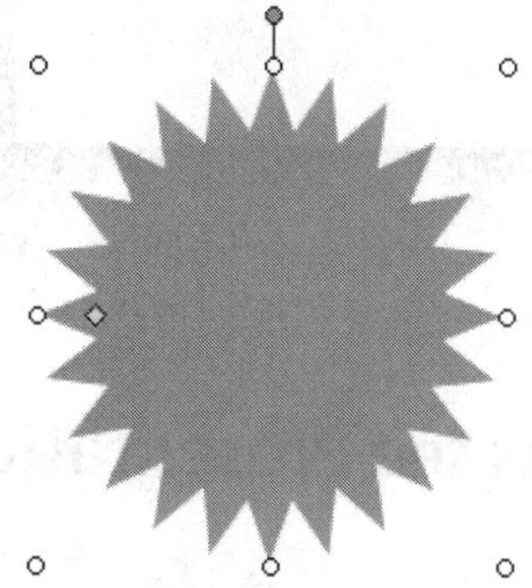

Figure R-5 A selected drawing object.

SEE ALSO *Clip Art, Drawing, WordArt*

Ruler

PowerPoint will add a ruler to the PowerPoint program window so you can carefully measure and position text and objects on your slides (see Figure R-6). To display the Ruler, choose the View→Ruler command. To remove the ruler, choose the command a second time.

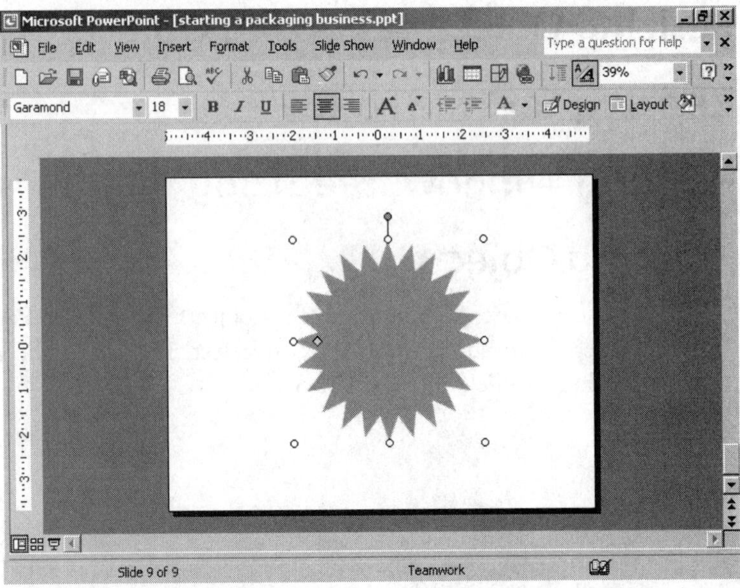

Figure R-6 The PowerPoint window with a ruler.

Saving Presentations see Presentations

Scrolling

You have several methods for scrolling, or paging, through the slides in PowerPoint presentation:

- You can use the slide pane's scroll bar. This scroll bar works like other scroll bars in Windows. You can click the arrows at either end of the scroll bar to scroll in the direction of the arrow. You can drag the scrollbar marker in the direction you want to scroll. You can also click above or below the scroll bar mark to move the marker in the direction you click.
- You can use the up and down arrow keys to move one line in the direction of arrow and the Page Up and Page Down keys to move one page up or down.
- You can click on a slide in the outline pane.
- If you're showing a slide show, you can also move to the next slide by press the space bar, by clicking a slide with the mouse, or by pressing the Enter key.

SEE ALSO *Go To*

Selecting Objects

Typically, you can select an object by clicking the object with the mouse. Note, though, that if another program (Excel, say) or another applet (WordArt, for example) created the object, you may need to double-click the object in order to simultaneously open and select the object for editing.

Selecting Text

You can select text in a variety of ways:

- To select individual characters or strings of text, click the first character you want to select and then drag the mouse to the last character you want to select. Alternatively, use the arrow keys to move the insertion point to just in front of the first character you want to select, hold down the Shift key, and then press the arrow keys or the Page Up and Page Down keys.
- To select a word, double-click it.
- To select a sentence, hold down the Ctrl key and click the sentence.
- To select a paragraph, triple-click inside the paragraph.
- To select the entire outline or entire table's text, click inside the text and press Ctrl+A.

Setting up a Presentation

To set up your presentation for a slide show, choose the Slide Show→Set Up Show command. When PowerPoint displays the Set Up Show dialog box, follow these steps (see Figure S-1).

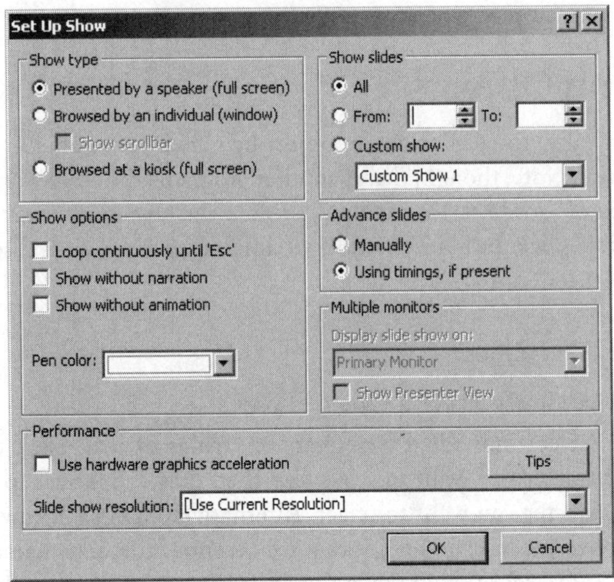

Figure S-1 The Set Up Show dialog box.

1. Mark the button in the Show Type area that corresponds to the way you will be presenting your presentation. If you will present the information in person, mark the Presented By A Speaker button. If you'll present the information by letting someone browse the slides of the presentation—in other words, you won't present the information but instead, audience members will view the information at their own pace—click the Browsed By An Individual button. If the information will be browsed at an unattended computer in a kiosk, click the Browsed At A Kiosk button.

NOTE *If you mark the Show Scrollbar check box, PowerPoint displays a scroll bar on the side of the Slide Show window. The Slide Show window that appears is available when you mark the Browsed By An Individual button. This scroll bar lets the individual browsing your presentation scroll through the presentation using the scroll bar.*

2. If you want the presentation to continue, or loop continuously, mark the Loop Continuously Until 'Esc' box. If you mark this check box, PowerPoint continues to display the slides in the presentation one after another until someone presses the Escape key. This means that after the last slide in the presentation is presented, PowerPoint redisplays the first slide.

3. If you want to include any narration you recorded for the presentation, uncheck the Show Without Narration box. If you don't want to record any narration, check the box. (Typically, a business professional user of PowerPoint won't record narration for a PowerPoint presentation.)

NOTE *To record narration for a presentation, you use the Slide Show→Record Narration command.*

4. To show your presentation without animation, mark the Show Without Animation check box. If you do want to include any animation you set up on slides, unmark this check box, of course.
5. Optionally, pick a pen color. PowerPoint lets you use a pen pointer if you want—you can draw on the slides using the mouse pointer during your presentation. You can use the Pen Color drop-down list box to pick the best color for your scribbling.
6. Use the Show Slides area and its buttons to specify which slides should make up the presentation. For example, if you want to use all slides in the open presentation, mark the All button. Alternatively, if you want to show only some of the slides, mark the From button and then enter the first slide number you want in the From box and the last slide number you want in the To box. If you set up custom slide shows for a presentation, you can also mark the Custom Show button. When you mark this button, PowerPoint lets you select the custom show from the Custom Show drop-down list box.
7. Use the Advance Slides buttons—Manually and Using Timings If Present—to tell PowerPoint how or when it should display the next slide. If you're going to present the slide in person, you will probably click the Manually button. If you click the Manually button, PowerPoint expects someone to tell it that it should display the next slide. You tell PowerPoint that you want to display the next slide by pressing the space bar or clicking the slide with the mouse. If you're not going to display or deliver a presentation in person, perhaps the slide show will be viewed at a computer in a kiosk, for example, mark the Using Timings If Present button. This tells PowerPoint that it should use the rehearsal timings you will have created as part of rehearsing for your presentation.

8. If you use multiple monitors on your computer, you can use the Display Slide Show On the box to select the monitor PowerPoint uses to display the slide show.
9. Optionally, tell PowerPoint to boost your computer's performance. The Performance area of the Set Up Show dialog box includes boxes you can use to boost the slide show speed. You may be able to boost the slide show speed by checking the Use Hardware Graphics Acceleration box. You may also want to boost the slide show speed by selecting a lower screen resolution from the Slide Show Resolution box.

SEE ALSO *Custom Slide Shows, Pack And Go Wizard, Rehearsing, Slide Shows*

Shadows

To add shadows to the selected text, choose the Format→Font command and check the Shadow box.

SEE ALSO *Fonts*

Shortcut Menus

Recent Microsoft programs, including Microsoft PowerPoint, make use of shortcut menus. A shortcut menu lists all of the common commands for working on a particular object or item. To display a shortcut menu, right-click the object or item.

Sizing Objects

Usually, you can size an object, such as a picture, a piece of WordArt, or a drawing object, by clicking the object to select it and then dragging the selection handles.

SEE ALSO *Clip Art, Pictures, WordArt*

Sizing Text see Fonts

Sizing Windows

You can size and resize the PowerPoint program window by clicking the Minimize, Maximize, and Restore buttons. These buttons appear in the upper right corner of the PowerPoint program window.

SEE ALSO *Active Presentation Window, Control Menu*

Slide

A *slide* is the basic building block you create using PowerPoint (see Figure S-2). If you were giving a slide show using, for example, a 35mm slide projector and you created your slides using PowerPoint, what you see in these figures would be what you display on a screen or wall.

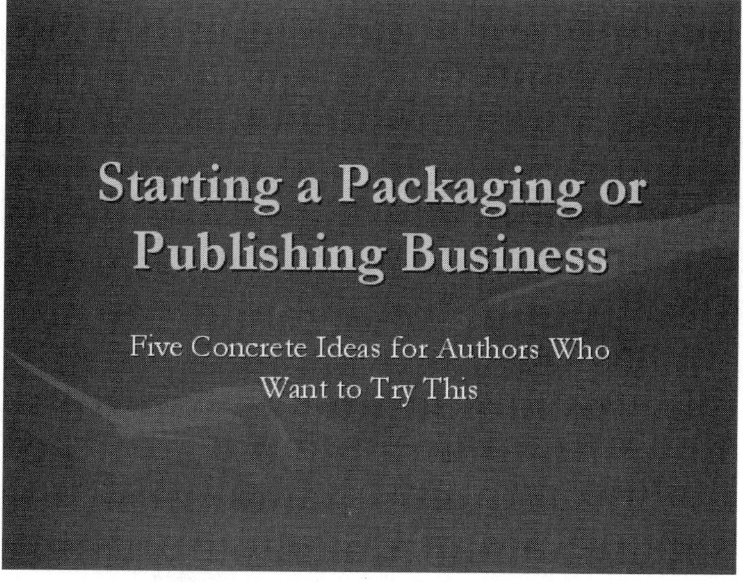

Figure S-2 A PowerPoint slide such as you might use to start a presentation.

Slide Layouts

PowerPoint supplies different slide layouts which you can use as frameworks or kits to build finished slides. Essentially, a slide layout is an empty slide with placeholders you use to add a title and items like text and graphic objects. When you choose the Insert→New Slide command, PowerPoint uses the task pane to display a list of common slide layouts (see Figure S-3). You choose the slide layout you want by clicking it. You pick a slide layout based on its placeholders.

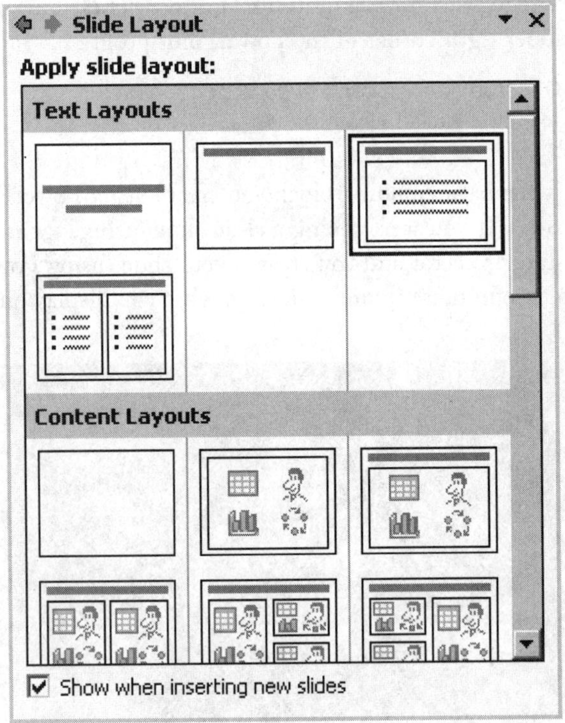

Figure S-3 The Slide Layout task pane.

SEE ALSO *Placeholders*

Slide Master see Master Slides

Slide Show

To view the slides in presentation, choose the Slide Show→View Show command. PowerPoint displays the first slide in the presentation.

To move to the next slide, press the space bar, press the Enter key, click on the slide with a mouse, or press either the Page Down or down arrow keys. After the last slide in the show, PowerPoint displays an empty blank slide. To end the slide show before the last slide, press the Esc key.

SEE ALSO *Setting up a Presentation*

Slide Transitions

If you don't specify otherwise, PowerPoint simply displays the next slide. In other words, PowerPoint uses no fancy or noticeable slide-to-slide transition. You can, however, specify that PowerPoint should use a slide-to-slide transition. To do so, take the following steps:

1. Display the presentation using Slide Sorter view by choosing the View→Slide Sorter command. PowerPoint displays Slide Sorter view (see Figure S-4).

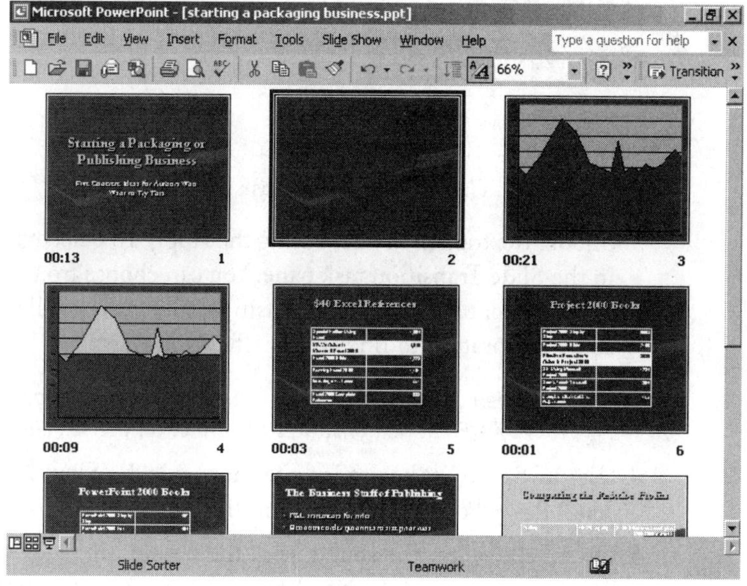

Figure S-4 Slide Sorter view.

2. To indicate you want to use a slide transition, click the Slide Transition button. PowerPoint displays the Slide Transition task pane (see Figure S-5).

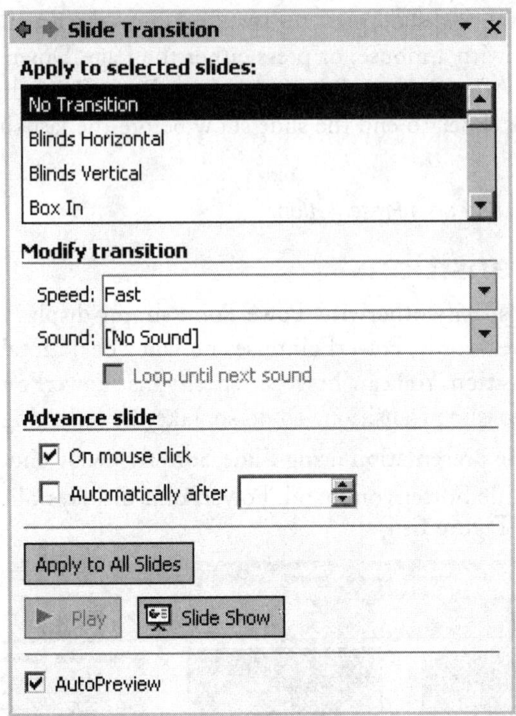

Figure S-5 The Slide Transition task pane.

3. Choose the transition effect using the Apply To Selected Slides list in the Slide Transition task pane. You can choose from more than fifty different slide-to-slide transition effects, so you'll need to do some exploration to find which effect you want.

NOTE *When you choose an effect from the drop-down list box, PowerPoint demonstrates the effect on the selected slide.*

4. Use the Speed list box to indicate how quickly (Slow, Medium, or Fast) PowerPoint should perform the effect.

5. Optionally, select the sound from the Sound drop-down list box. PowerPoint provides several transition sounds you can choose: Applause, [Breaking] Glass, Gunshot, and Laser, for example.

   You can also choose the Other Sound entry from the Sound drop-down list box. If you do, PowerPoint displays the Add Sound dialog box (see Figure S-6). You can use the Add Sound dialog box to choose some other sound for the transition. To use the Add Sound dialog box, first specify the location of the sound file using the Look In drop-down list box. Then, double-click the sound file from the list of files displayed in the list box area.

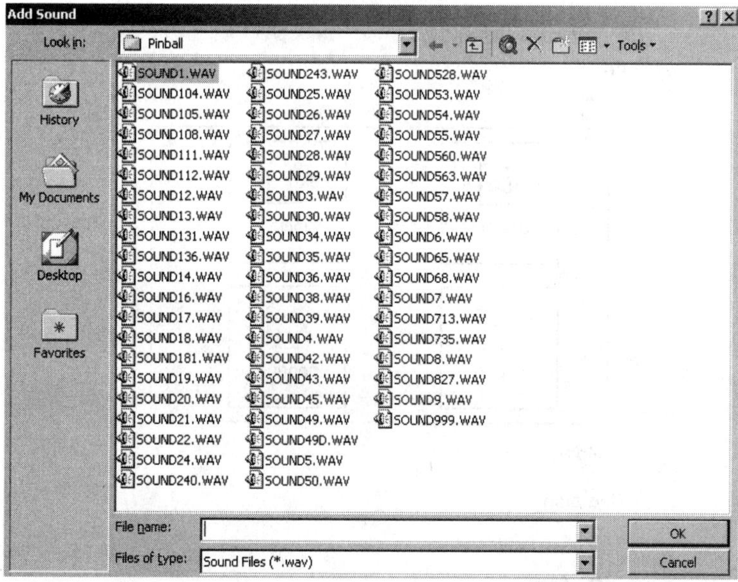

Figure S-6 The Add Sound dialog box.

6. Use the Advance Slide check boxes to tell PowerPoint what event should trigger or start the slide-to-slide transition. If you want PowerPoint to transition to the next slide when you click the mouse or press the space bar, mark the On Mouse Click check box. If you want to automatically transition to the next slide, mark the Automatically After check box and enter the number of seconds that PowerPoint should show the slide.

Sounds

To add sound to a PowerPoint slide, you either choose a sound from the PowerPoint Clip Gallery or insert a sound file stored somewhere else on your computer.

Inserting a Sound Clip

To insert or use a sound from the PowerPoint Clip Gallery, follow these steps:

1. Choose the Insert→Movies And Sounds→Sound From Media Gallery command. PowerPoint displays the Insert Clip Art task pane (see Figure S-7).

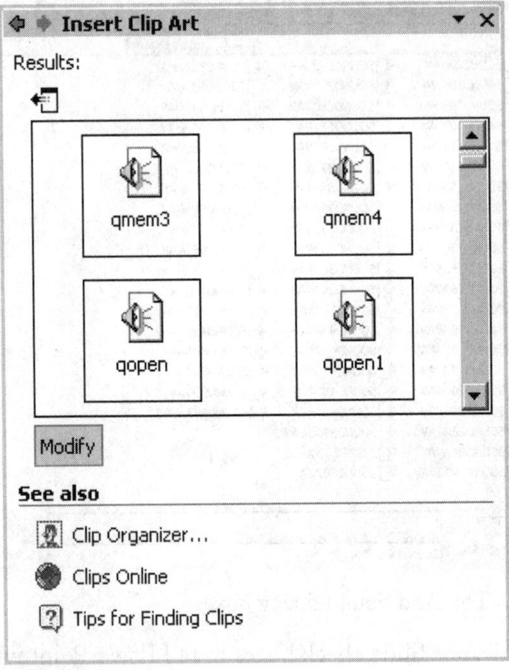

Figure S-7 The Insert Clip Art task pane.

2. Use the list box in the Insert Clip Art task pane to locate the sound you want. Or, you can click the Clip Organizer hyperlink and then use the Clip Organizer window to locate the sound you want.
3. To check a clip, right-click the sound and choose the Preview/Properties command. PowerPoint plays the sound and opens the Preview/Properties dialog box (see Figure S-8).

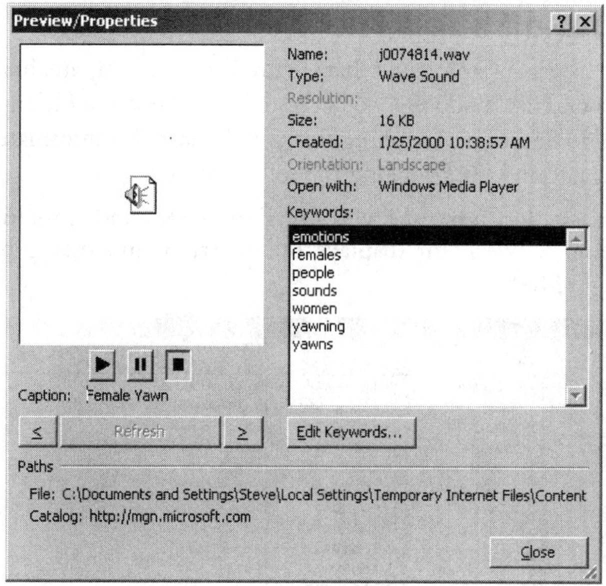

Figure S-8 The Preview/Properties dialog box.

4. When you locate the sound you want, right-click the sound and choose Insert from the shortcut menu. When you do, PowerPoint inserts the sound on the open or selected slide.

5. PowerPoint displays a message box that asks you when you want a sound played (see Figure S-9). If you want the sound to play automatically when you display this slide in your presentation, click the Yes button. If you don't want the sound to play automatically, click the No button. If you click the No button, you need to click the Sound File icon on the slide in order to play it.

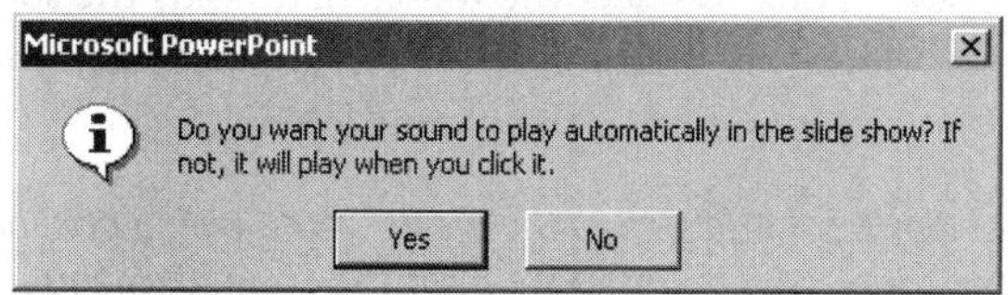

Figure S-9 The message box that asks when you want the sound played.

Using a Sound File

You can also insert a sound that is stored on your computer or network in a sound file. To do this, you need to know the sound file's name and its folder location. Assuming that you do have this information, you insert a sound file by taking the following steps:

1. Choose the Insert→Movies And Sounds→Sound From File command. PowerPoint displays the Insert Sound dialog box (see Figure S-10).

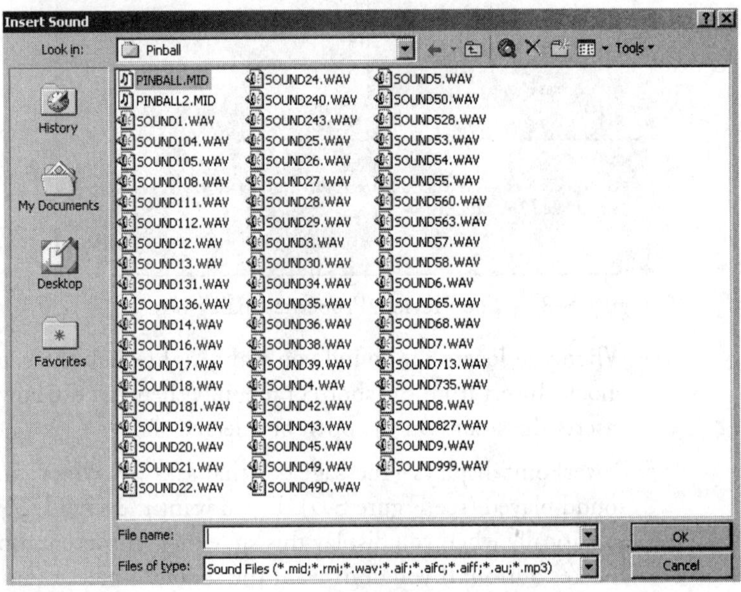

Figure S-10 The Insert Sound dialog box.

2. Use the Look In box to select the folder that holds the sound file. If the sound is really in a subfolder or in a sub-subfolder, you might need to first select and open the parent folder.

TIP *To play a sound listed in the Insert Sound dialog box, right-click the sound and choose Play from the Shortcut menu.*

3. When you've found the folder with the sound, double-click the sound file to insert the sound on your slide. PowerPoint displays a Message box that asks whether you want your sound to play automatically when the slide is displayed. Answer the question by clicking Yes or No.

Recording your own sound file

The Movies And Sounds submenu also displays a Record Sound command. You can use the Record Sound command to start a small Sound Recorder program (see Figure S-11). The Record Sound command lets you record sounds using your computer's microphone, and it works just like a simple tape recorder. After you record a sound and save it as a file to your computer's hard disk, you can insert the sound onto a slide, as described in the preceding sequence of numbered steps.

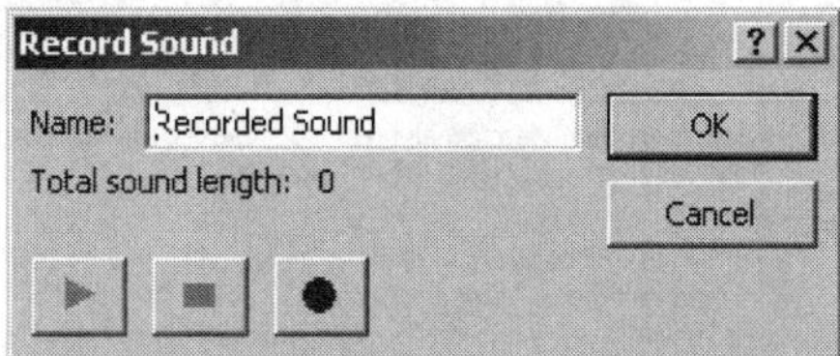

Figure S-11 The Record Sound dialog box.

SEE ALSO *Movies and Motion Clips, Music, Multimedia Effects*

Spacing Lines see Line Spacing

Speaking Notes

You can store your speaking notes with your PowerPoint presentation by using the Speaker's Notes pane (see Figure S-12). The Speaker's Notes pane, which appears beneath the slide pane, provides space for you to enter any notes you want to use as you talk about the selected or displayed slide.

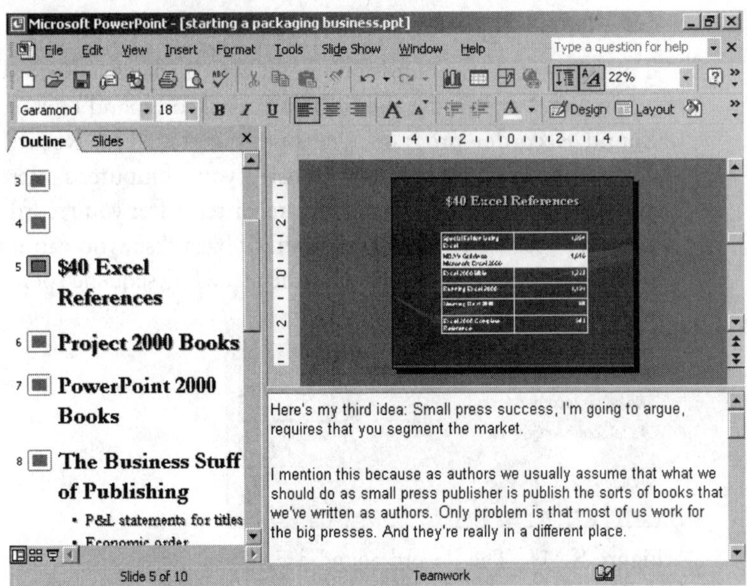

Figure S-12 The Presentation window showing the Speaker's Notes pane.

To enter your speaker's notes, display the presentation in Normal View, select the slide for which you want to record speaking notes, and then type your notes into the notes pane. All the same text-entry and text-editing techniques that work in the Outline pane also work in the Notes pane.

Speech Recognition

PowerPoint 2002 works with Office XP's speech recognition tool. This new tool requires some setup time and learning, but for many people, the effort pays off. Speech recognition can be a huge timesaver.

TIP *Speech Recognition requires a good quality headset microphone, at least a 400MHz computer and at least 128MB of memory.*

Setting Up Speech Recognition

To set up Speech Recognition, you need to configure your microphone and then train Speech Recognition to recognize your particular voice.

To do this, click Start, point to Settings and choose Control Panel. Then, double-click the Speech tool and click the New button, which appears on the Speech Properties dialog box. Windows first prompts you for your name. Windows next displays the Microphone Wizard dialog box (see Figure S-13).

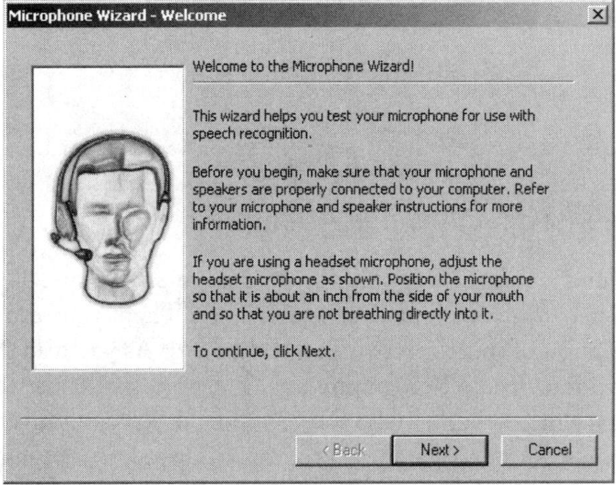

Figure S-13 The Microphone Wizard dialog box.

Put the headset on and position the microphone so that it's about an inch from your mouth. Then, click Next. Windows will instruct you to read some text to adjust the microphone volume and then, when that's done, Windows instructs you to read a simple sentence, "This papaya tastes perfect." Windows then plays a recording of you saying "This papaya tastes perfect." If the recording sounds okay, you're done and click Finish. If the recording sounds funny or garbled, move the microphone away from or closer to your mouth, and then try again.

When you finish configuring the microphone Speech Recognition starts voice training and displays the first Voice Training dialog box (see Figure S-14).

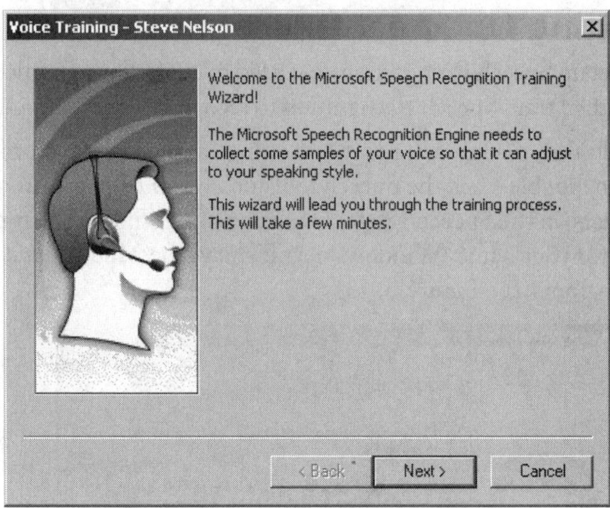

Figure S-14 The Voice Training dialog box.

To train the speech recognition tool to recognize your speech, you first answer questions about your age and sex. Then, you read a short description of speech recognition technology. As you read the short description, Speech Recognition highlights words as you say them and as it recognizes them. Make sure that Speech Recognition does this. If Speech Recognition doesn't recognize a word, try speaking more slowly and clearly. If you can't get Speech Recognition to understand your pronunciation of a word, click the Skip Word button.

NOTE *The reading you do to train Speech Recognition is very short. You can finish it in about five minutes. However, if you need to take a break, click the Pause button.*

Using Speech Recognition

Once you configure your microphone and train speech recognition to understand your voice, you can begin to dictate. Click the Microphone button and then the Dictation button, which appear on the Language Bar. Then, began speaking in a normal voice. As you talk, Speech Recognition interprets your words and enters them into the document at the insertion point.

NOTE *If you click the Microphone button on the Language bar and haven't yet configured the microphone, Windows walks you though the steps for both configuring the microphone and training Speech Recognition to understand your voice. In this case, you don't need to use the Control Panel's Speech tool to get to the Speech Properties dialog box.*

To begin a new line, say the word "Enter." To begin a new paragraph, say the word "Enter" twice.

NOTE *When you say a number, Speech Recognition spells out numbers less than twenty. For example, say "five" and Speech Recognition interprets this as the word "five," but say "twenty-five" and Speech Recognition interprets this as the numeral "25." Speech Recognition will recognize fractions. For example, if you say "one-half," Speech Recognition interprets this as ½.*

If Speech Recognition doesn't understand, click the Correction button and see if another interpretation of what you said is listed. If it is, select the alternative interpretation by clicking it.

Or, you can select the incorrect text and then begin speaking again. If speech recognition understands, it replaces the incorrect selected text with the new corrected text.

When you finish dictating, click the Microphone button again.

Punctuating Your Speech

Most of the words you say will be recognized as input as words. In the case of characters used for punctuation, however, PowerPoint assumes you mean punctuation. The table below shows punctuation symbols and lists the words you can use to enter them:

SYMBOL	WORD
.	Period or Dot
,	Comma
:	Colon
;	Semi-colon
?	Question mark
!	Exclamation point
&	Ampersand

<table>
<tr><td>*</td><td>Asterisk</td></tr>
<tr><td>@</td><td>At sign</td></tr>
<tr><td>\</td><td>Backslash</td></tr>
<tr><td>/</td><td>Slash</td></tr>
<tr><td>|</td><td>Vertical bar</td></tr>
<tr><td>-</td><td>Hyphen or Dash</td></tr>
<tr><td>—</td><td>Double dash</td></tr>
<tr><td>=</td><td>Equals</td></tr>
<tr><td>+</td><td>Plus or Plus sign</td></tr>
<tr><td>#</td><td>Pound sign</td></tr>
<tr><td>%</td><td>Percent sign</td></tr>
<tr><td>$</td><td>Dollar sign</td></tr>
<tr><td>_</td><td>Underscore</td></tr>
<tr><td>~</td><td>Tilde</td></tr>
<tr><td>…</td><td>Ellipsis</td></tr>
<tr><td>></td><td>Greater than</td></tr>
<tr><td><</td><td>Less than</td></tr>
<tr><td>^</td><td>Caret</td></tr>
<tr><td>[</td><td>Bracket or Left bracket or Open bracket</td></tr>
<tr><td>]</td><td>End bracket or Right bracket or Close bracket</td></tr>
<tr><td>{</td><td>Open brace or Curly brace or Left brace</td></tr>
<tr><td>}</td><td>Close brace or End curly brace or Right brace</td></tr>
<tr><td>(</td><td>Open parenthesis or Left paren</td></tr>
<tr><td>)</td><td>Close parenthesis or Right paren</td></tr>
<tr><td>“</td><td>Quote or Open quote or Close Quote</td></tr>
<tr><td>‘</td><td>Single quote or Open single quote or Close single quote</td></tr>
</table>

Using Voice Command

To use speech recognition for voice commands, click the Microphone button and then click the Voice Command button. Then, choose commands and select dialog box options by speaking. For example, to print your presentation, say, "File Print OK." To change the font used for the selected text to Helvetica, say, "Format Font Helvetica."

Customizing Speech Recognition

The Language bar's Speech Tools button displays a menu of commands you can use to customize the way that Speech Recognition works.

- To reconfigure your microphone or create a new speech profile, click the Options command. PowerPoint displays the Speech Properties dialog box—the same one you may have worked with to originally configure the microphone and train.
- To turn off the speech messages that Speech Recognition displays on the Language bar—messages that might say you're speaking too soft, too loud, or too quickly—choose the Show Speech Messages command. The Show Speech Messages command is a toggle switch. When speech messages show, a check mark shows in front in the command name.
- To further train Speech Recognition so it will do a better job at recognizing your words, choose the Train command. When PowerPoint displays the Voice Training dialog box, select one of the training sessions and then perform the reading. The more you train, the better Speech Recognition works.
- To add or delete words in the speech dictionary, choose the Add/Delete Words command. PowerPoint displays the Add/Delete Words dialog box. To delete a word, scroll through the list of words, click the word, and then click the Delete button. To add a word, enter the word into the Word box, click the Record Pronunciation button, and then say the word. To record your pronunciation of a word that Speech Recognition commonly misinterprets, select the word in the list, click the Record Pronunciation button, and then say the word.

- To permanently save the recorded speech—normally your recorded speech is only saved until you close the presentation—choose the Save Speech data command. The Save Speech Data command is a toggle switch. To later turn off the saving of your recorded speech data, choose the command again. (Note that you may also need to choose the Tools→Options command, click the Save tab, and then check the Embed Linguistic Data box to save your recorded speech.)
- To select another user's speech profile, click the Current User button and select another speaker profile from the list.

SEE ALSO *Handwriting Recognition*

Spelling

PowerPoint checks the spelling of your presentation outlines, underlining misspelled words with a squiggly red line (see Figure S-15). To fix a spelling error, right-click the underlined word. PowerPoint displays a menu that lists possible correct spellings. To make a suggested fix, select its menu command. If the word isn't misspelled, select the Ignore command from the shortcut menu (to just ignore this occurrence of the word), select the Ignore All command (to ignore every occurrence of the word in the document) or select the Add command to add the word to the dictionary of correct spellings (so that PowerPoint and other Microsoft Office programs will no longer show the word as misspelled).

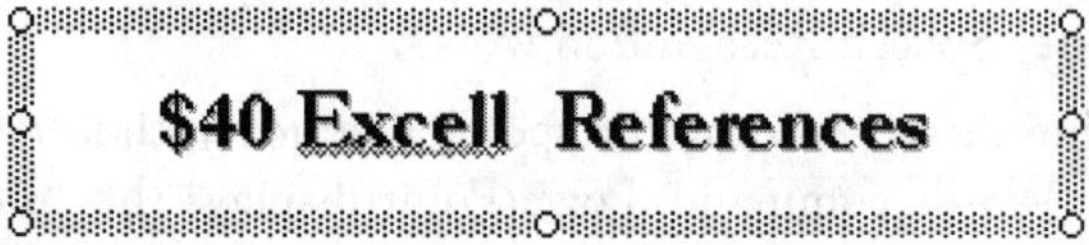

$40 Excell References

Figure S-15 Text in a PowerPoint presentation that the spelling checker has reviewed.

You can also choose the Tools→Spelling command to check the spelling of words in your outline. If PowerPoint discovers no misspellings, it displays a dialog box telling you simply that the spelling check is complete. That is what you want to see.

If PowerPoint finds one or more spelling errors, it displays the Spelling dialog box (see Figure S-16). PowerPoint will use the Not In Dictionary text box to identify the word that appears to be misspelled. PowerPoint selects this word in the outline. To fix the spelling, you can type the correct spelling in the Change To box. Or, you can select one of the words listed in the Suggestions list box. PowerPoint fills the Change To box initially with its best guess about the correct spelling.

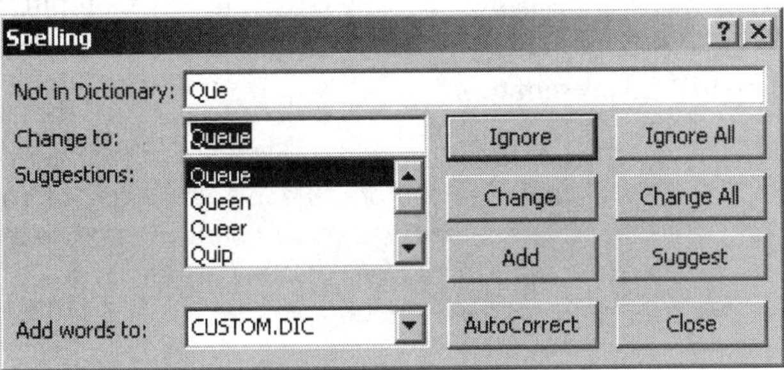

Figure S-16 The Spelling dialog box.

After you or PowerPoint have entered the correct spelling in the Change To box, click the Change button to correct the misspelling. Or, if you want to change the spelling everywhere it appears in the outline, click the Change All button.

If the word is not really a misspelling, you can click the Ignore button to ignore the single occurrence that was found or the Ignore All button to ignore every occurrence in the outline.

If you are using words that are correctly spelled but are not in the spelling dictionary—this might be the case if you are clicking the Ignore or the Ignore All buttons—you can click the Add button. When you click the Add button, PowerPoint adds the word shown in the Not In Dictionary box to its custom spelling dictionary. You typically add things like people's names and specialized business or industry terms to the custom spelling dictionary.

If the Spelling command identifies a misspelling but doesn't identify the correct spelling using its Suggestions box, you can try to get additional suggestions. To do this, enter another guess at the spelling into the Change To box, and then click the Suggest button. PowerPoint will use the word you entered into the Change To box to look for other suggested spellings.

Starting PowerPoint

You can start the PowerPoint program in several ways. You can click the Start button, point to the Programs item, and then select the PowerPoint program item from the menu that Windows displays. You can click the Start button, point to the Documents item, and then select a PowerPoint document from the Documents submenu that Windows displays (this both starts PowerPoint and opens the document). You open a PowerPoint document using either the My Computer window or Windows Explorer (again this starts both the PowerPoint program and opens the presentation).

NOTE *You can also create shortcuts that point to the PowerPoint program or to PowerPoint documents. When you open a shortcut, Windows starts the program or opens the document that the shortcut points to. For information on creating and using shortcuts, refer to the Windows help file.*

SEE ALSO *Documents, Program Errors, Stopping PowerPoint*

Status Bar

At the bottom of the program window, PowerPoint displays a status bar. This bar provides information about the displayed slide and information about PowerPoint's background actions (printing or spell-checking).

Stopping PowerPoint

To stop the PowerPoint program, choose the File→Exit command or click the PowerPoint program window's Close box. The Close box is the small square marked with an "X" in the upper right corner of the program window.

SEE ALSO *Starting PowerPoint*

Symbol Characters

To use symbols in your outline and slides choose the Insert→Symbol command and click the Symbols tab (see Figure S-17). Select the font set that provides the symbol from the Font list box. Then, select the symbol you want and click the Insert button.

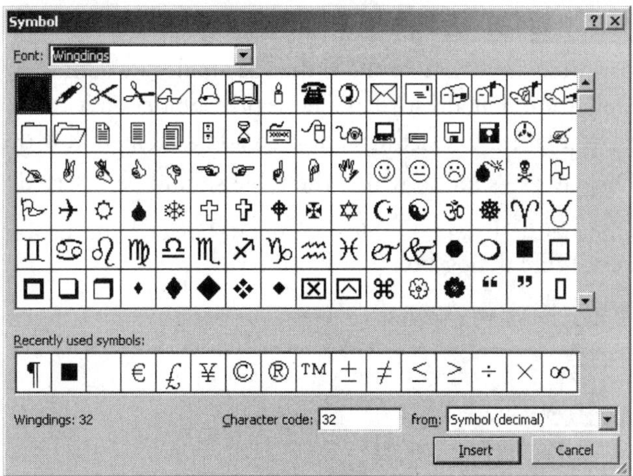

Figure S-17 The Symbol dialog box.

SEE ALSO *Fonts*

Tables

Tables arrange information into rows and columns, and you'll find them extremely useful for including slide information (see Figure T-1).

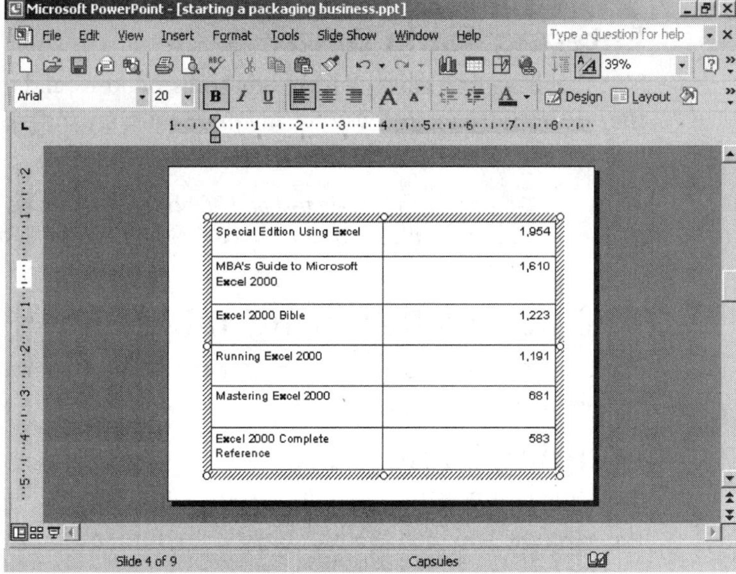

Figure T-1 A slide with a table

Adding a Table

Most often you'll create slides that use tables by adding a slide to a presentation that already has a table placeholder on it. You can, however, add tables to existing slides. To add a table, follow these steps:

1. Display the slide to which the table should be inserted.
2. Choose the Insert→Table command. PowerPoint displays the Insert Table dialog box (see Figure T-2).

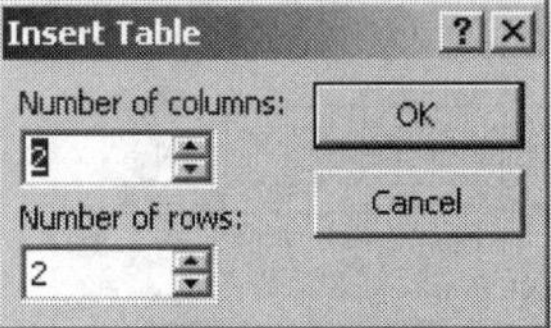

Figure T-2 The Insert Table dialog box.

2. Describe how many columns your table should have by entering a value into the Number Of Columns box.
3. Describe how many rows your table should have by entering a value into the Number Of Rows box.

TIP *You can enter a table into a table cell.*

Entering Table Data

To enter data into a table, click the table cells, or boxes, and then enter the information. You can also cut and paste and copy and paste information into a table's cells.

NOTE *Table cells can contain text and numbers, other tables, and even objects such as drawings, pictures, and bits of Clip Art and WordArt.*

Adding and Removing Table's Rows

If you right-click a table, the shortcut menu provides commands you can use to add and remove rows.

Merging Table Cells

To combine two cells or more in a table, select the cells, right-click the selection, and then choose Merge Cells from the shortcut menu.

Formatting a Table

If you right-click a table and choose the Borders And Fill command from the shortcut menu, PowerPoint displays the Format Table dialog box (see Figure T-3).

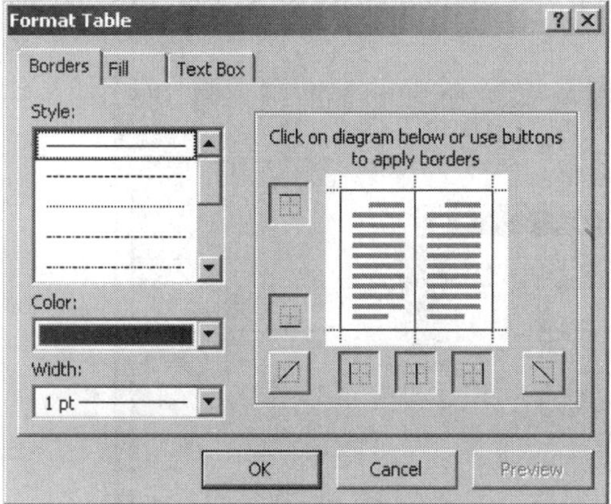

Figure T-3 The Borders tab of the Format Table dialog box.

The Borders tab lets you pick a border line style, color and thickness for the table's borders.

The Fill tab of the Format Table dialog box lets you pick a color for the table (see Figure T-4). To use a fill color, check the Fill Color box and then select the color from the Fill Color drop-down list box.

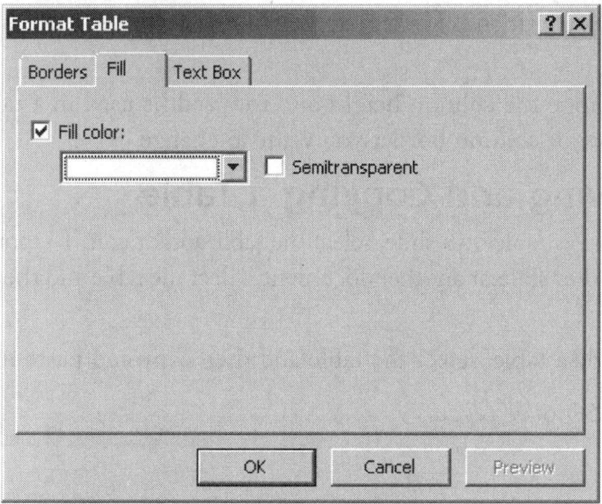

Figure T-4 The Fill tab of the Format Table dialog box.

The Text Box tab of the Format Table dialog box lets you specify how text should align in the cells, or boxes, of the table and what margins PowerPoint should use for the table cell contents (see Figure T-5). Select the alignment you want using the Text Alignment box. Use the Left, Right, Top and Bottom boxes to set your internal cell, or box, margins.

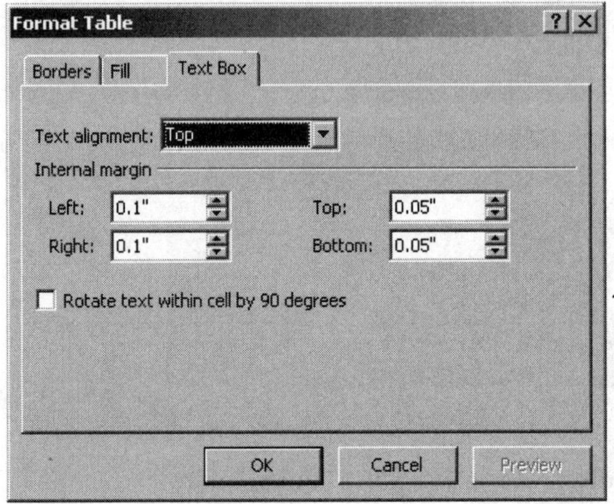

Figure T-5 The Text Box tab of the Format Table dialog box.

Resizing Tables, Columns and Rows

To resize a table, right-click the table and choose Select Table from the shortcut menu. Then drag the table's selection's handles to resize it.

To change the column height and row widths used in a table, drag the row or column border you want to change.

Moving and Copying a Table

To move a table on a slide, select the table and drag it. To move a table to another slide or another document, select the table and then cut and paste it.

To copy a table, select the table and then copy and paste it.

SEE ALSO *Slide Layouts*

Taskbar

The Windows taskbar displays the Start button, which you can use to display the menus you'll use to start PowerPoint or open a recently-used document, or presentation. The taskbar also displays buttons for the open PowerPoint presentations. You can switch between open presentations by clicking the buttons on the task bar.

Task Pane

PowerPoint 2002 displays a task pane along the right edge of the program window (see Figure T-6). PowerPoint attempts to fill this task pane with commands and options relevant to whatever you're doing with PowerPoint. For example, if you choose the File→New command, PowerPoint displays a list of commands and options for creating new documents.

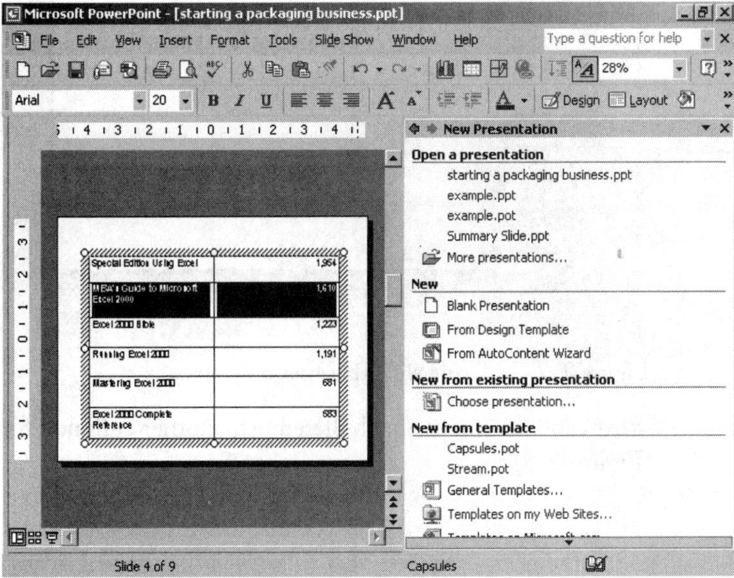

Figure T-6 The PowerPoint program window showing the New Presentation task pane.

You can remove the task pane by clicking its Close box. You can later display the task pane by choosing the View→Task Pane command.

To change what the task pane shows, click the task pane's Other Task Panes buttons (this is small arrow which is just to the left of the Close box) and select another task pane.

Text

Text *is* the most common element you'll use on your slides. Commonly, for example, you'll use only text on your first slide to introduce the presentation and the presenter to the audience (see Figure T-7).

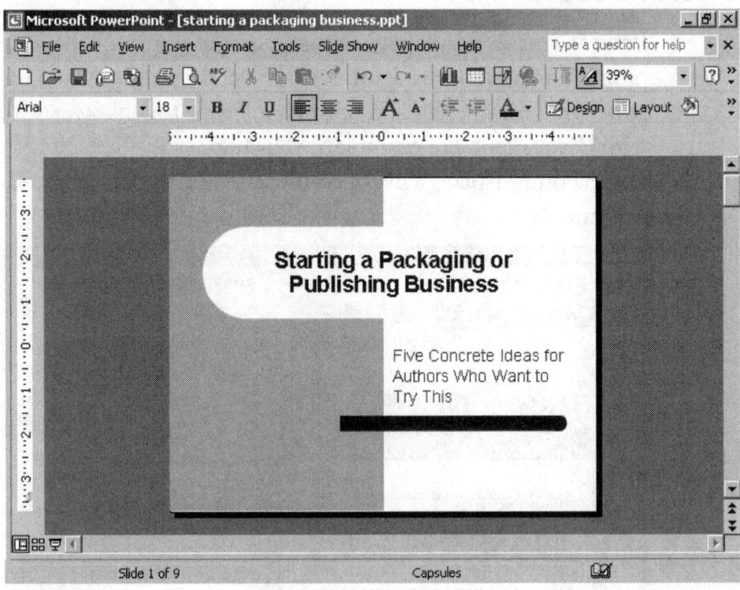

Figure T-7 A title slide that uses only text.

Text can also appear in a bulleted list, another common format (see Figure T-8).

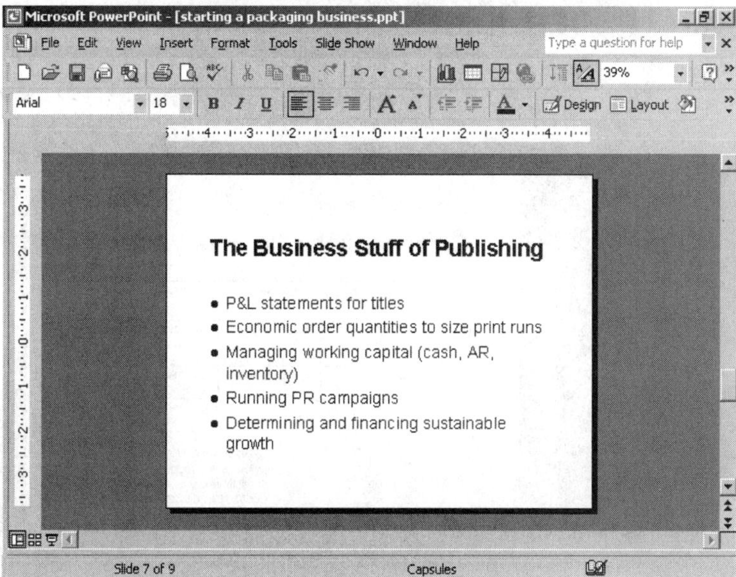

Figure T-8 A slide that shows a bulleted list.

You enter and edit text in PowerPoint in the same basic way as you enter and edit text in most other programs. Entering and editing text in PowerPoint works the same way it does in Microsoft Word. You can type using the keyboard, you can copy and move text from some other location, and you use the Speech Recognition or Handwriting Recognition tools.

SEE ALSO *Copying Text and Objects, Fonts, Moving Text and Objects, Selecting Text*

Text Boxes

A text box is a box with text (see Figure T-9). To add a text box to your presentation, display the Drawing toolbar (if necessary), click the Text Box tool, draw the box, and type the type.

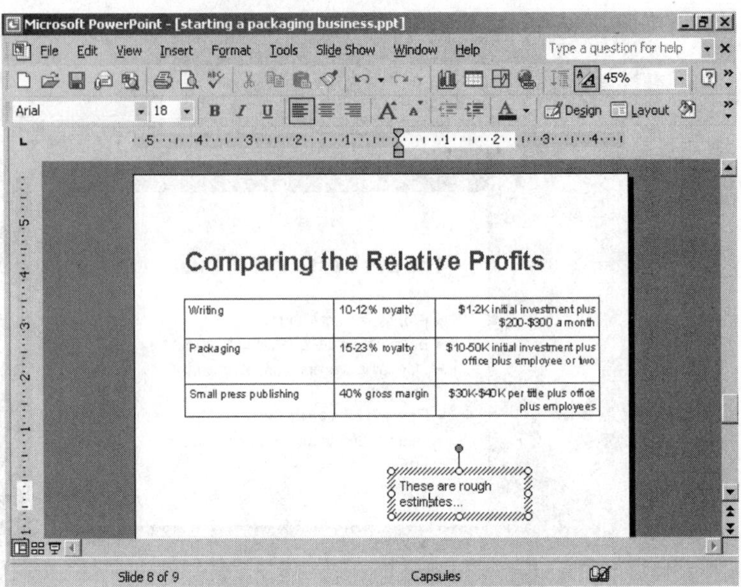

Figure T-9 A slide with a text box that says, "These are rough estimates…."

NOTE *Text box text doesn't appear in the presentation outline.*

SEE ALSO *Drawing*

Templates

PowerPoint supplies several dozen templates—almost-built and largely-formatted presentations—that you can use to produce your presentations more quickly and more easily. To create a new presentation based on a template, follow these steps:

1. Choose the File→New command. PowerPoint displays the New Presentation task pane.

2. Click the General Templates hyperlink. PowerPoint displays the Templates dialog box (see Figure T-10).

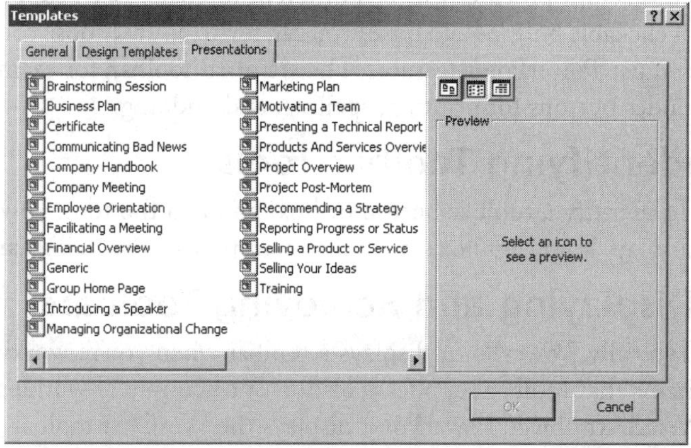

Figure T-10 The Templates dialog box.

3. Click the Presentations tab, if necessary.
4. Double-click the template icon that matches the presentation you want to create. PowerPoint opens a new presentation based on the template.
5. Enter and edit the outline text and then add any other required slide objects.

NOTE *You can create your own presentation templates. To do so, save a presentation using the presentation template format. If you want to see the presentation on the Templates dialog box, save the template in the Office templates folder. You may need to do a bit of searching to find this folder, but it will be easy to spot because it'll contain the other presentation templates shown in Figure T-10.*

Toolbars

PowerPoint provides thirteen different toolbars. Each supplies a set of clickable buttons and boxes you can use to easily choose commands and use PowerPoint features. The standard toolbar, for example, includes buttons for printing, spelling, and undoing.

Identifying Toolbar Tools

To identify a toolbar button or box, point to the tool. PowerPoint displays a pop-up box, called a screentip, with the tool's name.

Displaying and Removing Toolbars

Typically, PowerPoint displays a toolbar when you're working with items that toolbar supplies tools for. For example, if working with a WordArt object, PowerPoint displays the WordArt toolbar.

You can also control when a toolbar is displayed. Simply choose the View→Toolbars command and then select the toolbar you want. The commands listed on the Toolbars submenu are toggle switches. PowerPoint places a checkmark in front of those toolbars that are displayed. To remove a toolbar, choose the View→Toolbars command and select the displayed toolbar you want to remove.

NOTE *If you turn on PowerPoint personalized menus and toolbars, that setting also affects how toolbars appear. Refer to the Personalized Menus and Toolbars entry for more information.*

Customizing a Toolbar

To add buttons to a toolbar, follow these steps:

1. Make sure the toolbar is currently visible.
2. Choose the Tools→Customize command and click the Commands tab (see Figure T-11).

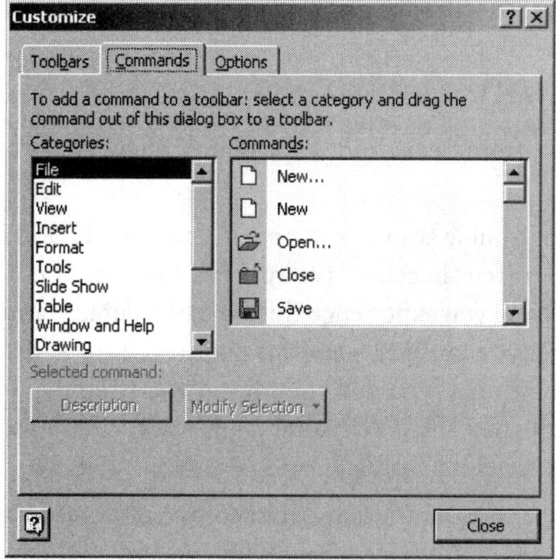

Figure T-11 The Commands tab of the Customize dialog box.

3. Select the command category from the Categories list box that includes the command you want to add to a toolbar.
4. Scroll through the Commands list box. When you see the command you want to add to the toolbar, drag it to the toolbar.

NOTE *You can also customize a toolbar by clicking on the arrow button at the very right end of the toolbar, choosing the Add Or Remove buttons command, and then the name of the toolbar. For example, to customize the Formatting toolbar, click the arrow button and choose Add Or Remove Buttons and then Formatting. PowerPoint displays a complete list of the buttons commonly placed on the toolbar. To add a button, select it from the list.*

To remove a button from a toolbar, follow these steps:

1. Click on the arrow button at the very right end of the toolbar.
2. Choose the Add Or Remove buttons command, and then the name of the toolbar. For example, to customize the Formatting toolbar, click the arrow button and choose Add Or Remove Buttons and then Formatting.
3. When PowerPoint displays a complete list of the buttons commonly placed on the toolbar, select the button you want to remove. PowerPoint identifies which buttons are already on the toolbar by marking them with a checkmark.

SEE ALSO *Personalized Menus and Toolbars*

Troubleshooting

You can suffer from two types of trouble when you work with PowerPoint.

The first type of trouble amounts to operational trouble working with the program—often because you're still learning how to use PowerPoint. When you experience this type of trouble—and assuming you can't get your answer from this book—use the Office Assistant to ask a question. If you don't get the answer from the first set of help topics that the Office Assistant suggests, try rephrasing your question using different words.

The second type of trouble stems from software problems with the PowerPoint program itself or perhaps with one of the other programs running on your computer. Surprisingly, you often can solve software problems, too, if you visit Microsoft's Knowledge Base web site. The Microsoft Knowledge Base web site provides troubleshooting information about solving all sorts of mechanical problems and bugs working with PowerPoint.

To use the Microsoft Knowledge Base Web site, open your web browser and enter the following URL into the Address box:

http://search.support.microsoft.com/kb/c.asp

When your Web browser opens the Knowledge Base search form, Select Microsoft PowerPoint from the My Search Is About box, type your question into the My Question Is box, and press Enter (see Figure T-12). The search results page that the Knowledge Base server displays will display a list of Knowledge Base articles that provide troubleshooting information related the problem you describe.

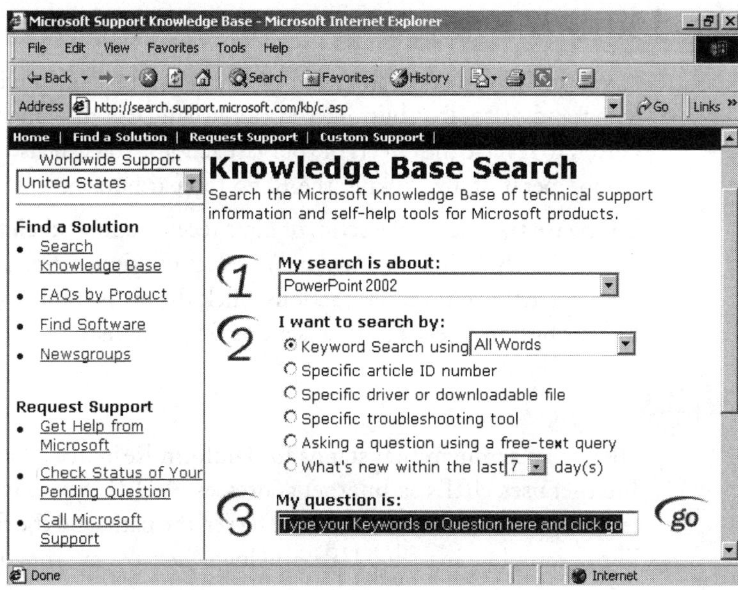

Figure T-12 The Knowledge Base search form.

SEE ALSO *Office Assistant*

Undeleting Presentations see Presentations

Underlining

Within PowerPoint, you have two tools for underlining the selected text. You can click the Underline button on the Formatting toolbar. You can also choose the Format→Font command and check the Underline box.

SEE ALSO *Font*

Undoing Mistakes

If you make a mistake in entering or editing text or in choosing a command or toolbar button, you can usually use the Undo toolbar button to reverse the effects of your last actions. You can also undo the Undo operation by clicking the Redo toolbar button.

To reverse the effects of a series of most recent actions, click the arrow beside the Undo toolbar button and select multiple actions from the list. To redo a series of last actions, click the arrow beside the Redo toolbar button select multiple actions from the list.

URLs

URL is an acronym that stands for Uniform Resource Locator. The Internet uses URLs as Internet addresses. A URL typically includes four components: the protocol, the server, the path, and the file name. For example, in the URL below, *http://* is the protocol, *www.redtechpress.com* is the server, */tocs/* is the path, and *mbaexcel.pdf* is the name of the file.

http://www.redtechpress.com/tocs/mbaexcel.pdf

NOTE *http:// is one of the protocols used to display Web pages.*

You can use URLs when you save and open files if you have permission to use the Web server. To do this, simply enter the complete URL into the File Name box on the Save As or Open dialog box. The Web server you're referencing will probably ask you for a password.

SEE ALSO *File Extensions, File Names, Pathnames*

Views

PowerPoint provides several different ways to look at your presentation. The Normal View is the default way to work with and look at your presentation (see Figure V-1). To view a presentation using the Normal View, choose the View→Normal command.

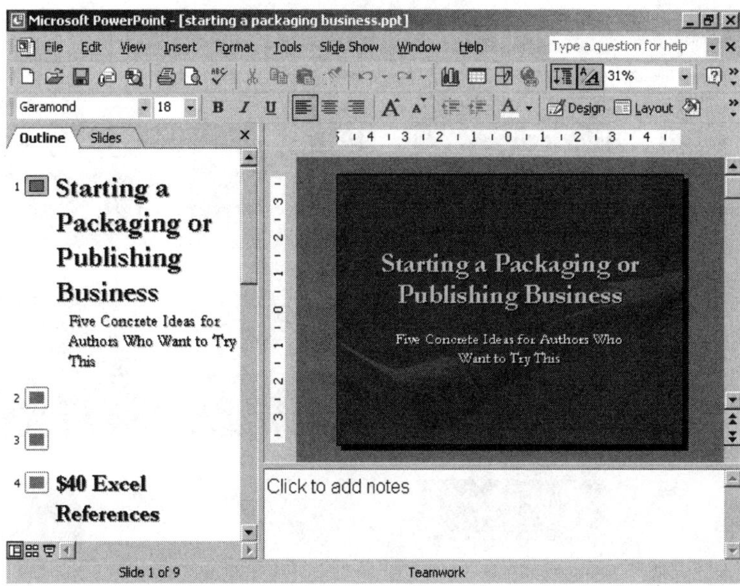

Figure V-1 The Normal View of a presentation.

The Slider Sorter View displays thumbnail images of all the slides in your presentation so you can easily rearrange the order of your slides and to make it easy to add transition effects (see Figure V-2). To view a presentation using the Slide Sorter view, choose the View→Slide Sorter command.

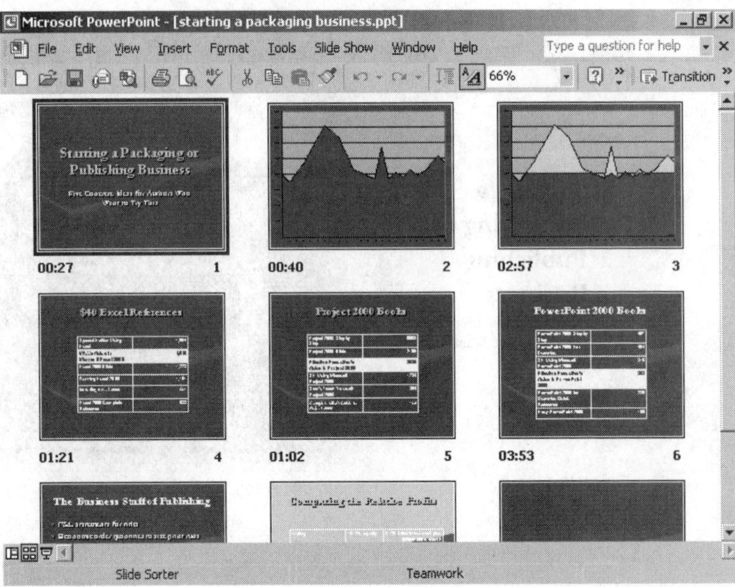

Figure V-2 The Slide Sorter View of a presentation.

The Slide Show View is the view someone sees when you show the presentation (see Figure V-3). To view a presentation using the Slide Show view, choose the View→Slide Show command.

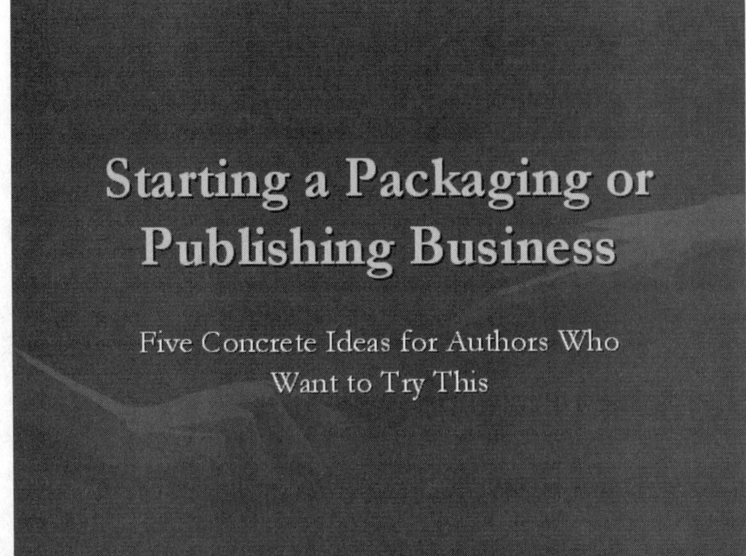

Figure V-3 The Slide Show View of a presentation.

The Notes Page view is a picture of the Notes Page that you might talk from when you give a presentation (see Figure V-4). To view a presentation using the Note Pages view, choose the View→Notes Page command.

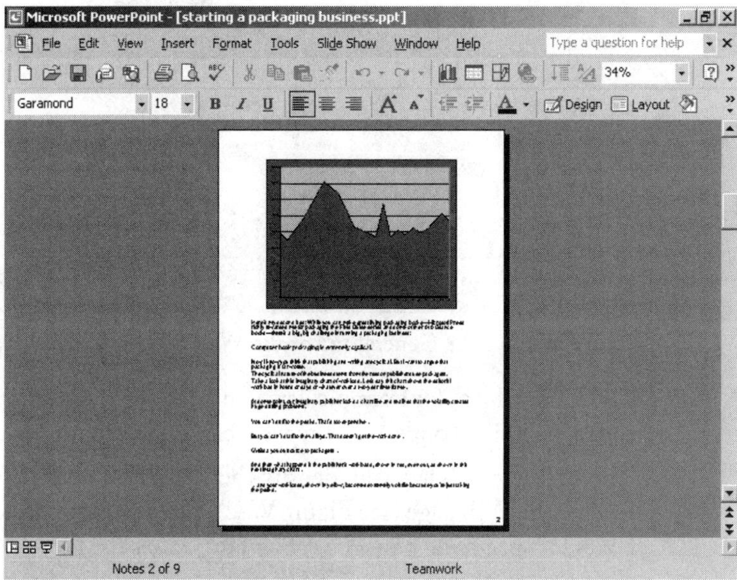

Figure V-4 The Notes Pages View of a presentation.

Visual Basic

Microsoft builds a programming language, called Visual Basic for Applications into the PowerPoint program. Unfortunately, Visual Basic for Applications isn't simple to use like some other macro tools. To write programs in Visual Basic, you need to know how to program.

Web Options

If you choose the Tools→Options command, click the General tab, and click the General tab's Web Options button, PowerPoint displays the Web Options dialog box (see Figure W-1). This dialog box provides several tabs that you can use to specify how Web pages you create using PowerPoint should appear.

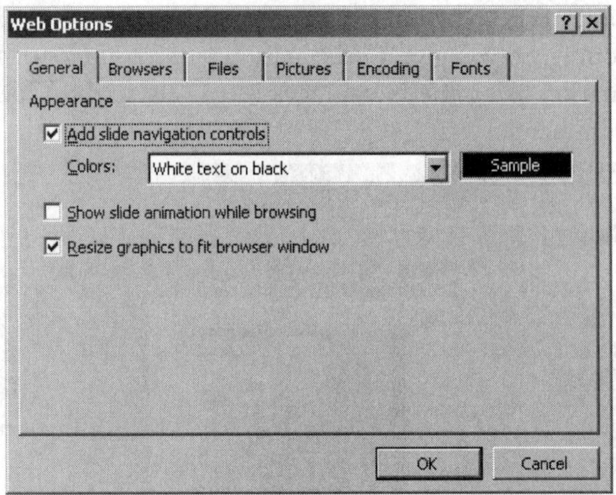

Figure W-1 The General tab of the Web Options dialog box.

The General tab, for example, lets you tell PowerPoint it should add slide navigation controls to any web-based presentations you create.

The Browsers tab lets you identify the Web browser people will use to view the Web page (see Figure W-2). The Files tab includes check boxes for specifying how PowerPoint organizes the files that are necessary to create web pages. The Pictures tab includes check boxes for specifying how PowerPoint should handle any pictures you use in your web pages. The Encoding tab includes check boxes for specifying what language code PowerPoint should use for the web pages. Finally, the Fonts tab includes boxes for specifying which fonts PowerPoint should use for the web pages.

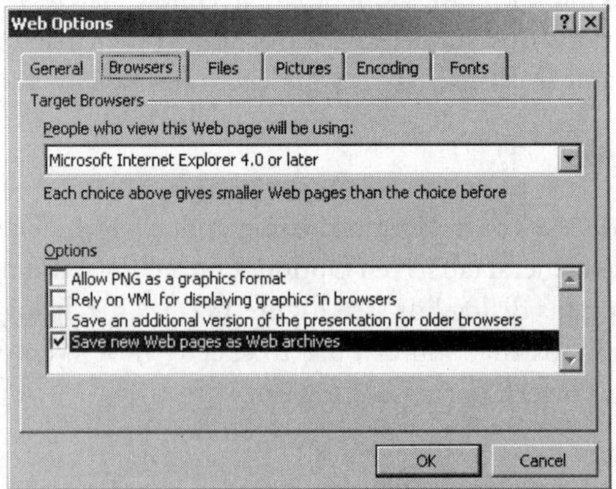

Figure W-2 The Browsers tab of the Web Options dialog box.

SEE ALSO *Web Pages*

Web Pages

You can save a PowerPoint presentation as a set of web pages. To do so, use the File→Save As command to save the presentation in almost the usual way—except use the Save File As Type box to indicate that you want to save the presentation as a web page (see Figure W-3) and click the Publish button.

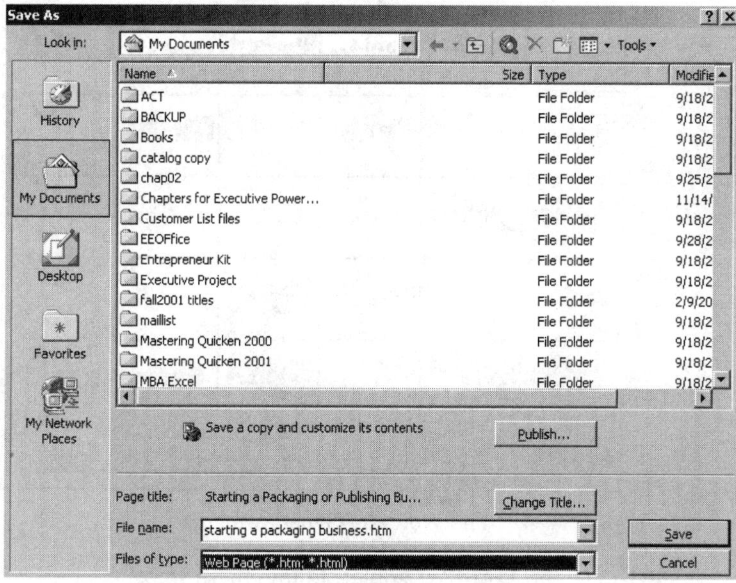

Figure W-3 The Save As dialog box as it appears when you save a presentation as a web page.

TIP *You can enter a pathname that uses a URL into the File name box.*

SEE ALSO *Web Page Options*

WordArt

You can turn text into a graphics object. To do this, you use the WordArt applet. WordArt, like Microsoft Graph, is a miniprogram, or applet, that comes with Office programs including Microsoft Word.

Creating a WordArt Object

To create a piece of text using WordArt, choose the Insert→Picture→WordArt command. PowerPoint starts the WordArt program and you see the WordArt Gallery (see Figure W-4). This window shows you the various ways you can display the selected text as a graphics image.

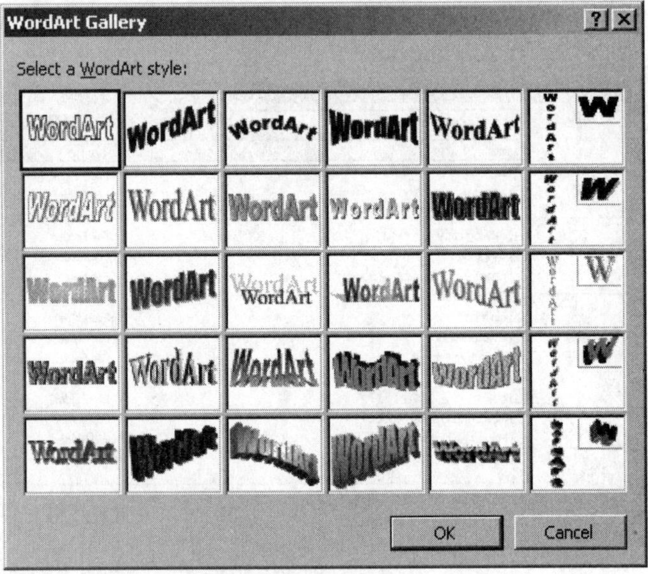

Figure W-4 The WordArt Gallery window.

To use the WordArt applet, follow these steps.

1. Select the WordArt style you want your object to resemble by clicking on an image shown on the WordArt Gallery window. Then click OK. WordArt displays the Edit WordArt Text window (see Figure W-5).

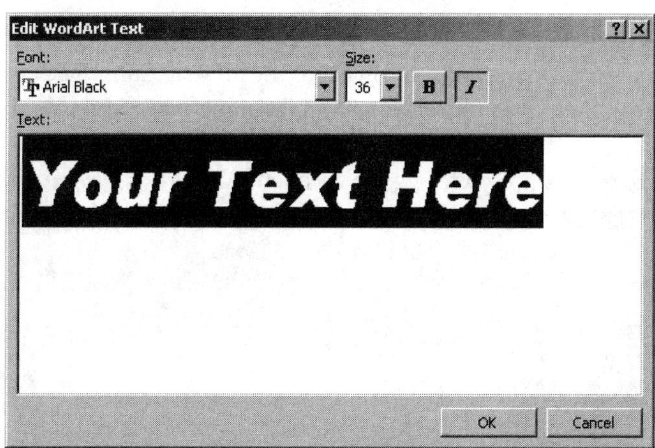

Figure W-5 The Edit WordArt Text window.

2. Enter the text that you want to turn into a WordArt object.
3. Use the Font list box to select the font you want to use. You can click the button at the right end of the Font list box to display a list of available fonts. The Text box shows you how your font selection looks—this is the preview area beneath the Font and Size boxes and the Bold and Italic buttons.
3. Use the Size box to specify the point size you want WordArt to use for the text.
4. Click the Bold and Italic buttons to boldface or italicize the text. The Bold and Italic buttons are toggle switches: To un-bold and un-italicize the text, click the buttons again.
5. After you've specified the font, size, and any boldfacing and italicization, click the OK button. WordArt adds the WordArt object to the slide.

NOTE *You can double-click the new WordArt image to redisplay the Edit WordArt window. This time, however, it provides a Preview button. You can click the Preview button to see what your WordArt style or text looks like on the slide. You may need to move the window to see the preview image on the slide.*

Moving and Resizing WordArt Objects

After WordArt adds the object to the presentation, you can move and resize the object by clicking and dragging (see Figure W-6). To correctly position the WordArt object, drag it to the appropriate location. To resize the object, drag the selection handles that surround the object.

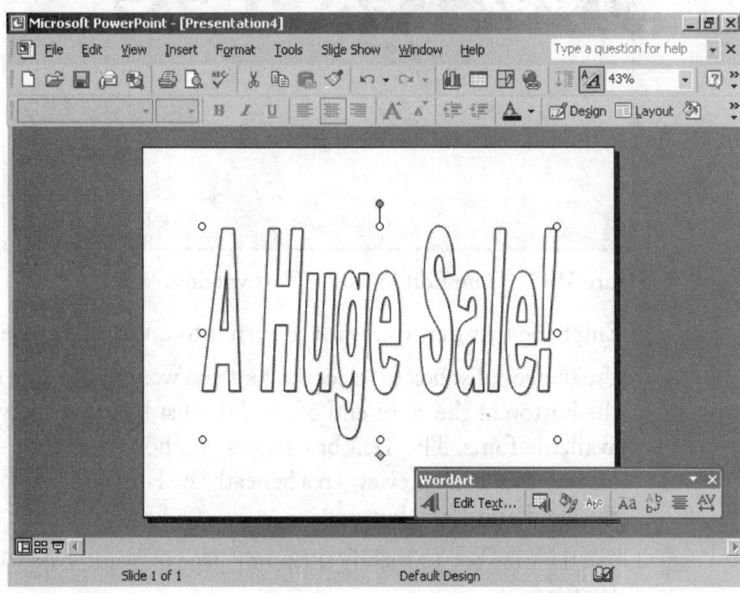

Figure W-6 A WordArt object.

Editing WordArt Text

The Edit Text tool, available on WordArt toolbar, redisplays the Edit WordArt Text window so you change the font, size, boldface, and italics specifications for the WordArt object or so you can edit the WordArt text.

NOTE *The WordArt toolbar also provides an Insert WordArt tool, which you can use to add another WordArt object to your presentation.*

Formatting WordArt Objects

The WordArt toolbar provides several tool for formatting WordArt objects:

The WordArt Gallery button, available on the WordArt toolbar, lets you select a new gallery setting for the existing, selected WordArt object using a WordArt Gallery window similar to the one shown in Figure W-1.

The Format WordArt button on the WordArt toolbar lets you change the color used for the WordArt object; the line, color, and style used to draw the WordArt object; and the size and layout of the WordArt object. When you choose the Format WordArt button, WordArt displays the Format WordArt dialog box (see Figure W-7). You can use its Colors and Lines tab to change, predictably, the color and lines used to create the WordArt object. To make changes, simply use the tab's drop-down list boxes to select different colors, line styles, and so on.

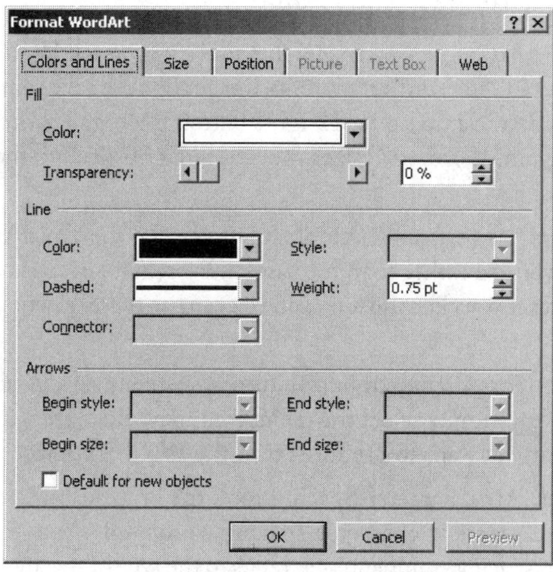

Figure W-7 The Colors and Lines tab of the Format WordArt dialog box.

Other Format WordArt tabs work in a similar fashion: Use the Size tab to change the dimensions of the WordArt object. Use the Position tab to describe how the WordArt object should be positioned on a page in relation to other objects.

The WordArt Shape button displays a menu of pictures you can choose from to select the shape of the WordArt object, (see Figure W-8). You simply click the shape you want the WordArt object to take.

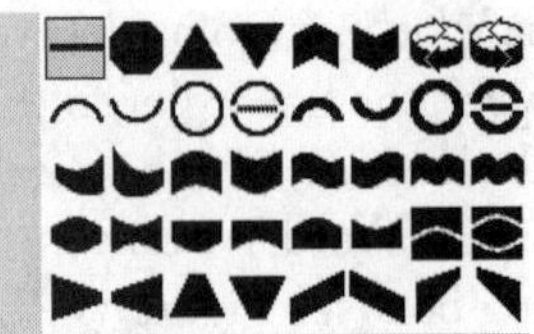

Figure W-8 The WordArt Shape menu.

The Free Rotate button, if clicked, adds selection handles to the WordArt object. You can use these Rotate selection handles to rotate, or spin, the WordArt object on the page.

The WordArt Same Letter Heights tool lets you tell WordArt that each letter in the WordArt graphics image should be the same height. The WordArt Same Letter Heights button is a toggle switch. If you click it again, WordArt resizes the letter heights back to their original sizes.

The WordArt Vertical Text toolbar lets you flip the WordArt text so that it's vertical rather than horizontal. WordArt also adds selection handles after you click the tool, and you can use these selection handles to rotate the object.

The WordArt Alignment button displays a menu of text-alignment options. You simply select the menu command that refers to the text alignment you want to use for text in the WordArt object.

The WordArt Character Spacing tool, the last one on the toolbar, displays a menu of character-spacing commands. You choose the character-spacing command that refers to the type of spacing you want for the text that makes the WordArt object.

Zoom

The Zoom box, which often appears on the Standard toolbar, lets you magnify or reduce the size of the presentation that shows in the window to some percentage of its actual size. To use the Zoom box, enter a percent in the Zoom box or open the Zoom list box by clicking its arrow and select a zoom percentage from the list.